GENDER | *in the Mirror*

Cultural Imagery and Women's Agency

OXFORD
UNIVERSITY PRESS

2002

DIANA TIETJENS MEYERS

OXFORD

UNIVERSITY PRESS

Oxford   New York

Athens   Auckland   Bangkok   Bogotá   Buenos Aires   Cape Town
Chennai   Dar es Salaam   Delhi   Florence   Hong Kong   Istanbul   Karachi
Kolkata   Kuala Lumpur   Madrid   Melbourne   Mexico City   Mumbai   Nairobi
Paris   São Paulo   Shanghai   Singapore   Taipei   Tokyo   Toronto   Warsaw

and associated companies in
Berlin   Ibadan

Published by Oxford University Press, Inc.
198 Madison Avenue, New York, New York 10016

Oxford is a registered trademark of Oxford University Press

Library of Congress Cataloging-in-Publication Data
Meyers, Diana T.
Gender in the mirror : cultural imagery and women's agency / Diana Tietjens Meyers.
p. cm. — (Studies in feminist philosophy)
ISBN 0-19-514040-0;   ISBN 0-19-514041-9 (pbk.)
1. Sex role.   2. Self.   3. Self (Philosophy)   4. Women—Social conditions.
5. Sex discrimination against women.   6. Feminist theory.   I. Title.   II. Series.
HQ1075 .M494   2002
305.42 — dc21   2001036805

3 5 7 9 8 6 4 2

Printed in the United States of America
on acid-free paper

In memory of my father, R. TIETJENS

My work is to inhabit the silences with which I have lived and fill them with myself until they have the sounds of brightest day and the loudest thunder.
—Audre Lorde, *The Cancer Journals*

Women have served all these centuries as looking-glasses possessing the magic and delicious power of reflecting the figure of man at twice its natural size.
—Virginia Woolf, *A Room of One's Own*

These quotations strike two themes that have always fascinated me—silence and voice, and mirroring and images. For me, what is so galvanizing about these themes is that they converge on questions about reflection and self-determination. How does one understand who one is and how one should live? How does self-understanding depend on speaking in one's own voice? How does one find one's own voice? And, supposing that one does, how then does one get heard? How does one translate one's self-understanding into action? How does one lead a life that is one's own?

Audre Lorde speaks of silences—her silences about her own experience and cultural silences about those who are marginalized, inferiorized, subordinated, and despised. These silences are not quiet, however. Cultural noise fills the aural void and covers it up. Discourses of derogation and cooptation generate an incessant, nullifying blather. This book is about that cultural noise pollution, its pernicious impact on women's lives, and what needs to be done to detoxify our social habitat.

One of the most lethal forms of this cultural pollution is the system of imagery that encodes gender stereotypes and norms. Virginia Woolf speaks of looking glasses and the images that play upon them. Women are captives of mirrors that are manufactured in patriarchal shops. When women aren't being reflected back as narcissists enamored with their own faces, they are drafted into service as reflecting surfaces for male egos. The mirrors that give women their self-images lie—they tell women they are ugly, fat, ungainly, worthless. The mirrors that women are expected to be erase their self-images—instead they beam back flattering images of men.

Women need mirrors that show them as the complex, distinctive, three-dimensional individuals they are. To find those mirrors, women must shatter the silvered glass of entrenched gender imagery and create their own self-imagery. They must break the silence; they must tune out the cultural racket; they must speak their own lives. This book theorizes that emancipatory undertaking.

A Note on the Dedication

Although my father was a postwar, middle-class suburbanite, luckily for me he was in some respects a rather eccentric one. Unlike most of my girl-friends' fathers, he had wide-ranging cultural interests, and he took it upon himself to supplement my classroom education. I feel it is particularly fitting that this book be dedicated to his memory because, more than any of my previous books, this one bears the impress of his distinctive influence. Chapter 5, for instance, begins with some remarks about my experience studying ballet and goes on to theorize the twists and turns of successive retellings of the myth of Narcissus and the history of pictorial representations of women with mirrors in Western art. My father, who valued and enjoyed ballet, arranged for me to study at a first-rate ballet school and took me to many ballet performances. And long before the public schools got around to it, my father introduced me to mythology by reading me tales from Bullfinch's compilation. At a time when art education meant little more than finger painting, my father frequently took me to the Art Institute of Chicago and regaled me with his understanding of and his delight in all manner of art forms. I enjoyed and appreciated these attentions and excursions while I was still a child, and they endowed me with lasting interests and pleasures. It is, then, with untold gratitude and deep love, that I dedicate *Gender in the Mirror* to the memory of R. Tietjens (1906–2000).

ACKNOWLEDGMENTS

I have many generous and astute friends to thank for help with this book. Sandra Bartky, Susan Brison, Lisa Cassidy, Wendy Donner, Jennifer Heckard, Phillip Koplin, Lewis Meyers, Hilde Nelson, Jennifer Radden, Sally Ruddick, Margaret Urban Walker, and Chandra Wells gave me invaluable suggestions for improving drafts of various chapters, and Linda Lemoncheck, the former editor of this series, provided extremely helpful comments on the entire manuscript as well as unflagging encouragement. In addition, I would like to thank the whole staff of the interlibrary loan service at Homer Babbidge Library, with special thanks to Lynn Sweet. Lynn and her colleagues cheerfully and expeditiously provided me with extensive and indispensable assistance.

I also thank the University of Connecticut for a sabbatical leave during spring 2000, which gave me the luxury of working exclusively on this book at a crucial point in my thinking, and the NYU Department of Philosophy for hosting me as a visiting scholar during my sabbatical, which enabled me to complete my research at the Bobst Library.

Finally, I wish to express special gratitude to Jan Balascak, the manager of the News Cafe on University Place in New York City. While I was on sabbatical and working on this book, Jan and the friendly staff of this café—not to mention the excellent coffee, comfy back banquette, and congenial music—provided me with an ideal place for long hours of caffeine-enhanced manuscript revision. To be sure, a room of one's own is essential for writing, but so too, I find, is a pleasant roomful of strangers.

Parts of this book have appeared in other forms. I wish to acknowledge these previous publications and thank the publishers for allowing me to use this material. They include: "The Family Romance: A Fin-de-Siècle Tragedy," in *Feminism and Families*, edited by Hilde Nelson (Routledge, 1997); "Tropes of Social Relations and the Problem of Tropisms in Figurative Discourse," in *Norms and Values: Essays in Honor of Virginia Held*, edited by Mark Halfon and Joram Haber (Rowman and Littlefield, 1998); "*Miroir, Memoire, Mirage*: Appearance, Aging, and Women," in *Mother Time: Ethical Issues in Women and Aging*, edited by Margaret Urban Walker (Rowman and Littlefield, 1999); "Intersectional Identity and the Authentic Self? Opposites Attract!" in *Relational Autonomy*, edited by Catriona Mackenzie and Natalie Stoljar (Oxford University Press, 2000); "The Rush to Motherhood—Pronatalist Discourse and Women's Autonomy," *Signs* (Spring 2001); "Marginalized Identities—Individuality, Groups, and Theory," in *Marginal Groups and Mainstream American Culture*, edited by Yolanda Estes, Arnold Lorenzo Farr, Patricia Smith, and Clelia Smyth (Kansas University Press, 2000); and "Feminism and Women's Autonomy: The Challenge of Female Genital Cutting," in *Metaphilosophy* (October 2000).

New York City   D. T. M.
May 2001

CONTENTS

GENDER IN THE MIRROR

CHAPTER ONE

Gender Identity and Women's Agency: Culture, Norms, and Internalized Oppression Revisited

What diverse women are like and how individual women go about conducting their lives are issues that go to the heart of feminism. Because patriarchal societies consider women inferior beings, and because these societies severely constrain women's choosing and acting, all feminists—theorists and activists alike—regard the questions of why women suffer these wrongs and how they can can be righted as crucial. Not surprisingly, then, the issues of women's identity and their agency inspire intense critical engagement not only with social conventions but also with the philosophical canon. The result has been a veritable cavalcade of theoretical advances.

Strangely, though, outbreaks of intellectual mischief and perhaps even obtuseness also tend to cluster at these sites of inquiry. As a number of commentators have observed, feminist theory is now and again marred by aberrant, unfeminist subtexts. Humanistic feminist Mary Wollstonecraft indulges in some quite unsympathetic, moralistic finger wagging at so-called womanly virtues. For Wollstonecraft, these qualities merely enshrine women's craven adaptation to a subordinate position. Likewise, a rather grandiose metaphysical hauteur surfaces in Simone de Beauvoir's existential feminism. Portraying women as mired in banal domestic routine and self-abnegating caregiving, de Beauvoir gives them no credit for their labor, nor does she disguise her contempt for what she terms women's "immanence." Whereas Wollstonecraft and de Beauvoir characterize women's identity as a trap and emphasize the tightness of its clasp to the point of seeming misogynist, traces of a baffling, cavalier triumphalism are detectable in Judith Butler's poststructuralist feminism. According to Butler, gender identity is a pesky phantasm that we can dispatch without too much trouble — say by delighting in the "deviant" gender performances of drag queens. Emphasizing the superficiality of gender identity, as Butler does, seems to make light of women's subordination.

In my judgment, each of these theorists has a major insight regarding women's identity and agency but casts it in curiously exaggerated terms. Although this rhetorical strategy serves the useful purpose of magnifying a problematic aspect of women's lives, it also makes it difficult for ordinary women to recognize their lives in theories about them. In noting the flawed tenor of these views, however, I am neither disputing nor discounting these theorists' overall contributions. Rather, I wish to highlight the treachery of the identity/agency terrain.

Feminist theorists find the topics of women's identity and agency vexing, I submit, because a pair of dilemmas structures these issues. To acknowledge women's gender identity together with the history of women's subordination seems to entail ascribing a host of ingrained defects to women and thus to call for a radical transformation of feminine identity. Yet, since masculine identity leaves much to be desired, there is reason to valorize feminine identity as a locus of suppressed yet genuine values and as a desirable form of relationally grounded selfhood and subjectivity. With regard to women's agency, it seems that if women are systematically subordinated, their ability to choose and act freely must be gravely compromised. Yet, if feminist theorists are to respect women's dignity and if they are to defend women's capacity to emancipate themselves, it seems they must counter that women's agency has been concealed or overlooked, not diminished.

In this chapter, I explore the relations among norms encoded in gender discourse, gendered identity, and women's agency. A number of feminist theorists argue that gender is a feature of social structures or linguistic classification systems, but that who one is or what one is like need not be gendered. Rightly shunning a false universalism about gender, these theorists externalize gender and sever it from identity. Against this view, I argue that gender is internalized and does become a dimension of women's identities (Section 1). However, I also urge that the developmental process in childhood and beyond is not merely a process of internalization. It is also a process of individualization. Thus, women's identities are both gendered and individualized. Still, it is important to recognize that individualization does not fully protect women's agentic capacities from damage. That women's identities are gendered in patriarchal cultures does impede women's ability to function as self-determining agents. Yet, major philosophical accounts of self-determination either underestimate the seriousness of internalized oppression or address this problem in ways that underrate women's agency within patriarchal societies (Section 2). In my view, then, feminist theory needs a different approach to self-determination.

A number of feminists have begun the project of reconceptualizing self-determination by developing what I call *feminist voice theory* (Section 3). Feminist work on the relation between speaking in one's own voice and leading one's own life is invaluable, for it calls attention to culturally entrenched narrative templates and representational conventions — figures of speech, mythic tales, and pictorial images — that invade women's stories and crowd out alternative versions of their lives. Still, feminist voice theory fails to furnish an epistemology that differentiates speaking in one's own voice from speaking in the patriarch's voice. Thus, I propose an account of self-determination that connects women's voices to their lives as well as to their emancipatory potentialities. Self-determination, I argue, is best understood as an ongoing process of exercising a repertoire of agentic skills — skills that enable individuals to construct their own self-portraits and self-narratives and that thereby enable them to take charge of their lives. Construing self-determination this way demonstrates women's need for expanded agency, for it discloses how patriarchal cultures illegitimately interfere with women's agentic skills (Section 4). However, this view of self-determination does not divest women of agency within patriarchal cultures, for it is undeniable that women exercise some agentic skills despite this hostile environment.

1. Internalized Oppression, Identity, and Individuality

People do not choose their gender (or, for that matter, their race, ethnicity, sexuality, stage of life, or class).[1] These are thrust upon us. Nor is it within one's power as an individual to expel gender from one's life. That our society and the people we associate with classify us according to gender is not controversial. Likewise, few would dispute that access to many goods, including social, economic, and political opportunities, differs depending on gender. Yet, in recent feminist theory, a controversy has erupted about whether women have gender identities. Perceiving racism within feminism, women of color object to white, middle-class feminists' universalization of their own experience of gender. Perceiving vestiges of the Enlightenment in feminism, postmodern feminists deny that people have stable individual identities and object to feminist theories that "essentialize" gender in the process of delineating a core gender identity. Responding to these critiques, a number of feminist theorists seek to justify solidarity among women while fully acknowledging women's diversity (e.g., Spelman 1988; Alcoff 1994; Young 1994; Haslanger 2000). Some of these scholars deny that social institutions and cultural traditions instill gender in our cognitive, emotional, and motivational infrastructures—that is, in our identities—and defend other rationales for feminism. I take issue with the move to exclude gender from individual identity. I argue that internalized oppression is a reality that feminists must address, but I do not defend a universalist view of internalized oppression and gender identity. Instead, I urge that subordination is internalized and becomes integral to individualized, subordinated identities.[2]

According to Iris Young, a leading exponent of the anti-identity view of gender, women as women are members of what we might call a *group precursor*, as opposed to a full-fledged group, but they do not necessarily have a gender identity. To explain gender (or sexual orientation, class, race, or nationality), Young invokes Jean-Paul Sartre's idea of seriality (Young 1994, 731–732). A social series or group precursor is "a social collective whose members are unified passively by the objects around which their actions are oriented or by the objectified results of the material effects of the actions of others" (Young 1994, 724). In more familiar terms, a series is constituted by a behavior-directing, meaning-defining institutional and social environment. The lives of series members are affected by being assigned to particular social series, for serial existence is experienced as a "felt necessity" that leaves individuals feeling powerless (Young 1994, 726). Thus, people feel impelled to act in ways that conform to their series memberships. Yet, series membership *"does not define the person's identity in the sense of forming his/her individual purposes, projects, and sense of self in relation to others"* (Young 1994, 727; emphasis added). Indeed, individuals can *choose* to make none of their serial memberships important for their individual identity (Young 1994, 733).

One difficulty with this proposal is that it seems to replace essentialist accounts of gendered psyches and bodies with an essentialist account of gendering social structures. Young indicts two culprits: compulsory heterosexuality and the sexual division of labor (Young 1994, 729–730). But if these structures differ in different societies during different historical periods, which they do, and if these structures also differ in different racial, ethnic, sexuality, age, and class groupings within a society, which they do, there is no reason to believe that all of the women whose lives are partly organized by these variable structures belong to the same series. As Susan Moller Okin points out, a sexual division of labor that prohibits women from working outside the home even if they have no other way to survive and provide for their children is different in kind from a sexual division of labor that disproportionately burdens women who are employed outside the home with childcare and other domestic tasks (Okin 1995, 285–286). An externalized essentialism cannot salvage unity among women any more plausibly than an internalized one can.

In my view, however, the more serious problem with Young's view is that it is premised on a false dichotomy: Either social positioning is constitutive of individual identity, and all similarly positioned individuals share a common identity, or else social positioning is external to individual identity, and no woman's identity is gendered unless she decides to let gender in. Since it is indisputable that women do not share a common identity—the same can be said of members of racial, sexuality, life-stage, class, and ethnic groups—Young opts for the voluntarist position. One is a member of this or that social series whether one likes it or not. One becomes a member of a social group only when one elects to join one. Series membership shapes one's identity only if one allows it to do so.

The alternative to this individualist voluntarism is not gender (race, sexuality, life-stage, class, or ethnicity) essentialism and a common feminine (racial, sexual, class, age, or ethnic) identity. The alternative is gendered *and* individualized identities. At one point, Young seems to concede this very point. No woman's identity "will escape the *markings of gender*," she observes, "but how gender marks her life is her own" (Young 1994, 734). I agree—identities are individualized. But I hasten to add that how gender marks a woman's (or a man's) identity will not be entirely her (or his) own choice. Gender worms its way into identity in ways that we may not be conscious of and in ways that we may not be able to change, no matter how much we try.

Sandra Lee Bartky's essays on women's bodily self-discipline and women's masochistic sexual fantasies are classics in the literature of internalized oppression. For Bartky, to internalize material is to incorporate it into the structure of the self, that is, into the modes of perception and self-perception that enable one to distinguish oneself from other selves and from other things (Bartky 1990, 77; for related discussion, see Cudd

1998). These modes of perception and self-perception reflect how others behave toward the individual; they amalgamate concepts, interpretive schemas, and thought patterns that are circulating in the individual's social milieu; they include skills that delimit what the individual knows (and does not know) how to do. Internalization is inevitable and can be innocuous. But to internalize oppression is to incorporate inferiorizing material into the structure of the self—to see oneself as objectified, to value and desire what befits a subordinated individual, and to feel competent and empowered by skills that reinforce one's subordination.

Bartky analyzes the feminine body as an instance of internalized oppression. Through obsessive dieting and exercising, restricted movement and posture, unreciprocated smiling, elaborate makeup and skin-care routines, and alluring ornaments and clothing, women "discipline" their bodies (Bartky 1990, 66–71; for related discussion of feminine narcissism, see Chapter 5). An undisciplined female body is defective, and yet a properly disciplined female body is a body with "an inferior status inscribed" upon it (Bartky 1990, 71–72). The attractive woman is "object and prey" for men, for feminine beauty plays up fragility, weakness, and immaturity (Bartky 1990, 72–73). Feminine comportment and demeanor are typical of lower-status groups (Bartky 1990, 73–74). In contrast to expansive masculine ease, women are instructed to cross their legs, keep their arms close to their torsos, listen attentively, and smile ingratiatingly. Severe penalties are attached to shedding this identity—"ugly," unfeminine women are scorned by men and denied employment (Bartky 1990, 76). To take one notorious case, when Ann Hopkins was evaluated for partnership at the accounting firm Price Waterhouse, she was criticized for not wearing makeup and for lacking feminine charm (Valian 1998, 111). Despite her superb record of attracting lucrative accounts to the firm and working high-volume billable hours, Hopkins was denied partnership (Valian 1998, 291). Although she sued for employment discrimination and ultimately won, she was obliged to undergo this ordeal simply because she failed to conform to feminine body norms.

Yet, incessant self-policing earns women no respect. On the contrary, feminine women are often ridiculed for their "obsession" with clothes, makeup, and other "trivial" details of appearance (Bartky 1990, 73). Still, few women are merely putting on a show. Most are becoming "docile and compliant companions of men" (Bartky 1990, 75). Moreover, what they are doing and what they are making themselves into seems entirely voluntary and natural. Indeed, when feminists criticize these practices and urge women to abandon them, most women give this suggestion a chilly reception. In Bartky's view, this reluctance to forgo feminine self-discipline is not merely a result of the negative sanctions women can anticipate. It also stems from the embeddedness of the aesthetic of feminine beauty and the routines of self-beautification in women's identities. Everyone finds the thought of undergoing a radical transformation of self—in the popular idiom, of becoming a different person—unnerving. Thus, women recoil from feminist critiques of feminine bodily norms because they find the idea of repudiating values that are constitutive of their sense of self and skills that give them a sense of mastery too unsettling (Bartky 1990, 77). An important virtue of Bartky's account of internalized oppression is that it makes sense of this reaction—it is reasonable for many women to feel deeply threatened by feminism, and it is understandable, though not desirable, that some of them reject it.

One reason that feminist critiques of the feminine body are so disquieting is that physical appearance and comportment are integral to women's sexual identity (Bartky 1990, 77). Bartky pursues the issue of sexual identity further in an essay on the psychosomatics of women's eroticism. Bartky asks us to consider a feminist, P, whose sexual pleasure depends on conjuring up masochistic scenarios (Bartky 1990, 46). As a feminist, P is convinced that this imagery replicates male dominance in the sexual register, and she is ashamed of and disgusted by its recurrence in her fantasy life (Bartky 1990, 51–52, 54). Still, moral reproach and psychotherapy do not alleviate her need for this debased imagery, nor do they diminish the pleasure it yields. P has internalized a subordinated vision of feminine sexuality, and she is powerless to extirpate it. As Bartky puts it, "We cannot teach P . . . how to decolonize the imagination" (Bartky 1990, 61). Fixed in indecipherable unconscious desire and manifest in discordant, yet tenacious sexual fantasies, subordination infests many women's identities.

Consider one more form that internalized oppression takes. In an essay examining the social construction of African-American manhood and womanhood, Patricia Williams focuses on the 1987 incident in upstate New York in which an African-American teenager, Tawana Brawley, turned up dazed, unclothed, burned, and smeared with feces and indicated that she had been raped and tortured by white police officers. Near the end of the essay, Williams recounts the following episode:

> At the height of the controversy, Tawana attended a comedy show at the Apollo Theater in Harlem. One of the comedians called attention

to her presence in the audience and, in a parody of the federal antisex and antidrug campaigns, advised her to "just say no next time." As the audience roared with merriment and the spotlight played on her, Tawana threw back her head and laughed along with the crowd. She opened her mouth and laughed in false witness of this cruel joke. It is the only image I have of Tawana with her mouth open—caught in a position of compromise, of satisfying the pleasure and expectations of others, trapped in the pornography of living out other people's fantasies. (P. Williams 1991, 177)

Throughout her essay, Williams's theme is the silencing of Tawana Brawley—by inept, if not corrupt and malign, legal officials, by the sensationalized press coverage, and by her African-American advisors. Never allowed to speak for herself and tell her own story, she enacts everyone's script but her own. At the Apollo, she becomes the girl who delights in the comedian's irony although the humor is at her expense. Relieved, perhaps, to elude the media discourse that has revolved around racist imagery of the insatiably lustful, venomous black whore, Brawley embodies the sexist imagery of the fetching, acquiescent girl of unblemished reputation. In the "sanctuary" of the Apollo Theater, Brawley's gender identity is rehabilitated, but her identity is one that others have contrived for her.

To be sure, gender does not exhaust any woman's identity and sense of self. Still, Bartky's and Williams's work demonstrates that gender is constitutive of who we are—our personalities, our capabilities and liabilities, our aspirations, and how we feel about all of these dimensions of identity. Yet, there is no attribute that all women or that all men share. The same is true of other subordinated and privileged identity categories. How is this possible?

Nancy Chodorow uses psychoanalytic theory to make sense of individualized, gendered identities. Psychoanalysis explains how individuals "personally animate and tint . . . the anatomic, cultural, interpersonal, and cognitive world we experience" (Chodorow 1995, 520; also see Chodorow 1999, Chapter 3). One's affective dispositions, unconscious fantasies, and interpersonal relationships filter the culturally entrenched conception of gender one encounters. Through various psychological processes—projection and introjection together with the defense mechanisms—gender acquires a "personal meaning" that is inspired by but that does not wholly replicate culturally transmitted strictures and iconography (Chodorow 1995, 517). I hasten to add that it is not necessary to posit a psychoanalytic developmental model to explain this process. Any developmental theory that accounts for enculturation along with individuality will draw the same conclusion. As Chodorow somewhat paradoxically puts it, each woman creates "her own personal-cultural gender" (Chodorow 1995, 518).

It is a mistake to picture attributes like gender as toxic capsules full of norms and interpretive schemas that individuals swallow whole and that lodge intact in their psychic structure. The diversity of individuals' experience of gender belies this view. But it is also a mistake to picture attributes like gender as systems of social and economic opportunities, constraints, rewards, and penalties that never impinge upon individual identity. The seeming naturalness of enacting gendered characteristics, the passion with which people cling to their sense of their own gender, and 10) 11 the intractability of many gendered attributes when people seek to change them testify to the embeddedness of gender in identity.

2. Subordination's Challenge to Autonomy Theory

The phenomenon of internalized oppression presents two opposed temptations for accounts of self-determination or, in other words, theories of autonomy. On the one hand, latitudinarian, value-neutral accounts of autonomy are attractive because they do not automatically impugn the ability of women who enact gender norms to make their own judgments and choices, and, consequently, they show respect for these women. On the other hand, restrictive, value-saturated accounts of autonomy, which deny that people can be both oppressed and autonomous, are attractive because, in claiming that internalized oppression blocks the self-determination of women in patriarchal cultures, they highlight the harsh, though often hidden, personal cost of living under oppressive social regimes. Neither of these approaches is ultimately convincing, however.

Preliminary to characterizing the weaknesses of these approaches, it is useful to review what an account of autonomy should accomplish. An account of autonomy aims principally to explicate an especially valuable mode of living. That mode of living is captured in a number of colloquial expressions: "She lives by her own lights," "She's always been true to herself," "I gotta be me!" and the like. Autonomous individuals are not mere conformists, of course, but they need not be eccentric. What is distinctive about them is that they rely on their own judgment. They know who they are—what really matters to them, whom they deeply care about, what their capacities and limitations actually are, and so forth—and they enact

GENDER IDENTITY AND WOMEN'S AGENCY

this introspective understanding of their "true" selves in their everyday lives. There is a good fit, then, between their identity, their attitudes toward themselves, and their conduct. Remarks such as "I feel at one with myself" and "I feel right in my skin" voice this sense of integration. As these idioms suggest, living autonomously is satisfying. Sometimes it is exhilarating. "At last I see what I *really* want!" might express the joy and excitement autonomy can bring. Subjectively, then, the value of autonomy stems from the fascination of self-discovery and the gratification of self-determination. Objectively, it rests on the dignity of the distinctive individual and the wondrous diversity of the lives individuals may fashion for themselves.

Explicating the nature of the personal and social costs of suppressing autonomy is another aim an account of autonomy should fulfill. Individuals experience lack of autonomy as a sense of being out of control or being under the control of others, whether other identifiable individuals or anonymous societal powers. At odds with themselves, at odds with their behavior, or both, nonautonomous individuals often feel anxious about their choices, contemptuous of themselves, and disappointed with their lives. "How could I have done that?" "Why did I give in?" or "Where on earth am I headed?" they may ask. Alternatively, they may simply feel hollow, for they may feel they have been made into vehicles for projects that they do not disavow but that are not their own. "What am I doing anyway?" or "What's the point of it all?" they may wonder. In one way or another, nonautonomous individuals suffer from alienation from self.

Societies that are not conducive to autonomy are objectionable because they diminish personal fulfillment. But this is not the only moral loss they incur. When a society discourages self-exploration and self-expression, it discourages attention to symptoms of discontent and shields social ideologies and institutions from probing examination and oppositional activism. A society that encourages autonomy exposes itself to criticism and equips people to pursue social change. By thwarting (or trying to thwart) dissent, societies that suppress autonomy perpetuate unjust social structures.

I shall not linger long over latitudinarian, value-neutral theories of autonomy, for their weaknesses have been diagnosed and elaborated elsewhere. Briefly, rational choice views take people's desires, values, and goals as givens and identify autonomy with organizing them into coherent, satisfaction-maximizing life plans (for critiques, see Meyers 1989, 76–79; Babbitt 1993, 246–253). But exempting an autonomous person's desires, values, and goals from critical reflection and fundamental transformation is plausible only if one assumes a background of social justice that is nowhere even approximated. Knowing what one wants and being able to figure out how to get it in a society that generally respects people's basic liberties is a travesty of autonomy when one's aims are misbegotten—contorted and cramped by structures of domination and subordination that basic liberties leave in place.

Hierarchical identification theories are also latitudinarian and value-neutral. They improve on rational choice theories, however, because they subject first-order desires—"I want an ice cream cone"—to scrutiny in light of second-order volitions—"You can't afford the extra cholesterol." To be autonomous is to reconcile the two levels and achieve a harmonious whole—wanting only fat-free snacks, I suppose (for critiques, see Meyers 1989, 25–41; Benson 1991, 391–394). Still, hierarchical identification theories neglect the possibility that an oppressive social context could subvert people's autonomy by imparting detrimental values that warp their second-order volitions. Perhaps the current wave of health consciousness is perversely ascetic, but from a feminist viewpoint a commitment to sexist and heterosexist norms is far more disturbing. What if a woman's first-order desire had been "I want an ice cream cone," her second-order volition had been "I'll die if I don't get married soon," and her resolution had been "Skip the cone because no one will want you if you look flabby in your bikini at the beach next month"? Here it is by no means obvious that achieving inner harmony constitutes a gain in self-determination. The possibility that internalized oppression fuels this individual's second-order volition raises doubts about her autonomy.

Value-neutral theories make inadequate provision for "authenticating" the concepts and commitments that structure one's interpretations and propel one's deliberations and choices. In contrast, restrictive, value-saturated accounts of autonomy, such as Susan Babbitt's and Paul Benson's, insist on the need to distinguish real from apparent desires and authentic values from spurious ones. They draw these distinctions by placing constraints on what people can autonomously choose.

According to Susan Babbitt, internalized oppression instills preferences and desires that do not adequately reflect an interest in one's own flourishing and that prevent one from pursuing one's "objective interests" even when one is aware that one has an option to pursue them (Babbitt 1993, 246–247). The problem, claims Babbitt, is the individual's "not possessing a sense of self that would support a full sense of flourishing"—that is, one has been deprived of a precondition for wanting to pursue one's objective interests (Babbitt 1993, 248). Although the oppressed have non-propositional knowledge—knowledge in the form of intuitions, attitudes, ways of behaving, and so on—that adumbrates their objective interests, this knowledge is inexpressible within the existing ideological regime and is not translatable into autonomous action (Babbitt 1993, 252–254). Mute and subjugated, these individuals' agency can only be salvaged through "transformative experiences" that, as it were, upgrade their selfhood (Babbitt 1993, 252–253).

I doubt, however, that oppression renders people's nonpropositional knowledge inexpressible. In fact, I think one of Babbitt's examples amply vindicates my dubiety. Commenting on Alice Walker's novel about domestic violence, *The Color Purple*, Babbitt claims that Celie's knowledge that she is a morally worthy person is nonpropositional and inexpressible. I would argue that Celie's knowledge indeed stems from nonpropositional sources: her feelings, attitudes, and perhaps her intuitions. But, as Babbitt reports, when taunted by Mister—"You nothing at all"—Celie trenchantly replies, "I'm pore, I'm black, I may be ugly and can't cook . . . but *I'm here*" (Babbitt 1993, 253; emphasis added). Babbitt is correct to say that the categories of Mister's ideology provide no direct, authoritative way for Celie to assert her moral status, but it is evident that Celie is able to give her knowledge a propositional form and to encode her knowledge in intelligible speech.

Oppression deprives Celie of conventions—readily available, generally accepted discursive formulas—through which she can articulate her convictions, protests, and aspirations (M. Walker 1998, 123–128). To articulate their self-knowledge, oppressed people must resort to circumlocution, devise figures of speech, and work to redefine the terms of intrapersonal understanding, interpersonal relations, and moral reflection. Thus, they must summon extraordinary imaginative and linguistic powers if they are to gain a rich understanding of who they are and why their needs and desires deserve respect. Nevertheless, in light of her defiant self-recognition and her poignant self-assertion, it seems doubtful that Celie lacks an "adequate" sense of self.

Still, it is undeniable that Celie's social context is doing everything possible to stifle her autonomy and to defeat her. For this reason, I expect, Paul Benson would argue that attributing autonomy to someone like Celie betokens a Pollyanaish confidence in her agentic capabilities.

According to Benson, "Certain forms of socialization are oppressive and clearly lessen autonomy" (Benson 1991, 385). There are two forms that oppressive socialization takes: (1) coercive socialization, which inflicts penalties for noncompliance with unjustifiable norms, and (2) socialization that instills false beliefs, which prevents people from discerning genuine reasons for acting (Benson 1991, 388–389). Autonomous people are "competent criticizer[s]" who can "detect and appreciate the reasons there are to act in various ways" (Benson 1991, 396, 397). But oppressive socialization systematically obviates and obfuscates victims' reasons for acting. As Benson puts it, oppressive socialization limits in "well-organized ways what sorts of reasons to act people are able to recognize" (Benson 1991, 396). Internalized oppression, it seems, can dragoon a person's entire life.

Presumably, Benson would conclude that, because of their socialization, the many women who do not repudiate subordinating feminine norms have defective reason-detection faculties—defective at least insofar as they are oblivious to the "decisive" force of the reasons against complying with these norms—and thus that they have been deprived of autonomy at least with regard to this aspect of their lives.[3] But I would urge that Benson's grim assessment of the sinister potency of oppressive socialization exaggerates the impact of socialization generally. It just isn't true that oppressive socialization always decreases autonomy. Some people become oppositional activists, and some of them flourish in that role. In cases of firebrand, adventure-loving resisters, one suspects they would have had a hard time fitting in and living autonomously if they had been born into a just society during peacetime. Other people carve out lives that enact "inappropriate" values in the interstices of society's constraints. They find pockets of lapsed surveillance or permissiveness within oppressive regimes and devise ways to express their unorthodox values and commitments in those spaces. Still others endorse at least some of the values upon which oppressive constraints are based and on balance accept the constraints and conform their lives to them. Undeniably, women in patriarchal cultures have much to overcome to attain autonomy. But it is hard to believe that where gender is concerned none of them ever chooses autonomously.

The fact is that we are all immersed in a culture at a historical moment. How do we know that some of us have attained adequate selfhood and thus have the epistemic perspective needed to grasp what full flourishing is like? How do we know that some of us have highly developed, acutely sensitive reason-detection faculties and thus have the epistemic skills needed to determine what cannot be a good reason to act or what is a dispositive reason to act? It seems to me that we would need far more consensus than we presently have (or are likely to get) about human nature and social justice before we could conclude that women who opt for compliance with feminine norms never do so autonomously. We would have to be persuaded, in other words, that all women's interests are such that this decision could not accord with any woman's genuine values and real desires under any circumstances. But if we are prepared to acknowledge that a woman who has undergone oppressive socialization but who rebels against its dictates may be accessing her "authentic" values and desires and acting autonomously, it seems to me that we cannot rule out a priori the possibility that a similarly socialized woman who chooses otherwise may be autonomous, too.

Restrictive, value-saturated accounts of autonomy are troubling because they promiscuously stigmatize women as victims and because they homogenize authentic selves and autonomous lives. The paradoxical effect of ahistorically, acontextually foreordaining what individuals can and cannot autonomously choose is to *deindividualize* autonomy and to overlook the agentic capacities that women exercise despite oppression. Yet, latitudinarian, value-neutral accounts of autonomy are troubling, too. According to this view, failures of autonomy are failures to obtain and take into account relevant information, or they are failures to integrate one's values, desires, and the like into a coherent outlook and a feasible course of action. To neglect the possibility that a well-integrated, smoothly functioning self could be in need of rigorous scrutiny and drastic overhaul is to deindividualize autonomy in a different way. This type of theory abandons the individual to the influence of a culture's prevailing beliefs and practices, oversimplifies self-alienation, and blunts autonomy's potential to spur social critique. Neither of these approaches offers a compelling theory of individualized autonomous living. A feminist view of autonomy must acknowledge that oppression impedes autonomy without stripping women of that autonomy which they have managed to wrest from a patriarchal, racist, heterosexist, ageist, class-stratified world.

3. Voice and Choice: A Feminist View of Autonomy

Wary of the individualist, antirelational bias in canonical autonomy theories, some feminists have repudiated autonomy (Jaggar 1983; Addelson 1994; Hekman 1995). Nevertheless, the history of depicting women as at the mercy of their reproductive biology and in need of rational male guidance together with the history of women's enforced economic dependence on men or relegation to poorly paid, often despised forms of labor argues against striking *self-determination* from the feminist lexicon. It is not surprising, then, that many feminist writers continue to invoke ostensibly discredited values like self-determination in unguarded writing about the needs of women and the aims of feminism, and a number of feminist scholars have reconceptualized autonomy and explicitly defended it as a feminist value (e.g., Nedelsky 1989, 7; Meyers 1989, 2000a; Govier 1993, 103–104; Benhabib 1995, 21, and 1999, 353–354; Weir 1995, 263). Other feminist scholars translate the issues that have traditionally occupied autonomy theorists into a vocabulary of voice.

Maria Lugones and Elizabeth Spelman observe that having a voice is "integral to leading a life rather than being led through it" and that "being silenced in one's own account of one's life is a kind of *amputation* that signals oppression" (Lugones and Spelman 1986, 19; emphasis added). Silencing disables agency, for the alternative to articulating your own experience and your own goals in your own way is to live someone else's version of you—to inhabit their definition of what you are like and their construal of what you think, feel, and want and consequently to find yourself enacting their story of how your life should go (Frye 1983, 105; P. Williams 1991, 166–178; M. Walker 1998, 127–128; Nelson 2001, Chapter 1). What motivates feminist voice theory is the fact that women are systematically denied the opportunity to discover themselves for themselves, to interpret themselves as they think fit, and to live their lives according to their own lights. These are the very same problems that animate autonomy theory—namely, self-determination and the role of self-knowledge and self-definition in securing self-determination.

Autonomy theory's propensity for polarizing people into free, paradigmatically male agents and incompetent, paradigmatically female dependents or victims justifiably gives feminists pause. So it makes sense to navigate around autonomy theory and address the issue of women's self-determination through a theory of voice and narrative instead. Still, voice theory presents characteristic problems of its own. A feminist voice theory must furnish an account of how one gets in touch with oneself and finds one's own voice. It is not enough to invent an interesting protagonist and spin a good yarn about her life. If it is true, moreover, that all women's psyches and bodies are liable to internalize oppression, it is necessary to distinguish when women are speaking in their own voices and when they are lip syncing the ominous baritone of patriarchy. In particular, a feminist voice theory must explain how to distinguish between a woman's ideologically oppressed voice and her emancipated voice and between the voice of a progressive feminist ideology and the voice of the individual woman. I shall refer to this as the problem of *voice authentication*. Two solutions to these epistemological puzzles suggest themselves.

One possibility would be to authenticate voices by checking on their original contexts of utterance. Arguably, the administrative assistant who laughs off her boss's lewd remarks while hoping for a promotion, the abused woman who forgives her batterer to keep the family's paycheck coming in, and the adolescent who yearns for love and complains about her fleshy female body do not speak in their own voices, for their social contexts relentlessly and forcefully pressure them to mouth a patriarchal line. In contrast, feminist separatist practices create safe enclaves in which no woman is penalized for rejecting a demeaning, distorting self-description and in which each woman is invited to conceive alternative means of articulating her sense of self and her aims (for related discussion, see Frye 1983, 105–107). Feminist standpoint theory suggests a related but somewhat different approach. The dialectic between political struggle and theoretical understanding might be seen as differentiating the oppressed voice from the emancipated voice (Hartsock 1997, 465). On this reading, the emancipated voice would be the one that has unmasked oppression-perpetuating falsifications by joining with others to challenge social structures, by analyzing how these structures maintain the status quo and who is benefiting from this set-up, and by envisioning a society free of repression and exploitation.

Neither of these proposals seems altogether satisfactory. While it is undeniable that feminist separatist contexts can authorize women to find their own voices, it is also advisable to bear in mind that separatist contexts can deteriorate into a dynamic of mutually reinforcing, escalating error and muddle. Insulation from opposed viewpoints can breed self-delusion. Yet, mandating oppositional politics as a prerequisite for the self-understanding needed to speak in one's own voice is insufficiently respectful of women's uniqueness as individuals, for many women have conflicting commitments or find other methods of getting in touch with themselves more in keeping with their personal style. An epistemology that does not do justice to women's individuality is hardly suited to a feminist account of self-determination.

Another possibility would be to conceptualize the emancipated, individual voice as one that expresses a set of objective values, such as flourishing, self-respect, and dignity (Babbitt 1993, 262). The trouble with this suggestion is that such values must be interpreted, and these interpretations are inherently contestable. Since the meaning of these values is not transparent, people are bound to disagree about whether an individual's self-description and self-narrative comport with them. Whereas some women identify flourishing with being a devoted mother and a reliable helpmate, others regard lives dedicated to homemaking as squandering women's potential. Now, if we extricate ourselves from such clashes of judgment by agreeing to disagree, congruity with objective values could not function as a criterion for authenticating women's voices. If anyone who frames her life story as a tale of flourishing, self-respect, and dignity is by definition speaking in her own voice regardless of how she is actually living, voice theory would lose both the power to discern internalized oppression and the leverage to critique alien, culturally ordained narratives. Appealing to objective values could only authenticate women's voices if the meaning of these values were indisputable.

Despite my qualms about these ways of filling the epistemological lacunas in voice theory, I am reluctant to dismiss them. Each strikes me as promising. Still, both views need supplementation, and neither should be privileged as the sole way of authenticating women's voices.

The attractiveness of these proposals depends, I believe, on unstated assumptions about women's agentic capacities. The worries that the insularity of a separatist context can foster misguided, possibly dangerous, convictions and that the values of flourishing, self-respect, and dignity are too indeterminate to provide touchstones for authenticating voices are allayed if we assume that the participants in separatist groups and the interpreters of these values exercise skills that enable them to express their feelings and ideas openly, to interact respectfully, to reflect intelligently, and to judge conscientiously. Likewise, undertaking to define flourishing, self-respect, and dignity sharply enough to make these values useful voice authenticators is less worrisome if we assume that women themselves are defining these values while exercising skills that attune them to conflicts between proposed interpretations and their own needs and aspirations, as well as skills that enable them to resist detrimental interpretations effectively. If I am right that my objections to authenticating women's voices by reference to the context or the content of their speech are neutralized when women are seen as endowed with agentic skills of the sort I have mentioned, it must be because these skills put women in touch with themselves and enable them to discern what they *really* want and care about and because they enable women to improvise ways to express their *own* values and goals, both in the medium of speech and in that of action.

To set out the agentic skills needed to provide feminist voice theory with a credible epistemology is to articulate an implicit theory of autonomy. A theory of how one can differentiate one's own desires, values, and goals from the clamor of subordinating discourses and overwhelming social demands and how one can articulate and enact one's own desires, values, and goals is a theory of self-determination. These are some of the skills that make self-determination possible:

1. Introspection skills that sensitize individuals to their own feelings and desires, that enable them to interpret their subjective experience, and that help them judge how good a likeness a self-portrait is

2. Communication skills that enable individuals to get the benefit of others' perceptions, background knowledge, insights, advice, and support

3. Memory skills that enable individuals to recall relevant experiences—not only from their own lives, but also those that associates have recounted or that they have encountered in literature or other art forms

4. Imagination skills that enable individuals to envisage feasible options—to audition a range of self-images they might adopt and to preview a variety of plot lines their lives might follow

5. Analytical skills and reasoning skills that enable individuals to assess the relative merits of different visions of what they could be like and precis for future episodes in their life stories

6. Self-nurturing skills that enable individuals to secure their physical and psychological equilibrium despite missteps and setbacks —that enable them to appreciate the overall worthiness of their self-portraits and their self-narratives, assure themselves of their capacity to carry on when they find their self-portraits wanting or their self-narratives misguided, and sustain their self-respect if they need to correct their self-portraits or revise their self-narratives

7. Volitional skills that enable individuals to resist pressure to capitulate to convention and enable them to maintain their commitment to the self-portrait and to the continuations of their autobiographies that they consider genuinely their own

8. Interpersonal skills that enable individuals to join forces to challenge and change cultural regimes and institutional arrangements

that pathologize or marginalize their priorities and projects, that deprive them of accredited discursive means to represent themselves to themselves and to others as flourishing, self-respecting, valuable individuals, and that close off their opportunities to enact their self-portraits and self-narratives

What I am suggesting is that autonomous people have well-developed, well-coordinated repertoires of agentic skills and call on them routinely as they reflect on themselves and their lives and as they reach decisions about how best to go on.[4] When a woman speaks in her own voice, then, she is articulating what she knows as a result of exercising these skills.

This view of autonomy and women's voices does not pigeonhole people as free agents, incompetent dependents, or helpless victims. On the one hand, it acknowledges that women achieve a measure of self-determination despite male dominance, for these agentic skills are commonplace and exercising them requires no esoteric knowledge. Still, since proficiency with respect to these agentic skills is a matter of degree, and autonomy often depends on whether or not one's chance circumstances are conducive to exercising these skills and on whether or not one is motivated to exercise these skills, it is safe to assume that, like everyone else, most women experience autonomy fluctuations over the course of time, peaking now and then. On the other hand, this view of autonomy acknowledges the institutionalization of male dominance and the gravity of internalized oppression, both of which impede women's ability to develop and exercise these skills. It does not collapse into despair or cynicism, however, for it also explains how women can recognize and resist subordination by marshaling their agentic skills.

Reconfiguring autonomy this way supplies a missing component in feminist voice theory while at the same time incorporating voice theory's key insights. As Lugones and Spelman urge, self-determination is inseparable from speaking in one's own voice.[5] If people cannot articulate what they are doing and what they stand for to themselves, their control over how they are engaging with the world is diminished. Moreover, they need to communicate what they are doing and what they stand for to others. Otherwise, people will rely on stereotypical images and scenarios to ascribe needs to them and to interpret their conduct. As a result, they may withhold respect and cooperation for no good reason, and they may oppose progressive social change. My skills-based, processual view of autonomy features the linguistic and interpersonal skills people need to accomplish these aims.

In addition, the view of autonomy I have sketched agrees with feminist voice theory that gaining a voice is an achievement and that social context affects women's ability to speak in their own voices. Not all contexts nurture agentic skills, facilitate exercising them, and authorize people to apply them to the task of rethinking and reconstructing values and norms. I would caution, however, that separatist groups and progressive political organizations are not the only autonomy-augmenting sites. Other settings include friendships and other intimate relationships, psychotherapy, and mentoring relationships (Friedman 1993, Chapters 7 and 8; Brison 1997, 20–31). At least since Virginia Woolf penned *A Room of One's Own*, moreover, feminists have championed solitude as a resource for finding one's voice, and it is important to notice that privacy, no less than companionship or professional assistance, is a socially conferred benefit. To privilege one of these contexts would be to ignore women's distinctive temperaments and priorities. Still, the underlying point of feminist separatist and standpoint theory remains: One cannot quell the din of internalized oppression simply by logging off patriarchy.com and clicking on women.com. Accessing one's own voice is a skilled, ongoing, and relational undertaking.

Any tenable theory of women's self-determination must accommodate the realities of enculturation and unconscious desire. Since enculturation shapes both the body and the psyche, and since unconscious desire influences both conduct and thought processes, it is necessary to eschew the dubious ideal of total individual control. On the view of autonomy I have advanced, the starting point is the embodied, socially situated, and divided self, and the object is to gain a rich understanding of what one is like and what one aspires to become and also to be able to adjust one's desires, traits, values, emotions, and relationships if one becomes convinced that one should. The autonomous individual is an evolving subject—a subject who is in charge of her life within the limits of imperfect, introspective decipherability and welcome, though in some ways intrusive (or downright harmful), physical experience and social relations, a subject who fashions her self-portrait and shapes her self-narrative through a process of skillful self-discovery, self-definition, and self-direction. Although pretending to have transcended the impact of an oppressive social regime is nothing but a masculinist affectation, agentic skillfulness does ensure that women's voices are not wholly subsumed by internalized ideology. Moreover, the prospect of developing these skills and expanding their range of application holds out the promise of intrepid, unprecedented essays in women's self-determination.

4. Patriarchal Cultures, Gender Normalization, and Women's Self-Determination

I have argued that internalized oppression is a systemic wrong for which feminists need to find remedies, but there is a view of culture that makes internalized oppression seem more like a paranoid fantasy that needs nothing more than a good debunking. Michelle Moody-Adams points out that successful cultures must preserve people's capacities for the exercise of judgment and discretion. "Any culture that worked to impair these capacities," she writes, "would be creating the conditions for its own demise" (Moody-Adams 1994, 307). I agree that a viable culture cannot turn its adherents into indoctrinated automatons who cannot question cultural beliefs and practices and who cannot instigate cultural change (Meyers 1993). Indeed, one implication of the account of autonomy I have been developing is that it is virtually impossible for a culture to be this repressive (for related discussion, see Chodorow 1999, Chapters 5–7). Still, I find Moody-Adams's confidence in the autonomy-preserving function of culture unduly sanguine, for I believe she underestimates the extent of cultural collusion in internalized oppression.

A thriving culture must evolve, but it must persist as well. If cultures are self-perpetuating systems, they must have built-in mechanisms that shield their beliefs and practices from criticism so zealous and damning that it triggers cultural decline or foments mass defection. Yet, the slightest acquaintance with human history confirms that cultures do not usually depend on the justice of their beliefs and practices to secure the loyalty of their adherents. What keeps them going?

Even the most unjust cultures have a willing coconspirator in human psychology's conservative bent. People commonly prefer the known over the unknown. Alas, they often prefer the security of having more or less mastered coping with a known evil over the risk of being thrown off balance by whatever might succeed it. This conservative disposition is culturally abetted. Cultures ward off the perils of internal dissension and disruption by circumscribing adherents' autonomy. Adroitly steering capacities for judgment and discretion into constructive pathways while limiting the scope of skepticism and critique enables cultures to evolve and endure. However, insofar as cultures corral autonomy skills in order to perpetuate unjust institutions and norms, they are not benignly guiding and modulating people's capacity for judgment and discretion. They are impairing it.

Cultures threaten autonomy in two principal respects. First, cultures lead people to notice some phenomena and overlook others, and they lead people to ascribe certain meanings to their experiences and to disregard other possible meanings. They do this by furnishing stock concepts and interpretive schemas that focus perception and organize reflection. Culturally entrenched concepts and interpretive schemas have countless functions, but for my present purposes the key one is framing self-portraiture and self-narration. As psychologist Jerome Bruner observes, "If the Self is a remembered self, the remembering reaches far back beyond our own birth, back to the cultural and language forms that specify the defining properties of a Self" (Bruner 1994, 53). Second, cultures valorize some agentic skills over others. They commend childrearing practices that nurture the favored skills and establish social structures that reward them, leaving other agentic skills to languish. For example, middle-class Euro-American culture prizes means/ends rationality and vigorously cultivates the skills needed to pick goals with high satisfaction yields and to plot successful goal-directed campaigns. In this culture, however, agentic skills are gendered. Although childrearing practices and reward structures do not extinguish means/ends rationality in middle-class Euro-American girls, their interpersonal skills are accentuated. The agentic skills one possesses and uses with ease secure a measure of self-understanding and self-determination. Lacking agentic skills or possessing agentic skills that are poorly developed or poorly coordinated with other skills constrains self-understanding and self-determination.

The agentic skills that a culture promotes match the social roles people are expected to play, and the stock concepts and interpretive schemas that a culture transmits provide input for these skills that is preselected and preprocessed in culturally congenial ways. Conversely, cultures suppress agentic skills that are likely to lead people to question the adequacy of culturally approved concepts and interpretive schemas and, perhaps, to condemn their cultural heritage or its core norms.

Internalized patriarchal oppression names the selections of culturally certified concepts and interpretive schemas together with the repertoires of culturally favored and disfavored agentic skills that recruit women into self-subordination. Since different cultures (and subcultures) structure women's agency differently, internalized patriarchal oppression is not uniform across cultures (or subcultures), and since different women process cultural materials differently, internalized patriarchal oppression is not uniform among women within the same culture (or subculture) either. In this book, I explore one cultural device that induces women to internalize patriarchal oppression. My focus is a subset of a particular culture's stock concepts and interpretive schemas—namely, the dominant system of tropes, mythic tales, and pictorial images that encode the various meanings of womanhood and norms applying to women in the United States today. (I shall sometimes refer to these different types of representation as *figurations of womanhood*.) My aim is to analyze how this component of gender discourse suffuses women's voices and undercuts their self-determination, to discover which agentic skills help women to repair this damage and increase their self-determination, and to identify changes in discourse and in social practices that would consolidate these gains.

I have chosen to focus on figurations of womanhood because I believe that their insidious role in internalized oppression and their egregious impact on women's self-determination have not been fully understood and theorized. What are generally taken to be the facts about gender within a given culture are encoded in captivating figurations that condense complex behavioral and psychological imperatives into memorable, emotionally compelling forms. The culturally entrenched tropes, mythic tales, and pictorial images that depict women serve as a kind of shorthand in which group norms are crystallized and through which these norms become embedded in the "geology of desire" (I borrow Barbara Herman's phrase; Herman 1991, 787). Indeed, it would not be inaccurate to say that these figurations *fossilize* gender norms in the geology of culture, for they integrate these norms into the corpus of common sense, where they are protected from criticism (Beauvoir 1989, Chapter 9; Kittay 1988; Rooney 1991). Mere social convention—normalized gender—is thus naturalized.

Phyllis Rooney quotes a passage from John Locke's *An Essay concerning Human Understanding* that is both revealing and alarming:

> All the art of rhetorick [*sic*], besides order and clearness, all the artificial and figurative application of words eloquence hath invented, are for nothing else but to insinuate wrong ideas, move the passions, and thereby mislead judgment . . . *eloquence*, like the fair sex, has too prevailing beauties in it to suffer itself ever to be spoken against. And it is vain to find fault with those arts of deceiving wherein men find pleasure to be deceived. (Locke, quoted in Rooney 1991, 84)

I agree with Locke's observation that the beauty of figurative language is beguiling and disarms rational disputation. I also agree that linguistic imagery (and its sibling, pictorial imagery) is liable to abuse. In subsequent chapters, I shall argue that there is no better illustration of how imagery can be used to "insinuate wrong ideas, move the passions, and thereby mislead judgment" than the ubiquitous figurations of womanhood in Western, patriarchal culture. However, figurations of womanhood are neither inherently misleading nor harmful, and I shall also argue that replacing patriarchal figurations with emancipatory ones is a vital feminist objective. Despite my quarrel with Locke's simplistic, unconditional condemnation of figurative language, I would urge that his central point is sound and that this passage is more insightful than he realized. In the same breath as Locke denounces the misleadingness of figurative language, he commits the sin of simile and analogizes the seductiveness of "eloquence" to the wiles of feminine charm (for more examples of philosophers relying on tropes to condemn figurative language, see Kittay 1988, 1). Ironically, his own rhetoric proves his thesis. Evidently, traditional gender imagery is *irresistibly* seductive.

The artifice of construing stereotypes as lists of prescribed or forbidden attributes and behaviors gives a false impression of how such concepts are disseminated. Figurations of womanhood convey complex ideas in an easily assimilable and nearly indelible form. Although we often have trouble taking in information and regulations, imagery sticks with us. Culturally entrenched representations of womanhood pass on gender norms without reducing them to explicit profiles of gender-compliant traits of character, explicit rules of gender-compliant comportment, and explicit edicts about gender-compliant aims. The vibrant immediacy of these figurations facilitates the transmission and retention of these messages. Thus, girls are often inducted into cultural expectations — their attitudes and behavior shaped — despite explicit instruction and parental role models to the contrary. Many parents who try to raise children in nonsexist ways are defeated by cultural influences that they are not conscious of and that consequently they cannot counteract (Valian 1998, 22–38, 58–59). In conventional households where gender norms are accepted, parental values and guidance are powerfully seconded by culture. Seductive as figurations of womanhood are, feminine norms are to a significant extent absorbed subliminally.

Figurations of womanhood carry a potent emotional charge. It is important to remember how children are introduced to this system of imagery — how one trembled when the witch appeared in a fairy tale and how one adored, perhaps revered, the kind, beauteous mothers in these stories. Children's lively imaginations and emotional susceptibility are thus enlisted to mesh norms with abiding affect. In addition, gendered tropes construct the Western world view—its conception of nature as "mother nature," its conception of creativity as "giving birth to an idea," its conception of good and evil as "the chaste woman" and "the lascivious whore."[6] Because figurations of womanhood symbolize disparate conceptual and experiential domains that concern the very fundaments of human existence, they help to unify these domains into an overarching philosophical vision. To repudiate the patriarchal stock of gender figurations is not merely to advocate women's equality and freedom, then. It is to challenge the regnant world view. As a result, cultural representations of womanhood galvanize emotional commitment and resist critique.

Encoded as a system of figurations, feminine norms are strict, yet adaptable. Figurations are open to interpretation, and this elasticity enables them to stretch to cover new situations. For instance, one might think that the mass entrance of white, middle-class women into the job market in recent decades would contradict and discredit hegemonic maternal imagery. But it didn't, for the vast majority of these female employees become mothers, and the problems of juggling competing career and parenting responsibilities are discursively represented as "women's problems" or "working mothers' problems," not "parents' problems" or "working fathers' problems" (Valian 1998, 45). Still, culturally entrenched figurations of womanhood are narrowly prescriptive, for imagery circumscribes interpretation. People who violate a culturally entrenched figuration, however derogatory it may be, provoke resentment and antagonism. A professional woman who is aggressively competitive is despised as much as a professional woman who is meek and ineffectual (Valian 1998, 291). Stuck in a no-win predicament, women cannot feel better about themselves or earn respect by conforming to masculine figurations. The constrained flexibility of gender figurations ensures their applicability in a wide range of circumstances, and this adaptability ensures their survival despite momentous social and economic change.

Lodged in women's cognitive, emotional, and motivational infrastructures—their psycho-corporeal economy—prevailing gender figurations provide the default templates for their self-portraits and their self-narratives (Haste 1994, 36–47). Unless a woman takes pains to construct her self-portrait and self-narrative in terms of unorthodox figurations of womanhood, she is likely to appropriate standard-issue, culturally furnished ones. If she does, she will perceive herself, recount her experiences, and anticipate future moves using the stock concepts and interpretive schemas that these culturally entrenched figurations encode. Sadly, though, when the system of figurations that she draws on is that of a patriarchal culture—a culture committed to the subordination of women—her self-portrait and self-narrative bespeak internalized oppression. This noxious influence notwithstanding, women who conform to norms of femininity commonly regard their lives as fulfilling natural feminine desires—their indwelling destiny as women—for their lives enact a conception of gender that has become integral to their identity and their sense of self.

Now, it might be thought that all that is needed to free women from this internalized oppression is to point out discrepancies between the idealized or vilifying cultural figurations of womanhood and the facts about women's actual characteristics and potentialities. However, it is not possible to expel a figuration from one's psycho-corporeal economy by noticing counterexamples or disconfirming statistics. Since these figurations frame women's self-portraits and self-narratives, freeing oneself from them means "drawing" one's self-portrait in a new style expressing new aesthetic values and "writing" one's self-narrative with a new plot line incorporating new themes. It means reconceiving one's identity. It comes as no surprise, then, that dry recitations of sensible reasons to disavow a subordinate role and subordinating values and desires seldom convert anyone who has internalized oppression. Since personal transformation is not so easily achieved, it is by no means obvious how women's self-determination can be augmented.

The question of how women can resist internalized oppression and increase their self-determination is the principal concern of this book. In the next five chapters, I take up a series of specific figurations of womanhood. Chapters 2 and 3 examine representations of motherhood and the mother/child relationship; Chapter 4 examines the Oedipal imagery of the family romance; Chapter 5 examines representations of feminine narcissism; and Chapter 6 examines symbolic associations between aging women and mortality. These figurations impede women's self-determination by stifling their voices and haunting their choices. In each case, I analyze the ambient murmur these figurations sustain and the ways in which this cultural noise pollution eats away at women's agentic health. In particular, I explicate how these figurations complicate the epistemology of self-knowledge —that is, the epistemology of self-portraiture and self-narration. I identify agentic skills that contribute to women's ability to displace patriarchal figurations and craft emancipatory counterfigurations; I propose social reforms designed to cultivate these skills; and I describe alternative cultural figurations of womanhood that would facilitate women's self-determination.[7] In Chapter 7, I consider the need for these changes from a different angle. Shifting from the value of self-determination for individual women to the value of justice for women as a social group, I argue that until feminist counterfigurations supplant patriarchal figurations of womanhood, women's social and economic gains will remain in jeopardy, for patriarchal figurations stoke misogyny and fuel antifeminist backlash. A culture-jamming, discursive politics must go hand-in-hand with feminist social and economic initiatives. As Audre Lorde so wisely remarked, "For women, then, poetry [in my terms, counterfiguration] is not a luxury" (Lorde 1984, 37).

CHAPTER TWO

The Rush to Motherhood: Pronatalist Discourse and Women's Agency

No choice has a more profound impact on a woman's life than her decision whether or not to become a mother.[1] Bound up with sexuality and gender identity, choices about childbearing and motherhood are emotionally gripping and socially pivotal. They affect one's attitude toward oneself: self-esteem may be enhanced, or it may suffer. They condition others' judgments: although very young women, aging women, and poor women are discouraged from becoming mothers, women who prefer not to have any children under any circumstances are commonly reproached for selfishness or pitied for immaturity. They position women with respect to a fundamental social structure and moral situation: the family. As a legal institution, the family sanctions some childbearing decisions and censures others. As a customary nexus of affection and sustenance, it assigns distinct tasks and responsibilities to different family members. Through motherhood decisions, then, women assume an indelible social and moral identity and incur or disavow various caregiving obligations. Moreover, since the family does not exist in isolation from other social systems, women's motherhood decisions have implications for their extradomestic aspirations. As a result of the interpenetration of the family and the economy and the organization of the economy to suit a prototypical employee, who is supposed to be exempt from caregiving obligations, maternity usually limits women's employment opportunities, their prospects for promotion, and their long-range earning power. In sum, a woman's motherhood decision is crucial to her personal well-being, definitive of her social persona, and predictive of her economic horizons.

Because motherhood decisions are singularly personal and unsurpassably important, feminists have long struggled to secure women's autonomy over these decisions. Demanding that women's right to procreate be respected, feminists have opposed coercive methods of curbing fertility, such as forced sterilization and withholding welfare supplements for new babies. In addition, they have campaigned for the right to choose *not* to procreate—that is, for fully funded contraception and unrestricted access to abortion.

One result of these initiatives in the United States is that women's motherhood decisions are now surrounded by a highly voluntaristic rhet- oric. Arguing that women should be free to choose whether to bring a pregnancy to term, the abortion rights movement dubs its position *pro-choice*. Similarly, the expression *family planning* presumes that the timing of reproduction is a matter of choice. It is worth noticing, however, that the conception of choice invoked by advocates of reproductive freedom is lopsided. The idea is to empower women to delay or space out childbearing. The option of altogether abstaining is seldom, if ever, explicitly mentioned. Indeed, it is implicitly denied. Since the current (albeit outmoded) paradigm of the family is a social unit composed of a heterosexual couple and their children, the concept of family planning does not include refusing to have children, for that would amount to family prevention, which sounds like blasphemy in an era of pietistic pronouncements about "family values." Evidently, the scope of socially condoned autonomy with respect to motherhood is far less extensive than it initially appears to be. Indeed, I am convinced that even where both the right to procreate and the right to refrain from procreating are tolerably secure, women's decisions about childbearing and motherhood are seldom as autonomous as they could be. In my judgment, then, winning these legal guarantees, although absolutely vital, still falls short of achieving feminist emancipatory goals.

Certain features of the view of gendered, individualized identity and the skills-based view of self-determination I developed in Chapter 1 make them especially well suited to the task of analyzing women's motherhood decisions. My account of self-determination is designed to accommodate a socially and relationally situated self. Autonomous individuals are enculturated. For women, this means that they internalize oppression—that is, subordinating norms influence what they are like and what they aspire to be and do. Still, as individuals, they assimilate these norms in distinctive ways. Thus, my view of gendered, individualized identity allows us to recognize the impact of subordinating reproductive imperatives on women's deepest sense of self without assuming that all women have identical attitudes toward motherhood. Moreover, my skills-based view of self-determination enables us to understand not only how patriarchal noise can overwhelm women's voices and choices but also how women can find their own voices and make their own choices. Women's capacity to interpret and to autonomously enact or resist subordinating norms depends on their agentic skills. Likewise, the extent of their self-determination depends on which agentic skills they possess, how well developed and coordinated these skills are, and whether these skills are applied to a particular decision. Thus, my account of self-determination differentiates degrees of autonomy both when the individual elects a conventional path and when the individual heads out on an uncharted route. Agentic skills endow women with the capacity to fashion self-portraits and self-narratives in their own voices and to lead their own lives. Limited or idle agentic skills deprive women of their own voices and undermine their self-determination whether they opt for motherhood or against it.

I begin this examination of motherhood decisions by listening to women. I review and interpret women's testimony about their decisions to become or not to become mothers, and I urge that women's autonomy in this respect is often compromised (Section 1). In response to this rather bleak assessment, an objection might arise to the effect that I am demanding more autonomy over motherhood decisions than anyone could realistically have or want. I address this concern by arguing that autonomy over whether or not to become a mother is possible as well as desirable (Section 2). To grasp how such autonomy can be gained, it is necessary to identify the social conditions that commonly defeat it and the strategies some women have used to overcome these constraints. Thus, I diagnose a substantial social obstacle to women's autonomy over motherhood decisions—I call it the discourse of *matrigyno-idolatry* (Section 3). After showing how some women have used agentic skills to circumvent this pronatalist onslaught, I recommend two ways in which feminist politics can contest this hostile discursive environment and expand the scope of all women's self-determination (Section 4).

1. Women's Testimony

The prevalence of talk of reproductive freedom and choice notwithstanding, there is abundant evidence that women's motherhood decisions—decisions not to have children as well as decisions to have them—are lacking from the standpoint of autonomy.[2] While it would be wrong to claim that no woman ever makes a fully autonomous reproductive decision, it is important to recognize that the women who do are exceptional. Most women's reproductive autonomy seems quite severely compromised.

Autonomy can be difficult to detect, for it takes various forms, and the threats to autonomy vary with people's circumstances. Many childbearing decisions are collaborative decisions that bring into play the peculiar psychodynamics of particular couples and, in many cases, the power imbalances that commonly shadow heterosexual relationships. When heterosexual couples make these joint decisions, it is not unusual for the women to suspect that they are being unduly influenced by their partners and to feel that they are going along with plans and projects less out of conviction than out of habitual deference or a desire to minimize friction.[3] Yet, since the autonomous subject is neither insular nor static, and since autonomous individuals are equipped to cope with changing circumstances, finding oneself in a new, possibly distressing situation can clarify what one cares about most deeply and what one really wants to do. As Anne Donchin observes, some women who are not aware of having made a conscious decision—even, I would add, some women whose pregnancies are due to contraceptive failure—might nevertheless "rejoice in their pregnancy and affirm it as their own" (Donchin 1996, 483; also see Veevers's discussion of becoming aware of an "implicit decision" not to have children, Veevers 1980, 23–25). The possibility of retrospective autonomy compounds the difficulty of detecting autonomous motherhood decisions (Meyers 1989, 54–55). The standard picture of autonomy is prospective. An individual has an array of options and, after thoughtful consideration of each, picks one. However, since one can retrospectively realize that spontaneous, perhaps uncharacteristic, behavior that was not thought out in advance aptly expressed one's values and sense of self, autonomy can be conferred on past actions. Autonomy must accommodate the dense texture of human lives—the give-and-take of relationships, the need for self-knowledge to keep pace with an evolving self, and the circuitous pathways to self-definition. Although this labyrinthine complexity may erode confidence in our ability to discriminate precise degrees of autonomy, it does not follow that we cannot use the notion of skillful self-determination to estimate approximate levels of autonomy or to compare different individuals' autonomy.[4]

Unfortunately, the tendentiousness of the social psychological literature on motherhood decisions makes it quite difficult to figure out how women are thinking about this issue. Researchers focus on "abnormal" phenomena—women who opt out of motherhood and, more recently, teenage mothers and women who pursue motherhood through technological means. Reports about the decision-making experiences of women who choose to have children and who easily become pregnant are scarce. Moreover, studies of women who choose not to have children and studies of women who resort to reproductive technologies in order to have children seem bent on proving either that these decisions are truly free, legitimate, and even admirable, or else that these women are hapless victims. They seem to be in the grip of the polarization within autonomy theory that I criticized in Chapter 1. Also, work on adolescents is more concerned with how to prevent pregnancy or which services are most beneficial to needy mothers than it is with these women's decision-making processes. In these studies, the bureaucrat's managerial orientation displaces the value of enhancing women's autonomy. Methodological debates over models of choice further complicate the picture. Some investigators are eager to demonstrate the influence of childhood experience on identity consolidation and adult choice, while others seek to show that the constellation of opportunities and constraints and the balance of likely rewards and penalties that an adult woman faces overpower childhood socialization and determine reproductive outcomes. None seeks to identify or assess the skills women bring to bear on their decisions. Plainly, these empirical investigations cannot be taken at face value.

I seek to compensate for the deficiencies of these research reports by focusing mainly on the quoted interview material and by analyzing correspondences between narratives of "abnormal" motherhood experiences and the narratives of "normal" motherhood experiences I was able to locate.[5] I have concluded that, despite the researchers' divergent models and aims, several consistent findings can be extracted from their work. Before I proceed, however, a caveat is in order. To make an accurate assessment of any individual's autonomy, it is necessary to know far more about how adept she is in using agentic skills and far more about how she did (or did not) put them to use in reaching her decision than these studies usually reveal. Thus, my approach in this section is to draw attention to patterns in women's comments that show up across a number of studies, and I shall argue that these patterns point to autonomy deficits—that is, curtailed use of agentic skills—in many women's decision making about motherhood. But to anticipate my discussion in Section 4 and to avoid painting an overly gloomy picture, I shall briefly note some exceptions to these patterns at the end of this section.

An arresting feature of much of the testimony is that it clusters either around the pole of casualness or around the pole of adamance. Some women regard having children as an inevitable part of life:

> "I can't remember if I ever thought I had a choice. I think I thought you just did it. You grow up and you have children." (Ireland 1993, 70)

> "When I was a child, I assumed I would have children. It was one of those 'of course' kinds of things." (Lang 1991, 96)

> "I don't remember a time when I didn't want to be a mother. . . . I never dreamed there was anything like an alternative lifestyle to being a mother." (Ireland 1993, 32)

Such nonchalance seems to be the rule. Most people presume that children are necessary to personal fulfillment and never consider not having children (Veevers 1980, 40–41; Rogers and Larson, 1988, 48). Culturally transmitted mythologies of rapturous motherhood subsidize this blithe refusal to reflect (Veevers 1980, 42). Barbara Omolade points out, as well, that cultural idealizations of marriage influence young, African-American women's procreative choices (Omolade 1995, 274–275). Presumably, these reassuring matrimonial images also fuel the procreative choices that women of other races and age groups make. In fact, a study of women who expected to become mothers found 70 percent of them "extraordinarily illusionistic" about what being a mother and caring for a child is actually like (cited in Lang 1991, 82).[6] Heedlessly imbibing cultural attitudes valorizing procreation together with a romanticized image of motherhood and heterosexual partnership removes motherhood from the realm of choice and preempts exercising agentic skills.

For some women, though, this casualness is an out-of-reach luxury. Two groups of women express vehemently positive and negative attitudes toward childbearing. When women have difficulty conceiving, they often display a monomaniacal dedication to infertility treatment and evince heartrending angst about the possibility of failure:

"We'll sell the car, the house even, if it comes to it. . . . There was nothing I wouldn't give up if it meant we could have a child." (Lasker and Borg 1994, 11)

"We both feel like eunuchs." (Ireland 1993, 21)

"Pain doesn't really explain it. It is a hollow, empty feeling of not being good enough." (Ireland 1993, 37)

The flip side of automatic childbearing is obsession, anxiety, and despair. It seems, then, that the casual assumption that one will become a mother masks a desire that has the rigid, obdurate character of a compulsion. Asked what she feared most when she was in eighth grade, one interview subject mentions no threat to her safety or to her opportunity to develop her talents. Rather, she recalls dreading "not being able to have children" (Ireland 1993, 33).[7]

Still, there is a group of women who do not share the assumption that childlessness implies defect and ensures dissatisfaction. These women, who have been termed *early articulators*, decide against motherhood well before marriage and express intransigent opposition to having children:

"I have never, not even for a second, ever wanted to have a child." (Lang 1991, 77)

"I don't feel like this [not having children] was ever a decision. . . . It's just never been an issue with me . . . and I'd say I've felt this way since I was about twelve." (Lang 1991, 79)

"Even as a young child, I knew I would never have children. I just knew I wouldn't. . . . I even broke up my second engagement because I could see he really wanted a family." (Lang 1991, 76)

This tiny minority of nonconformist women are certain that they want nothing to do with having a child and that having one would wreak havoc with their lives.

The vast majority of women are absolutely sure that having a child is one of the most important things in life (quite possibly *the* most important thing in life) and that not having a child would be devastating. What these typical women have in common with early articulators, though, is that a strong desire about childbearing is in place at an early age. The early formation of these desires would pose no obstacle to self-determination if women used their agentic skills later to consider whether to act on these desires. But most women experience desires about motherhood as psychic postulates that govern the course of their adult lives. Thus, desires about motherhood are generally formed well before women are equipped to make autonomous decisions, and, implacable as these desires are, they are subsequently insulated from open-minded reflection and modification.

Most women seem impelled into or away from maternity; however, there is a group of voluntarily childless women who do not fit this profile. This group, which is about twice the size of the early articulator group, has been dubbed the *postponers*. Ambivalence and indecision mark the postponers' relation to maternity:

> "I have periodically gotten into a big stew about it . . . and I feel I can't keep on doing that forever. . . . It pulsates." (Landa 1990, 152)

36) 37

> "I fear I wouldn't be a fulfilled woman, that I'll wake up at fifty and say, 'You blew it.' But I go through entire days thinking of what I'm able to do because I don't have children." (Safer 1996, 57)

> "I really *want* to want children. . . . I keep hoping that, when the time comes for me to have a family, I'll just automatically get ready. . . . I really hope I will be a happy mother someday . . . because it's so much of a hassle to make a decision *not* to have the family." (K. Gerson 1985, 133)

> "I always took it for granted that I'd have kids . . . [but having kids] always seemed like something I would do in the future. I think I was waiting to really want to do it. . . . Really, I was waiting for the desire to make the decision for me, I guess. But it didn't. I don't *not* want to have children. . . . It has started to look as though not making the decision to *have* kids was the same as making the decision *not* to." (Lang 1991, 85)

> "Am I feeling bad because it's something I really wanted and don't have? or is it feeling bad because it is something other people have and I always have to say I don't? I just don't know." (Ireland 1993, 65)

> "Sometimes I feel like I was gypped, even though I wasn't gypped. It was my own choice, but I feel, why did I choose this? What made me choose not to have children when I really in my heart want to have children? . . . How did this happen?" (K. Gerson 1985, 143–144)

The principal reason postponers give for forgoing childbearing is the value they place on self-determination (Houseknecht 1987, 377; Landa 1990,

148; Safer 1996, 104). Yet, terms like *drift, passivity*, and *unconscious* recur in analyses of these women's choices, and these quotations lend support to these characterizations (Ireland 1993, 42; Lang 1991, 73; K. Gerson 1985, 135). Unable to acknowledge their doubts about motherhood or unable to figure out how to reconcile motherhood with their other aims, postponers tell themselves that motherhood will eventually happen. But it doesn't, and many of them are left feeling confused and sometimes regretful. Spared the inexorable desires that propel most women to become mothers and some women to avoid it assiduously, postponers end up in limbo, unable or unwilling to use their agentic skills to sort out their values and desires and hence unable to finalize their decision. Bewilderment is no less inimical to self-determination than compulsion.

It might seem that I have not given postponers enough credit. They may not be deluding themselves into thinking that they are merely delaying motherhood. Perhaps they are clearheadedly putting off making a decision about motherhood—keeping their options open until they are sure what they really want to do. Or perhaps they are cleverly outfoxing norms linking femininity and motherhood by representing themselves as postponers rather than refusers.

It is possible that complete interview transcripts would disclose such complex motivations. However, to judge by these excerpts, neither of these readings is likely to be substantiated. These women speak of wanting to want children, hoping a desire for children will overtake them, and feeling cheated because they really want to have children but never did. If these women are autonomously transgressing gender norms, they evidently cannot admit it, even when they are guaranteed anonymity. Nor do they lay claim to a strategy of autonomous delay. Some of them speak of the desire for motherhood as something that may eventually happen to them and make the decision for them. If these women are mobilizing their agentic skills and taking charge of this issue, they are keeping it a secret. Indeed, if being able to tell one's own story in one's own voice is a mark of self-determination, these women's autonomy is suspect. However, other postponers speak of seemingly irresolvable conflicts within their value systems and between their nonmaternal status and social expectations. Although these women are now deeply divided, it is altogether possible that they will apply their agentic skills to these conflicts and eventually reach an autonomous decision.

A study of teen mothers opens another window on women's shaky grip on autonomy vis-à-vis motherhood. None of the subjects in this study said she intended to become pregnant (Horowitz 1995, 153). But as their pregnancies progressed, all of them eventually said they intended to become mothers (Horowitz 1995, 155). If Horowitz's analysis is reliable, however, there is no reason to regard their professed intentions as autonomous. (Unfortunately, Horowitz does not quote extensively from her interviews with her subjects, and so we cannot hear their stories in their voices.) Neither abortion nor adoption were considered serious options (Horowitz 1995, 153). Moreover, the pregnant women "were *instructed* by peers and mothers that they were *expected* to 'intend' to become mothers" (Horowitz 1995, 153; emphasis added). Since social norms foreclosed the only ways to refuse motherhood, and since the people closest to them were prodding them to embrace motherhood, it appears that these women were immersed in a social milieu that provided little or no support for skillful self-interrogation and individualized decision making. Thus, their commitments to motherhood seem more like socially engineered default positions than autonomous choices.

While the women Horowitz studies are subjected to a veritable deluge of blatant promaternal pressure, there are less overt, more universal social pressures that parallel the ones these young women face. In the United States today, having children promises to solve two perennial human problems, namely, meaninglessness and loneliness. For the countless people who find their jobs neither interesting nor fulfilling, children represent a way to infuse value and significance into everyday life (Omolade 1995, 279). Also, since society is splintered into family units, and since social interaction is organized around family life in many communities, children ward off isolation. Of course, meeting one's needs for meaning and companionship is extremely important and, in principle, entirely compatible with self-determination. The threat to self-determination stems from the fact that many people have little choice about *how* to meet them.[8] In view of the fact that social structures make having children the only feasible way for many people to satisfy these needs, it is reasonable for them to opt for parenthood. Still, if most people found their work more worthwhile and found it easier to maintain deep, long-term friendships apart from parent-child networks, there would be more reason to think women were choosing motherhood for its intrinsic value and special rewards and less reason to consider their autonomy with respect to motherhood at risk.

Whether because imperious desires about motherhood exert a seemingly despotic power over women's lives, because women's feelings about motherhood are so repressed or so conflicted that they cannot figure out what they want, or because social expectations, personal privations, or cultural myths stifle women's self-reflection, self-determination is elusive.[9] There are exceptions, of course. To become mothers, lesbians who have not had children in a heterosexual relationship must overcome formidable obstacles—the cultural stereotype that excludes them from maternity as well as the resistance of adoption agencies and reproductive technology clinics to assist them. Thus, lesbians cannot avoid making a conscious choice, and there is evidence that their choices are often carefully considered—that they examine their motives for having children and that they think through their plans for raising their children before they become parents (Weston 1991, 190–191). Still, such sober, indepth reflection is neither universal in the lesbian community, nor is it confined to this group. In a rich and candid autobiographical narrative, Jeanne Safer, a married heterosexual, relates the lengthy and complex reflective process through which she decided against becoming a mother (Safer 1996, 7–42). Safer's attunement to her feelings, her honesty about her needs and goals, her lucid and affectionate interpretation of her relationship to her parents, and her efforts to gain a realistic grasp of what mothering would be like argue for the autonomy of her choice. In the same vein, describing the conclusion of her decision process, one of Mardy Ireland's childfree subjects offers a tantalizing glimpse of the satisfaction that self-determination can bring: "The knowing started as a kind of intellectual acceptance, then it sank down into my heart with emotional acceptance, and finally came down into my belly. . . . the deep knowing is a great relief" (Ireland 1993, 81).

These autonomous lesbians and their heterosexual counterparts are hardly typical, however. When asked why they want or don't want to have children, most people are flummoxed. Highly articulate individuals lose their fluency, grope for words, and stumble around, seizing on incompatible explanations and multiplying justifications (Veevers 1980, 15; Lasker and Borg 1994, 14–15).[10] Overt defensiveness about motherhood is also common. Mothers and childfree women alike glorify their own choices and scorn the other group's choices (Veevers 1980, 122; K. Gerson 1985, 190; Horowitz 1995, 153). If anything, such awkwardness in accounting for oneself and testiness about one's chosen course bespeak autonomy deficits. If women were autonomously becoming mothers or declining to, we would expect to hear a splendid chorus of distinctive, confident voices, but instead we are hearing a shrill cacophony of trite tunes.

2. The Scope of Autonomy: Can/Should Motherhood Decisions Be Autonomous?

That decisions about motherhood combine mind-boggling complexity with daunting momentousness militates against supposing that these decisions can ever be autonomous. Unconscious forces are opaque and indecipherable yet, for all one knows, decisive. Darwinian mandates seem to hold sway, yet the relation between genetic coding, on the one hand, and subjectivity and desire, on the other, seems unfathomable. Likewise, disentangling one's own desires and values from internalized social ideology seems vital, yet any boundary demarcated between them seems artificial, arbitrary, and fragile. Disquieting, too, is the fact that choosing to become a mother is irrevocable, although no one can accurately anticipate and fully appreciate the consequences of this choice.[11] The possibility of autonomously deciding whether or not to become a mother might be rejected, then, because reproduction is assumed to be biologically programmed, because being a mother is considered an incontrovertible value, because the lifelong ramifications of the decision seem to be beyond individual powers of comprehension, or because the individual is thought to be too enmeshed in her social context or too driven by her unconscious motives to be self-determining. Nevertheless, I shall argue that autonomy with respect to motherhood is both possible and desirable.

Most of the time, settled, virtually indisputable values preempt critical reflection. That is why, for many people, "To be, or not to be?" does not seem like a reasonable question to pose every morning before breakfast. All the same, it might be thought that people can and should rationally judge whether life is worthwhile. But once one has made this determination and incorporated it into one's value system, it need not be reconsidered and reaffirmed unless reasons to doubt its wisdom come to light. Although advance value certification of this sort often makes sense, it is unconvincing in regard to the value of life, for under reasonably auspicious conditions, reaching the conclusion that life is worth living is all but inevitable. Moreover, any reasons one might adduce to support it pale in comparison to the brute inexorability of the life urge and the sheer obviousness of the desirability of living. It is hard, then, to see what makes this conviction autonomous, for going through the motions of rationally endorsing life is fatuous, if not pathological—reminiscent of Woody Allen's hilarious, angst-stricken monologues, but hardly convincing as an exercise in autonomy.

Where there is only one real option and no self-conscious choice, autonomy may seem beside the point. I believe that this assessment seems self-evident, however, because of the prevalence of a hyper-cerebral understanding of autonomy. Contrary to this view, it seems to me that values can be (and often are) embodied—embedded in the flesh and enacted by a body that is sensitive to somatic cues and skilled both in preserving states of well-being and in relieving states of uneasiness or discomfort. The unthinking embodiment of values that are all but incontrovertible— so universal, so indispensable to enjoying other goods, and so seldom in conflict with other values—is advantageous. It is just as well that people usually are not capable of deciding that life is not worth living, for, if they could easily reach this conclusion, some would surely make disastrous mistakes. In addition, it is plausible to think that people are doing what they really want to do when they take ordinary measures to sustain themselves or protect themselves from harm. Although they seem to lack control over what they are doing because their course of conduct has not been preceded by a process of rational deliberation and planning, their value-imbued flesh is directing their conduct, and I see no good reason to exclude value-imbued flesh from the true self. The subject of autonomous action is not a mind that contingently inhabits and supervises a body. Autonomy skills draw on and integrate mental and physical capabilities. Were it not for the "somatophobia" bred of the misogyny-spiked, metaphysical dualism that has so powerfully influenced the course of Western philosophy (I borrow Elizabeth Spelman's evocative term [1988, 30]), the marvelous capabilities of the human body, including its receptivity to values and its ability to enact them, would surely have been noticed and discussed in connection with autonomy before now.[12]

Still, when life goes tragically awry, people are obliged to weigh the value of life. Terrible personal misfortune, such as severe, unrelievable suffering or debilitating, fatal illness, or social cataclysm, such as genocide or the rise of a totalitarian leader, call the superordinate value of continued existence into question. Under these circumstances, there is nothing absurd about deliberately renewing or repudiating one's commitment to life, and it is crucial for autonomous subjects to get a critical purchase on this issue.

My comments about autonomy and the value of life bear on the autonomy of women's decisions about whether or not to become mothers in several respects. First, if the value of motherhood is embedded in women's bodies, and if, therefore, women's critical reflection about becoming mothers is usually superfluous, it must be shown that being a mother is an all but incontrovertible value comparable to life itself. I shall take up this question in more detail shortly, but let me suggest at this point that elevating motherhood to this status would amount to reinstating the doctrine that motherhood is women's destiny. Second, that people can and sometimes do autonomously make life and death decisions shows that neither the momentousness nor the irreversibility of a decision entails that it cannot be made autonomously. Whatever the obstacles to autonomously making such life-defining decisions may be, then, they are not insuperable. However, third, if the superfluousness of regular critical reflection on whether to go on living stems in part from a biologically programmed drive to survive, it might seem that women's critical reflection on motherhood decisions must be superfluous, too. If embodied values derive from instinct (or biological programming), if instinctual behavior lies outside the scope of autonomy, and if there is a procreative instinct, thoughtful weighing of motherhood decisions would be a better subject for a stand-up comedienne's routine than it is for autonomous women.

Although I am not sure exactly what instinctual behavior is or which types of behavior qualify as instinctual, I am confident that some types of behavior that many people would consider instinctual do not entail values that autonomous subjects must enact. For example, copulation and other erotically pleasurable behavior is widely regarded as instinctual, and yet celibacy is an ascetic spiritual discipline that has a long and transcultural history. Likewise, most cultures prescribe sexual continence, if not total abstinence, for unwed women. Admittedly, there is much to be said against these practices of deprivation and these norms of chastity—they are unhealthy, they are unfair to women, and so forth. My point is not to endorse them. Rather, my point is that, despite the fact that the drive for sexual gratification seems likely to count as instinctual, these practices and norms presuppose that sexual desire is amenable to autonomous regulation, even repudiation. Agentic skills can override instinct.

Still, sexuality is a fascinating case. Although sexuality seems inextricable from our biological makeup, there is no reason to suppose that in every respect sexuality is biologically determined. On the contrary, there is good reason to suppose that in many respects it is socially constructed, and yet people experience it, by and large, as a given. Few ever question the desirability of sexual satisfaction. Few see switching sexual orientation as feasible. Even the content of erotic fantasy has an obsessional, intractable character. For most people the arena of autonomy with respect to sexuality is sharply circumscribed. However, it is doubtful that we should be complacent about this limitation.

Sandra Bartky's discussion of women's masochistic sexual fantasies highlights a troubling dimension of this pervasive sexual heteronomy (see Chapter 1, Section 1). Bartky, recall, describes the predicament of P, a feminist who is beset by masochistic sexual fantasies (1990, 46). According to P's feminist analysis, such fantasies eroticize male dominance and thus help to perpetuate oppressive gender relations. Yet, P's sexual pleasure depends on imagining scenes of mortifying defilement. Her principles at odds with her desire, P is estranged from herself. But her desire remains invested in these fantasies despite moral suasion and psychotherapy. As Bartky observes, feminism lacks "an effective political practice around issues of personal transformation," and consequently women are not in a position to "decolonize" their own imaginations (1990, 61). Lamentably, P cannot achieve autonomous control over her erotic imagination.

Biological dispositions do not necessarily preclude autonomy. Social strictures can thwart autonomy. The issue is not nature versus culture. The issue is malign compulsion, such as P's patriarchally induced masochistic fantasies, versus benign desire, such as one's sexual orientation.

It is clear that having children is not a malign compulsion. Although some feminists trace women's subordination to childbearing and/or childrearing and urge women to eschew motherhood, the vast majority of feminists regard motherhood as compatible in principle with feminist ideals and focus on critiquing social attitudes and policies that devalue and penalize women's reproductive activities. I agree that there is no inherent conflict between feminist aims and motherhood. There is, however, a manifest conflict between feminism and the pronatalist dogma that motherhood is necessary to fulfillment as a woman, and there are numerous reasons to consider women's gaining autonomous control over motherhood decisions a prime feminist objective.

First, if individuals are unique, and if their personalities and talents are enormously diverse, having children cannot be the best route, or even a viable route, to personal fulfillment for every woman. For some women, motherhood proves to be a persistent source of frustration and anguish as well as a lifelong distraction from more compelling interests and goals.

Second, motherhood continues to economically disadvantage women. Adolescents who bear children and assume responsibility for raising them have difficulty completing their education and finding decently remunerated work. The 1996 gutting of the federal AFDC (Aid to Families with Dependent Children) program in the United States has increased the economic peril of solo mothers exponentially. Moreover, mothers who live with male partners and who do not work outside the home are vulnerable to impoverishment in the aftermath of separation or divorce. Yet, working outside the home does not adequately protect mothers from this hazard, for they often find career advancement stalled. Since mothers serve as the primary caregivers in most families, they are obliged to take time off to meet their children's needs or to fill in when paid childcare arrangements fall through. In addition, their "leisure" time is typically consumed by homemaking tasks—cooking, cleaning, and, of course, caring for the children. Job performance and hence salary increments are often casualties of this physically and emotionally grueling domestic regimen. Despite expanded paternal participation in childcare in some social sectors and despite some employers' parent-accommodating programs, such as on-site daycare and flextime, the economic costs of motherhood remain substantial. Feminists should continue to campaign against these socially inflicted liabilities. However, since these costs and the specter of poverty are unlikely to be eliminated in the foreseeable future, feminists should also be concerned with ensuring that women do not assume that motherhood is an incontrovertible, embodied value and that they are empowered to make autonomous decisions about whether they want to become mothers.

It might seem that once these injustices have been overcome—if society fulfilled its obligation to support children and if communal childrearing practices were in place—autonomy with respect to becoming a mother would cease to be of paramount importance. In my view, however, autonomy would take on a quite different complexion, while remaining as important as ever. Just as many women are now using their agentic skills to autonomously negotiate various kinds of coparenting schemes, women in a postpatriarchal society would need to use their agentic skills to autonomously create and sustain childrearing communities. Likewise, just as women who can now trust their prospective coparents to do their share and whose economic advantages relieve them of worries about paying a child's expenses can concentrate on the intrinsic values of bringing a child into the world and the personal meanings that act and the ensuing mother-child relationship have for her, so too women in a postpatriarchal society could set aside nuts-and-bolts exigencies and focus their attention on core issues of value and meaning. I would also expect conversations about the meanings a new child would have for the parental partnership or for the childrearing community to be salient for many women. If mothers were no longer assigned sole responsibility for childcare and devalued for this work, their autonomous decision making would undoubtedly assume a more relational mode.

Still, it does not follow that women should relinquish their autonomy and submit to a partner's or a group's wishes. On the contrary, for the same reasons that postpatriarchal societies should guarantee women's right to abortion, it would remain desirable for women to marshal their agentic skills when participating in deliberations about becoming mothers. Moreover, we must not forget that some women will not want to have children or join childrearing collectives under any circumstances. A feminism that is responsive to women's diversity must accord these women's interests equal respect, and their interests confirm the need for feminists to regard women's autonomy over motherhood decisions as a prime and ineliminable concern.

Third, becoming a mother can pose a threat to women's health. Pregnancy and birth are not without danger. Mortality rates for abortion in the United States are considerably lower than for giving birth.[13] More serious still, by playing on infertile women's feelings of inadequacy and shame, the predatory reproductive technology industry peddles painful, risky, and expensive treatments that are frequently ineffective.[14] Lack of autonomy makes women easy targets for these blandishments. In addition, there is evidence that childcare can be instrumental in the onset of psychological disorders, such as depression (Oakley 1981, 80). Plainly, childbearing and childrearing can be detrimental to the well-being of individual women. Again, to the extent that better health policy could ameliorate these harms, feminists should be advocating appropriate reforms. But women's health is not all that is at stake; their control over which risks they assume is also in question. Thus, feminists should be working to secure women's autonomy over motherhood decisions, while also working to minimize the health risks women face.

Along with these personal considerations, childbearing raises issues of social morality. On the one hand, fascism, racism, and militarism converge ideologically on pronatalism. "Our" women's alleged duty to bear children not only offsets high birth rates among "inferior" peoples, it fills the ranks of the infantry. Thus, the xenophobic French politician, Jean-Marie Le Pen recently reminded "French" women—in his parlance, this category excludes French women of Jewish or African descent—of their duty to procreate. On the other hand, despite recent worldwide drops in fertility rates, overpopulation, when properly extricated from racist undercurrents, remains a serious problem. Although famines have been caused by avoidable distributional bottlenecks as opposed to unavoidable supply shortages, and although we have the agricultural and industrial capacity to sustain many more people than presently exist (Sen 1990), pollution and crowding are not negligible problems, and it is doubtful that we can rely on technological advances to solve them. To condemn the cruelty of coercive restraints on procreation is not to absolve individuals of their responsibility to confront the ecological and social consequences of their own childbearing decisions.

Motherhood is by no means a malign compulsion, for there are plenty of good reasons why a woman might want to have children. But neither is motherhood simply a benign desire that should be accepted without question. Since there are both prudential and social reasons to question the desirability of becoming a mother, maternity is not an all but incontrovertible embodied value. Moreover, even if most women are biologically disposed to want to have children, we have seen that it does not follow that autonomous reflection and choice are impossible. Since there is ample evidence that few women make fully autonomous decisions about whether or not to become mothers, and since there are compelling reasons for women to gain autonomous control over these decisions, it is puzzling that feminists have given little attention to theorizing how motherhood could be brought within the scope of autonomous reflection and action.[15] In my judgment, it is incumbent on feminists to contest the social conditions that prevent so many women from making fully autonomous decisions about becoming mothers.

3. Pronatalist Discourse—Matrigyno-idolatry

Plainly, I cannot address all of the social issues that the problem of autonomy and motherhood raises here. What I propose to do is to revisit the theme of voice and self-determination and to focus my remaining remarks on the ways in which culturally entrenched tropes, mythic tales, and pictorial images that bond womanhood to motherhood usurp women's voices and endanger their autonomy. What is so pernicious about pronatalist discourse, in my view, is that it harnesses highly directive enculturation to unconscious processes and protects the resulting psychic structures from change by codifying and consecrating them in standard-issue self-portraits and self-narratives. In pursuing this line of thought, I shall rely on work in psychoanalytic theory to link the cultural context to the individual woman and her decision-making capacities, and I shall urge that a feminist account of autonomy and a pro-autonomy feminist agenda must be concerned with women's capacity to contend with the pronatalist figurative regime.

The discursive setting of women's decisions about motherhood is overwhelmingly pronatalist. Heterosexuality is not only normative, it is imbued with a procreation imperative. Diverse religious traditions mandate procreative heterosexuality by condemning "barren" marriages. Moreover, they figure the woman as the mother. Marian imagery, for example, powerfully identifies womanhood with motherhood and represents the mother as a beatific, munificent dispenser of love and forgiveness. Freud's twentieth-century narrative of femininity outfits this theological gender ideology in secular, psychological garb (for details, see Chapter 5, Section 3). His account of the emergence of the "normal" woman is simultaneously the story of her erotic attraction to men and the story of her desire to bear children. Curiously, few feminist psychoanalytic revisionists sever this link. In the arena of social ideology, the doctrine of "true womanhood," which declares childbearing to be women's destiny, and the "cult of domesticity," which elaborates this destiny into a childrearing function, have deep roots in the baleful history of reproductive politics in the United States (Petchesky 1985, 74–82; May 1988, 135–161).[16] This heritage is regularly refurbished and revitalized for image consumers. Popular media, such as magazines, television, and movies, fortify the pronatalist juggernaut by depicting motherhood as the only creditable form of fulfillment for women (Franzwa 1974; Peck 1974; Kaplan 1994, 258–267). This vast system of representations collapses womanhood into motherhood and idolizes the mother. Hence I call this pronatalist discourse *matrigyno-idolatry*.[17]

Ever resilient, matrigyno-idolatry flourishes despite (maybe because of) women's political and economic advances. Ever adaptable, matrigynist figurations proliferate to beguile a changing audience. As one interview subject comments, "I think the only reason I'm considering having children right now is because it's *heresy* not to consider having children" (K. Gerson 1985, 164; emphasis added). She knows whereof she speaks.

Regrettably, feminists have sometimes colluded in matrigyno-idolatry. Margaret Sanger famously proclaimed, "Woman must have her freedom — the fundamental freedom of choosing whether or not she will be a mother and how many children she will have" (Petchesky 1985, 89). Yet, to gain acceptance for contraception, Sanger capitulated to her medical coalition partners, who took the position that doctors should have the exclusive right to dispense birth control and that dispensation should be limited to cases in which pregnancy would be harmful to the woman's health (Petchesky 1985, 90). Contemporary feminists have proven no more sensitive to the dangers of pronatalist discourse. Possibly the most blatant instance of "feminist" matrigynism is Luce Irigaray's stunning declaration: "It is necessary for us to discover and assert that we are always mothers once we are women" (Irigaray 1991, 43). More subtle, but no less egregious, matrigynist formulations can be found in other current feminist scholarship.

Negative stereotypes of childfree women match and buttress idealized matrigynist figurations.[18] Through the figure of the witch who consorts with the forces of evil, the childless woman is portrayed as an outcast, and her freedom and vitality are branded wicked. In psychoanalytic phraseology, the witch represents the woman with a "masculinity complex"—the selfish, hard-driving career woman, lately vilified as the "corporate bitch/ ball-breaker." Defanged, the witch becomes the more ambiguous figure of the spinster. As the spinster, the childless woman is portrayed as a failure, for she has achieved neither of the defining feminine goals, namely, marriage and motherhood. Yet, she seems more pathetic than odious— narrow, rigid, and dry, to be sure, but effectively neutralized in her aseptic isolation. While the spinster issues an unmistakable warning to girls and young women—"See how dreadful it is to miss your chance for procreative, heterosexual bliss"—she is as much an object of pity as contempt.

It is noteworthy, as well, that the feminist social psychological literature on childbearing choices has not expunged this enmity toward childfree women. Veevers's influential analysis of her data on voluntary childlessness divides her childfree subjects into two categories and implicitly valorizes one of them (Veevers 1980, 158–159). On the one hand, there are the life-negating "rejectors"—those narcissistic, child-hating antiparents whose faults are memorialized in the stereotype. On the other hand, there are the life-affirming "aficionados," who are so enthralled with other projects that they haven't had children, but who are flexible and might have children if their circumstances changed. Most childfree individuals, Veevers argues, are aficionados, and aficionados are "more similar to parents." I suppose Veevers thinks she is doing the childfree population a service by dispelling the myth that they are all sour, maladjusted misanthropes. But inasmuch as she legitimizes voluntary childlessness by assimilating it to the psychology of parenthood, she contributes to a retrograde current of normalizing matrigynist sentiment. Motherhood is the sine qua non of womanhood, and even childfree women (the healthy ones, at any rate) are mothers at heart.

Feminist psychoanalysts argue that the key figurative culprit in matrigyno-idolatry—the trope that undergirds the familiar imagery inventoried so far and the trope that ultimately carries the weight of manufacturing the "choice" of maternity—is the image of mother-child fusion (Kristeva 1987, 234–236; Bassin 1994, 163). Recently scientized and vernacularized in the sonography-facilitated trope of mother-fetus bonding, this emotionally galvanizing signal trope posits an original state of unfailing succor, harmony, and security. The baby-centric tendencies of psychoanalytic theory bias it toward narrating the tasks of separation, individuation, and agency that this original union poses for the developing child. Let us reverse our perspective and look at this trope, instead, from the standpoint of women. To them, this ubiquitous trope represents pregnancy and infant care as a utopia and, moreover, a utopia in which the mother is all-powerful and perfectly beneficent. Biology bestows this unsurpassable possibility on women and withholds it from men. What a temptation! Is it any wonder that historically subordinated, devalued women seize the opportunity to become mothers? Is it any wonder that many of them embark on motherhood with drastically unrealistic ideas of being a mother? Is it any wonder that they have a lot of trouble articulating plausible reasons for their choice? The siren song of fusion forecloses self-determination and marshals antagonism to the very idea that self-determination with respect to motherhood might be a good thing.[19]

Feminists have not been immune to the influence of this trope either. In her account of the reproduction of mothering, for example, Nancy Chodorow comes alarmingly close to resurrecting this fantasy as feminine psychic structure and to condoning the resulting usurpation of women's self-determination. Endowed with a relational self that has "permeable ego boundaries," women become mothers not only because they are emotionally equipped to do it well and to find it satisfying but also because they long to recreate the experience of being mothered and to reexperience that unmediated interpersonal bond (Chodorow 1978, 206–209; for her reservations about nonautonomous motherhood, see Chodorow 1974, 60). Yet, as Donna Bassin cautions, surrender to the allure of the trope of fusion comes at an exorbitant, or rather, a ruinous, price: "If motherhood is taken on for nostalgic reasons, . . . the mother can experience herself only as an object" (Bassin 1994, 172).[20]

Patriarchal cultures immerse women in a sophisticated system of matrigynist figurations. This discourse singles out women's preferred course and trumpets its attractions; it conceals the drawbacks of embarking on this course and quells apprehension; it scolds and humiliates those who dare to contemplate any alternative. Both in virtue of its cunning coordination of inducements and admonitions and in virtue of its pervasiveness, it constitutes a concerted attack on women's autonomy with respect to motherhood.

4. À la Recherche des Voix Perdues: *Pronatalist Discourse and Discursive Insurgency*

In the previous section, I cited numerous cases in which feminist interpretations succumb to matrigynist distortions, not to condemn this work (in fact, I admire much of it), but rather to demonstrate how transfixing this discursive regime is and how extremely difficult it is to overcome it. How, then, does matrigyno-idolatry undercut women's self-determination with respect to motherhood decisions?

From the standpoint of women's self-determination, the trouble with matrigyno-idolatry is epistemological rather than metaphysical. It would be misleading to claim that this discourse determines women's choices. Matrigyno-idolatry notwithstanding, women's voluntary procreative outcomes range over a spectrum, and this diversity belies the charge of determinism. Moreover, although nearly all women do become mothers and although in a less directive discursive environment more women might refrain, to claim that women are determined to become mothers is to run roughshod over the indisputable fact that most women very much want to become mothers. To explain the harm of matrigyno-idolatry through recourse to the demon determinism is to miss its less obvious, more insidious impact, namely, its power to stifle women's voices by insinuating pronatalist imperatives into their self-portraits and self-narratives.[21]

One reason this discourse is objectionable is that it obfuscates women's motivations concerning motherhood.[22] As a result, women commonly lack the self-knowledge that is necessary for autonomous decision making. Matrigynist figurations frame women's introspection. They render promaternity feelings and inclinations vivid and compelling, while eclipsing doubts, misgivings, worries, and fears. Since matrigynist figurations trivialize or mute reluctance and resistance, many women who choose motherhood do so on the basis of doctored self-portraits, with pertinent information airbrushed out. Women who decide against motherhood by avoiding the issue and deferring closure maintain a never-enacted maternal self-image borrowed from matrigyno-idolatry. Their self-portraits out of alignment with their actions, these women suppress the disparity and sacrifice self-determination. Having confronted neither the possibility that some things are more important to them than motherhood nor the possibility that they are missing out on something that matters deeply to them, their self-knowledge is spotty, and their autonomy is impaired. Finally, matrigyno-idolatry puts the small group of women who explicitly reject motherhood on the defensive. Fearing (not unreasonably, I should think) that their resolve will be undermined if they open the issue of maternity to untrammeled reflection, many of these women concoct images of the mother as a repulsive grotesque instead of working on their own self-portraits. Thus, they often deny feeling any attraction whatsoever to motherhood and may also deny seeing any value in it. Again women's self-knowledge is curtailed, and their self-determination is called into question. All too often, women voice self-conceptions that are beholden to matrigyno-idolatry and never articulate richly individualized self-portraits. By confounding self-reading skills, matrigyno-idolatry suspends many women's self-determination.

Another way in which this discourse obstructs women's self-determination is that it funnels imagination into narrow channels. Options can be practically feasible and potentially desirable but subjectively unavailable to individuals. When options are not subjectively available—whether because one of them overshadows its anathematized rival, because irreconcilable needs are buried, or because alternatives are defensively shunned—self-determination is diminished. Pronatalist doctrine saturates women's consciousness and chokes off the options that are subjectively available to them (for helpful related discussion, see Mackenzie 2000 and LeVine 1984, 85–86).[23] Having children is the only motherhood scenario the vast majority of women can viscerally imagine in the first-person singular mode. Among women who want children, "baby lust" supplants autonomous choice.[24] Not having children is the only motherhood scenario a minuscule minority of "deviant" women can viscerally imagine in the first-person singular mode. They lock themselves into adamant refusal to treat motherhood as a viable option. Meanwhile, postponers who do not want children deceive themselves into believing that really they do, although they can never find time to fit it in. They cannot stop imagining themselves as mothers, but their self-image is merely a fantasy. In their case, imagination is disconnected from choice and action. Their imaginations disempowered by matrigyno-idolatry, many women find alternative paths agentically unintelligible and insuperably ineligible. Desires formed well before the age of consent then become women's destiny, for no other autobiographical narrative has enough credibility to be worth entertaining.

The damage inflicted by the hostile discursive environment I have described should not be underestimated. Yet, despite the corrosive ubiquity of matrigyno-idolatry, there are women who make solidly autonomous decisions about whether to become mothers, and, as I argued earlier, it would be good if more women were able to do so. Thus, it is necessary to inquire into the introspection and imagination skills that enable some women to outwit the matrigynist figurative regime that compromises so many women's self-determination in order to better understand how feminists might intervene in matrigynist discourse and break its hold on women's lives. After describing two strategies of dissident self-figuration that women have used to gain self-determination—lyric transfiguration and appropriation/adaptation—I shall outline several social and discursive changes that are needed to secure women's capacities for self-determination.

The strategy of lyric transfiguration involves exploiting literary techniques to fashion individualized imagery expressing one's subjective viewpoint and one's sense of one's identity. Julia Kristeva's poetic evocation of her experience of motherhood in "Stabat Mater" is a well-known example of lyric transfiguration (Kristeva 1987). Rejecting the personification of motherhood in the figure of the Virgin Mary, Kristeva creates a prose poem in which exquisite imagery of delicate sensuousness alternates with wrenching imagery of pain, turmoil, and dislocation. In capturing her unique apprehension of maternity, Kristeva's text transfigures motherhood for herself and for some of her readers, too. Those who are less gifted than Kristeva, however, might take encouragement from Jeanne Safer's model. Safer recounts a series of vivid dreams, which she interprets as bearing on her decision about motherhood (Safer 1996, 12, 22–25, 35, 36). The sequence culminates in a tableau of a garden "with a restored fountain and cantaloupes on the vine, growing on [her] parents' property in the dead of winter," which she construes as a metaphor for her decision not to have children (Safer 1996, 36). The water flowing from the fountain and the fruit ripening despite the cold represent her "new definition of fertility" without motherhood (Safer 1996, 37). By tapping into her personal nocturnal reservoir of imagery—a resource available to everyone—Safer escapes the grasp of matrigynist figurations and consolidates a positive vision of herself as a childfree woman.

A second approach—appropriation/adaptation—is taken by one of Mardy Ireland's subjects, whom she calls Judith. Judith, a photographer who has chosen not to have children, characterizes the help she gives younger women artists, such as selecting and preparing their work for exhibitions, as her "midwifery" (Ireland 1993, 82). In choosing this metaphor, Judith joins a tradition going back at least as far as Socrates in which women's service to one another in the birthing process is used to symbolize the assistance men give to other men in their creative labors. What is unusual about Judith's appropriation of this trope is that she is a woman. Whether because few women have historically been scholars, writers, or artists, or because women have lacked sufficient distance from their reproductive role to use it as a self-referential trope, women have seldom invoked their reproductive activities as metaphors for their own intellectual or aesthetic creativity (Kittay 1988, 78–80). But through appropriation/adaptation of this hoary trope, Judith carves out a spot for herself in the gender firmament and provides herself with a guiding image of her unorthodox life trajectory. To accomplish these aims, she becomes a discursive rebel. Not only does she refuse the matrigynist conflation of womanhood with motherhood, which would render her trope unilluminating, but she also filches a trope from the cultural storehouse and freely adapts it to suit her distinctive activities and self-concept.

Of course, appropriation/adaptation need not be confined to recycling procreative imagery. Indeed, this particular appropriation/adaptation must be viewed as a calculated risk. Symbolizing professional and artistic creativity as procreativity or symbolizing various generous practices, such as mentoring and volunteer work, as nurturance flirts perilously with reducing women's variegated accomplishments and contributions to sublimations of maternal impulses. To avoid replaying the essentialist matrigyno equation and reaffirming the antifeminist claim that no "true" woman can repudiate motherhood, women might be well advised to seek out images, allegorical tales, or exemplary biographical narratives that do not feature reproductive motifs. These, too, could be individualized and instated as psychic beacons.[25] Whatever literary forms are employed, though, what is important for women's self-determination is that, whether they choose to become mothers or not, they find discursive means to symbolize their particular relations to motherhood and through these self-figurations resist their homogenization in matrigynist ideology.

What Kristeva, Safer, and Judith have in common is that they augment their self-determination by finding their own voices. Firmly repudiating matrigynist imagery, they insist on casting their self-portraits in personal imagery. It is evident, then, that skills in interpreting and critiquing prevalent figurations of motherhood and skills in accessing and adapting figurative materials from diverse sources are necessary if women are to extricate themselves from matrigyno-idolatry and gain self-determination with respect to motherhood. Still, for purposes of self-determination, discursive innovation is not by itself enough. To enable self-determination, women's novel self-figurations must be screened for aptness and propitiousness:

1. Does a heterodox figuration better express the woman's sense of who she is and what matters to her?
2. Is it likely to facilitate her ability to undertake projects and pursue goals that she feels are truly her own?
3. Will it help her to explain herself to others and to gain their understanding, respect, and, perhaps, support?

To answer these questions, discursive insurgents must master the art of imaginatively trying on tropes (Meyers 1994, 108–115). They must anticipate what it would be like to inhabit a proposed figuration by constructing scenarios in which the figuration guides their conduct and by viscerally imagining themselves acting out those scenarios.

Those figurations that survive this vetting must become embedded in the cognitive, emotional, and corporeal structures that shape agency and that function as criteria of self-appraisal. To agentically integrate dissident self-figurations, women must command skills that enable them to invest emotionally in these tropes and to reconfigure their embodied values as well as their patterns of thought and volition in accordance with them (for discussion of the role of metaphor in self-knowledge and agency, see Kristeva 1987, 14–16, 276, 381). By devising imagery that expresses her identity and assimilating the imagery in this way, a woman enriches and individualizes her self-portrait, defines herself in her own terms, and makes her desire her own. Barring unforeseen countervailing circumstances, then, she gains a substantial degree of self-determination over a major life decision.

Since the skills I have described are learned, proficiency develops as a result of instruction and practice. Teaching these skills requires parental and pedagogical methods that encourage children to profit from idiosyncracy and reverie and that foster their receptivity to unfamiliar ideas and rhetorics, their originality and inventiveness, and their delight in individuality. Unfortunately, childrearing is currently geared to conformism—teaching children what is expected of them and how to meet those demands. Most children are subjected to repressive, deadening, incentive-driven practices that do little to cultivate the agentic skills women need and that crush children's potential when they do not turn them into angry, deracinated misfits. Unless childcare and schooling are reformed, then, women's autonomy with respect to becoming a mother will remain a privilege reserved for a lucky elite—typically, women brought up in enlightened households and affluent women who have access to progressive psychotherapists. To democratize women's self-determination, caregivers and educators must modify their practices and actively promote skills that enable women to discern the detrimental impact of matrigynist figurations on their lives, to envisage dissident figurations, and to entrust their lives to those figurations that augment their fulfillment and enhance their self-esteem.

It is not the case that any woman with enough gumption and native talent can bootstrap her way to autonomous control over whether or not to become a mother. On the contrary, women's procreative autonomy presupposes a social commitment to values and competencies that have heretofore received lots of lip service and scant tangible support. Redesigning childrearing to cultivate women's agentic skills is vital. Still, such reform addresses only part of the problem, for it does not directly challenge the overarching matrigynist discursive context.

Plainly, a discursive vacuum is not a viable antidote for culturally entrenched and transmitted matrigynist tropes. Having a child is too awesome an experience and too crucial to society for motherhood to be passed over in cultural silence. It does not follow, though, that feminists must stomach matrigyno-idolatry and its calamitous effects on women's self-determination. Feminist authors and artists can counter matrigyno-idolatry with matrigyno-iconoclasm, that is, they can generate alternative images of maternity and femininity to supplant matrigynist ones (for a general account of feminist counterfigurative politics, see Meyers 1994, 56–115). For instance, spotlighting the mother who laughs, the mother who knows sexual pleasure, and the mother who is angry would help to displace the baneful tropes of the beatific, selfless mother and mother-child fusion (Suleiman 1994, 278–281; Isaak 1996, 142; Hirsch 1989, 170; for additional alternatives to the fusion trope see Chapter 3, Section 3). I would add, too, that feminist images of mature women disassociated from motherhood—the woman who writes, the woman who performs, the woman who explores, the woman who leads, the postmenopausal woman doing anything(!)—are indispensable to the subversion of matrigyno-idolatry.

In the same way that masochistic imagery has colonized many women's sexual fantasy lives, matrigynist imagery has colonized many women's reproductive imaginaries. The aim of feminist counterfigurative initiatives is to fashion a benign discursive environment that offers women an array of self-images and that underwrites a wide range of values and aspirations. Coupled with efforts to ensure that individual women acquire the agentic skills they need to make selections from a pluralistic stock of tropes and to tailor those tropes to fit their distinctive needs, temperaments, capabilities, and hopes, this latitudinarian setting would secure a key social condition for the emancipation of women's self-visioning powers and thus for women's self-determination with respect to becoming mothers.

CHAPTER THREE

Gendered Models of Social Relations:
How Moral and Political Culture Closes
Minds and Hearts

Developmentally, the maternal identification represents and is experienced as the human for children of both genders. But, because men have power and cultural hegemony in our society, a notable thing happens. Men use this hegemony to appropriate and transform these experiences. Both in everyday life and in theoretical and intellectual formulations, men have come to define maleness as that which is basically human, and to define women as not-men.
— Nancy Chodorow, "Gender, Relation, and Difference"

By rendering a care perspective more coherent and making its terms more explicit, moral theory may facilitate women's ability to speak about their experiences and perceptions and may foster the ability of others to listen and understand. . . . The promise in joining women and moral theory lies in the fact that human survival, in the late twentieth century, may depend less on formal agreement than on human connection.
— Carol Gilligan, "Moral Orientation and Moral Development"

I will try to imagine what society would look like, for both descriptive and prescriptive purposes, if we replaced the paradigm of economic man with the paradigm of mother and child.
— Virginia Held, *Feminist Morality*

Psychologist Carol Gilligan became puzzled when she saw data purporting to show that girls and women think about morality in less sophisticated, less satisfactory ways than boys and men. After all, neither common sense nor crime statistics suggest that women conduct their lives any less morally than men. So Gilligan set about studying girls and women, and, in her intensive interviews with them, she detected a "different voice"—a system of framing concepts and thinking skills that she named the "ethic of care" (Gilligan 1982).

Answering the call of the different voice that Gilligan heard in the moral discourse of women, a number of feminist moral philosophers articulate and defend an ethic of care. Since exponents of care ethics use a distinctive set of framing concepts and thinking skills, theorizing their moral viewpoint hinges on reimagining and refiguring the moral sphere. Thus, care theorists move moral relations that philosophers had ignored or denigrated for centuries to the forefront of philosophical concern. Some care theorists focus on the intimacy and emotional bonds of friends and lovers. Others focus on the mother-child relationship. In this chapter, I examine the latter strand of thought, for it brings to light the way in which cultural representations of gender can interfere with autonomous moral and political judgment and occlude moral and political insight.

We have seen that culturally furnished imagery structures women's decisions about motherhood to a significant degree (Chapter 2). More broadly, gendered tropes structure perception and imagination, including moral perception and moral imagination. Since the seventeenth century, for instance, the image of the social contract has symbolically absorbed the concept of justice in Western societies. For many people today, the concept of justice is inseparable from the notion of a fair deal, an agreement that equal parties freely enter into. In light of this cultural mindset, politicians frequently couch their programs in the rhetoric of contracts, and the effectiveness of this vocabulary is indisputable. Indeed, so pervasive and so captivating is this rhetoric, not only in politics but also in philosophy, that it is sometimes forgotten that *homo economicus* is but one of many possible representations of human nature and that the social contract is a metaphor for justice and just relations. Philosophers who advocate a consent-giving procedure through which rational choosers would voluntarily assume (or do assume) an obligation to obey the laws of a particular society literalize the metaphor in practice, and philosophers who elaborate hypothetical social contracts literalize the metaphor in theory. But, in the words of Immanuel Kant, "It is the *Idea* of that act [the social contract] that alone enables us to conceive the legitimacy of the state" (Kant 1965, 80;emphasis added). Through the symbolism of a social contract struck among rational economic actors—not the event—people can envisage a just society and renew their allegiance to the state.

Where care theorists take exception to Kant's view is his claim that the social contract provides the sole tenable image of just social relations and legitimate political power. Metaphors assert identities. But since a particular metaphor is only one among many ways to describe a subject, the aptness of one metaphor does not rule out other apt metaphors (Frye 1990; Meyers 2000b). An affirmation of metaphorical identity is not a license for figurative imperialism. Thus, Annette Baier, Virginia Held, and Sara Ruddick give pride of place to mother-child imagery with its connotations of nonconsensual obligation and differential power, but they do not deny the value of liberty and equality. Conjuring with the image of the babe in arms, Baier notes that a disposition to trust is essential to the survival of individuals who are born helpless and dependent, and she goes on to disclose how morally fundamental trust between strangers as well as between close associates and family members is. Contracts themselves, she argues, presuppose a climate of trust (Baier 1994). Reflecting on pregnancy, birthing, and the mother-child relation that this process may bring about, Held maps out an alternative route to grasping the value of human life and discovers novel reasons to commit greater social resources to the welfare of children (Held 1987). The image of mothering prompts Ruddick to generate a system of dissident values, including holding and conserving life, humble acknowledgment of the limitations of one's power, resilient cheerfulness in the face of setbacks, innovative adaptation to change, and attention to the uniqueness of the individual (Ruddick 1997). She argues that these maternal values provide a far better framework for international relations than the values of competition, striving, and winning that presently govern world politics, for "maternal diplomacy" would lead to more evenhanded and stable international agreements (Ruddick 1987).

The metaphor of fairness in transactions between buyers and sellers of goods and services provides an invaluable corrective to state paternalism and invasiveness. But the hegemony of this commercial imagery fosters an exceedingly thin view of social justice—that is, the view that all is well once the state guarantees the liberties of the individual and respects individual choices (Baier 1987). Mother-child imagery challenges us to consider what values the social contract omits and whom the social contract marginalizes.

Although the mother-child paradigm and the social contract paradigm share similar weaknesses, which I shall spell out in Section 1, the mother-child paradigm meets considerable resistance. One aim of this chapter, then, is to analyze why the voice of care and specifically its mother-child imagery is usually silenced in political theory (Section 2). In my view, culturally transmitted representations of mother-child relationships activate anxieties that make it impossible for many individuals to contemplate a society structured according to a mother-child paradigm with any equanimity. Because their thinking is dominated by distorting and disturbing imagery, many individuals dismiss care ethics and care-based political theories out of hand. However, because I myself can find no good reason to suppress this "other" voice, I defend feminist discursive moves to counteract this silencing (Section 3). If the ethic of care is to receive the consideration it deserves, and if individuals are to fully avail themselves of their capacity for moral reflection and judgment, it is necessary to replace prevalent images of the mother-child relationship with images that respect the needs of both mothers and children. Finally, I argue that the indeterminacy of extended tropes like the social contract paradigm and the mother-child paradigm ensures the vitality of moral and political theory. Both the social contract paradigm and the mother-child paradigm support innovation and renovation in moral and political theory, for both paradigms allow for—indeed, require—extensive interpretation and elaboration (Section 4). In sum, the care ethic and the unorthodox imagery that underwrites this voice open a pathway to expanded self-determination in our moral and political thought and action.

1. Images of Social Relations: The Social Contract versus the Mother and Child

I regard care theory's proposal to replace the paradigm of economic man with that of the mother-child relationship for purposes of moral and political theory as one of its most radical and intriguing contributions. Yet, invoking mother-child imagery in this context raises alarms because: (1) it substitutes a new, narrow vision for an old, narrow vision; (2) it is gender specific, not universal; and (3) it appeals to a relationship that has been corrupted by patriarchy. Because Virginia Held takes pains to fend off these challenges, I shall base my discussion on her views.

Held qualifies her proposal for a paradigm shift in social thought in a number of ways. She denies that there should be just one paradigm of social relations (Held 1993, 195). She adds that it is the relation between post-patriarchal "mothering persons" and children, not the relation between

mothers and children under patriarchy, upon which she would model society (Held 1993, 202). She also takes the perils of metaphorization's
equivalencies into account. Aware perhaps that asserting that justice is a
mother-child bond might be misunderstood as ruling out all other
metaphors for just social relations, she switches to a simile and invites us
to contemplate how society and its goals would look if they were construed
as "*like* relations between mothers and children" (Held 1993, 195). Let us
imagine society as if its members were related as mothers and children
ideally are, she urges, but let us conceive this world undogmatically and
avoid closing our minds to other visions of social relations and the insights
they may afford.

It might be objected that, since the historical and cultural variability of
childrearing practices is well documented, there is no single paradigm of
the mother-child relationship, and thus to figure social relations as
mother-child relations is to relativize the concept of justice. Held responds
to this skepticism by insisting that she is invoking an idealization (Held
1993, 202). Just as social contract theorists base their accounts on an idealization of actual bargaining and contract-making practices, so she proposes to extract essential features of the mother-child relationship, to identify desirable child-caregiver bonds and desirable childrearing practices,
and to base her social and political account on them. She observes that the
mother-child relationship is inherently not voluntary, and she characterizes the mother's position as "affectional and solicitous" and the child's position as "emotional and dependent" (Held 1993, 204). She cites Sara Ruddick's view that standards implicit in childrearing practices constitute an
ideal that practitioners aspire to, as well as Charlotte Perkins Gilman's fic-
tional depiction of a society organized in accordance with the values of
motherhood (Held 1993, 187–188, 201–202). Undeniably, the exact features of the maternal ideal are disputable. One may agree, for example,
that any plausible account of childrearing must posit the survival of the
child as a goal. However, for Ruddick, the goals of childcare also include
developing the child's capacities for independent thinking and for responding compassionately to distant strangers as well as to dear friends
(Ruddick 1997, 593–595). But it is obvious that one can doubt that fostering this sort of freedom and goodness must be included in the ideal of maternal practice.

Such disagreement about the lineaments of the ideal might seem particularly damaging because, if there is disagreement about such basics, reflecting on this ideal will yield no definitive political prescriptions or man-

dates. People whose maternal ideals differ will envisage correspondingly different political ideals.

If controversy along these lines were fatal to the care ethic's mother-child imagery, however, it would be fatal to social contract theory, too. Social contract theorists agree that force and fraud nullify agreements, but they disagree about what constitutes coercion and deception. Whereas some see the disparities in the bargaining positions of business owners or managers and their nonunionized employees as violating the requirement that the parties to the agreement be equals and thus regard many wage agreements as coerced, others see nothing wrong with these agreements. Likewise, philosophical debates about what knowledge the parties to a Rawlsian original position should have are in essence debates about the conditions under which an agreement about political principles should be counted as fair (Rawls 1971, Chapter 3). Should these individuals know how risk averse they are? Should they know how talented they are? Should they know whether they endorse an individualistic or a communitarian conception of the good? Does blocking out this information invalidate the agreement they conclude, or does blocking it out validate their social contract? In addition, there are enormous discrepancies among the principles endorsed by different social contract theorists. John Rawls advocates civil liberties and redistributive taxation (Rawls 1971, Chapter 2). Norman Daniels claims that Rawls's premises entail far more economic equality than Rawls admits (Daniels 1975). Robert Nozick counters that any redistributive taxation at all is a grievous injustice that violates the natural right to property (Nozick 1974, Chapter 7). Evidently, disagreement about premises, indeterminacy of reasoning, and underdetermination of results are endemic to social contract theory.

The ethic of care and the mother-child trope hold no monopoly on controversy, and the controversies they raise, which parallel those that classical liberal political theory and the social contract trope raise, are no reason to reject the care ethic. Proponents of the ethic of care are not urging societies to replicate actual mother-child relations on a mass scale. Rather, they are arguing that the image of a social contract does not capture all of the human realities that a just society needs to address.

The care ethic's spotlight on mother-child imagery poses a striking contrast to the conceptual schema that structures most contemporary political thought. What seems a pivotal and perennial problem from within the social contract framework—for example, how to induce self-interested people to contribute to society—evaporates when the mother-child trope is substituted. Of course, mothers will try to create an environment that enhances their children's life prospects. What appears to be highly suspect social engineering to many social contract theorists—for example, transfer payments to poor families—seems an incontrovertible social imperative when the mother-child trope governs our thinking. Of course, society should meet the basic needs of poor children. Of course, poor mothers should not be forced to leave their children in understaffed, shabbily equipped daycare facilities. The mother-child trope brings new issues to the forefront and commends major reforms. However, pointing out the theoretical and practical implications of this reframing, substantial though they may be, underestimates the radicalism of the ethic of care.[1] To grasp the dimensions of this feminist transformation, it is necessary to examine the imagery behind the mother-child trope—in other words, the culturally entrenched figurations that shape our attitudes toward and our understanding of the mother-child relationship.

2. Imaginary Underpinnings of Mother-Child Relations

Held advocates using the mother-child trope to orient our moral and political reflection, but she advises us to adopt this strategy as an interim measure designed to compensate for the distortions of social contract theory. It is plain, though, that taking her suggestion seriously would revolutionize our thinking about society and social policy. As a result, the experiment she proposes prompts a good deal of dismay and sometimes outright antagonism, despite her stress on the provisionality of her recommendation. Held speculates that this overreaction may testify to widespread disrespect for and abuse of children—people naturally spurn the idea of importing this maltreatment into relations among adults (Held 1993, 213). No doubt, this is part of the explanation. I believe, however, that the problem goes even deeper.

Held's text makes a good starting point for this inquiry. Initially she endorses the image of the mother-child relationship, but eventually she offers a novel formulation: the mothering person–child relationship. As I understand it, the motivation for recasting the image in this way is twofold. First, Held wants to honor women's traditional role as caregivers. Hence she refuses to leave out the term *mother*, and she rejects gender-neutral terms like *caregiver*, *nurturer*, and *parent*. But second, she does not want to claim that men have never fulfilled this role, and she wants to enlist them in childrearing in the future. So, she speaks of mothering persons rather than mothers.

To my mind, this attempt to devise a gendered, yet nonsexist trope is a discursively untenable compromise. Either *mothering person* seems like a strange neologism that sets up disconcerting and irresolvable cognitive dissonance, for, in our present, which is to say, patriarchal, cultural context, mothering person is virtually an oxymoron. Or else it activates all of the gender-specific associations of maternal imagery and falls prey to our misapprehension of maternity and the tropes of maternity that perpetuate this misapprehension. The nonpatriarchal household is not a reality.[2] Since it does not yet exist—either in fact or in culturally approved representations of the future—it cannot serve as a figurative guide to restructuring social relations. Let's assume, then, that what people are reacting to is the mother-child trope. How does the discourse that encodes mother-child relationships undergird the defensive incredulity and hostility that Held and other care theorists have encountered?

Oscillating sentimentality and contempt with regard to motherhood and childhood fuel this problem. Maudlin overvaluation endows the mother-child relationship with an inflated preciousness and surrounds it with an aura of reverence that thwarts its transferral from the sanctuary of domesticity to the rough and tumble of social relations in general. Paradoxically, cruel disvaluation of mothers and children cements this segregation. If motherhood and childhood are conditions of imperfect personhood, as they are traditionally thought to be, no one would want to be figured as a mother or as a child in relations with other persons. This perverse constellation of attitudes is enshrined in and transmitted through a cultural stock of familiar figures of speech, stories, and pictorial imagery. I shall canvass three typical tropes that I have gleaned from psychoanalytic theory but that are well anchored in the popular imagination.

Nothing more poignantly expresses the deep ambivalence of the mother-child relationship than the prime trope of this relationship, namely, fusion. From the position of the child, it expresses uninterrupted and secure satiety—need is abolished, for it is anticipated and met before it can be felt. But fusion also represents a terrible threat to the child—to be fused with another is to have no independent identity of one's own and no alternative means of satisfying needs. Thus, the tie to the mother is associated with the dissolution, that is, the death, of the individual and also with subjection to another's absolute power, that is, tyranny. Neither is fusion imagery altogether benign with regard to the maternal position. On the one hand, fusion suggests boundless love and rapturous devotion, a joyful, ecstatic bond (for related discussion, see Chapter 2, Section 3). But, on the other hand, fusion is consuming. It symbolizes exorbitant responsibility for the other and living vicariously through the other. The mother's lot is deference and self-sacrifice. Note, moreover, that the consolations and anxieties of mother-child fusion are reciprocal but not identical. There are parallels between the way in which the trope of fusion represents the consolations and anxieties of the child and those that beset the mother, but the positions of the dependent and the caregiver cannot be psychically or agentically interchangeable. Thus, the succinct trope of fusion symbolizes a surfeit of conflict and anguish.

The trope of fusion is easy to mistake for a biological truth, for many people understand pregnancy as the symbiotic union of a woman and a fetus.[3] However, in culture and in fantasy, mother-child fusion represents much more than anatomical containment and physiological interplay. Since this image subsumes maternity, real mothers' active role in securing individuation for their offspring and in transmitting culture to them is eclipsed. Mothers represent the dedifferentiation of self and other and the suspension of the reality principle. Only fathers represent distinct identity, awareness of the external world, and social membership (Chasseguet-Smirgel 1994, 124). Fusion imagery turns maternal nurturance into a hazard and turns fathers into saviors—guarantors of selfhood in the face of the ever-present danger of maternal engulfment. In addition to stripping feminine imagery of any association with individuation and culture, the trope of fusion desexes mothers (Chasseguet-Smirgel 1994, 120). Dedicated to their children's comfort and thriving, mothers have no desires of their own, including sexual desires. It follows that they have no lives of their own. Cast as altruistic, nurturing attendants, women are not credited with independent selfhood and subjectivity, and unconscionable demands on their time and energy are seldom perceived as abusive (Chodorow 1980, 7–8; Chodorow and Contratto 1982, 63–71; Bordo 1993, 79). The trope of fusion is politically dangerous not only because it helps to vindicate practices that exploit and subordinate women but also because it represents a utopian condition that some people yearn to make real. Nostalgia and longing for the fantasized womb inspire some people to try to build a perfect community (Kristeva 1986, 205). Alas, the inevitable frustration of this fabulous but unfulfillable goal has historically led to authoritarian schemes to beat unruly human beings into submission and fabricate an illusion of harmonious social cooperation.

A second trope of the mother-child relationship, namely, the undischargeable debt, places the child in a more active but also a more burdened role. This image portrays the mother as bestowing the gift of life and the child as incurring a debt that cannot possibly be paid off, for the value of the gift is immeasurable. No matter what children do—no matter how loving, how attentive, how dutiful they may be—they never make any progress in reducing the balance in the debit column. Indeed, their maternal accounts will always be in arrears. It might seem that a truly generous benefactress would release her beneficiary from this debt. Unfortunately, the obligations of gratitude, the basic currency of this lugubrious emotional economy, cannot be cancelled by fiat. On the contrary, to forgive the original debt would be to swell the debt of gratitude. While the fusion trope negates children's agency and reduces them to passivity, the undischargeable debt trope channels their agency into the rituals of filial piety and stunts their creativity. It strangles the mother's agency, as well. Locked in her status as primordial benefactress extraordinaire, she becomes a strange beast—a holy loan shark—in patriarchal iconography.

Concluding her discussion of Derrida's autobiography, Kelly Oliver remarks, "Doesn't the acknowledgment of the debt of life always bring with it the danger of making the mother into a god? Of draining her blood and embalming her alive?" (Oliver 1997, 67). Psychoanalytic theorists term this mythic, marmoreal figure the *phallic mother* because the phallus symbolizes power. The phallic mother is an omnipotent, potentially deadly female figure, the engulfing aspect of the trope of fusion reborn as the phantasm of a terrifying colossus.

Many psychoanalytic theorists hold that fear of the phallic mother fuels misogynist prejudice and social practices that control and subordinate women (Chodorow 1980, 13–15; Chasseguet-Smirgel 1994, 124–125; for discussion of the phallic mother in relation to sexism, see Chapter 7, Section 2). By converting fear into contempt and hatred, the quaking child who is alive and well in everyone's unconscious defensively tames the imaginary maternal monster that the image of infinite indebtedness animates. A corollary of this dynamic is that girls and women dare not identify with feminine power (Chasseguet-Smirgel 1994, 122). As much as boys and men, they need to disavow the phallic mother and protect themselves from her. Turning to their fathers for safety, girls idealize them and defer to them. Ironically, idealizing the paternal figure undermines later heterosexual relationships, for no man can live up to this glorified image of masculinity (Contratto 1987, 139). Yet, because women are besieged by neediness for the security of affiliation with a man, they counterfeit a persona that fits what they believe men want, and they convert their disappointment with and anger toward their male partners into empathy and understanding (Contratto 1987, 152). The life-bestowing mother as power-hungry and insatiable benefactress gives men a pretext to subordinate women and induces women to collaborate in their own subordination.

The Oedipal trope—the blatantly baleful successor to the seemingly idyllic fusion trope—eroticizes the mother-child relationship and represents the mother as the child's first and most intense love. But since this sexualized love must remain unrequited, the mother-child relationship is transmuted into a symbol of the incest taboo, and frustration and reproach descend on the mother-child relationship. Worse still, the eroticization of the mother-child relationship bares its gender specificity. In a world of gender saliency, the mother-child relationship is either a mother-daughter relationship or a mother-son relationship. Just as there are no genderless mothers—in Held's parlance, mothering persons—so there are no genderless children. Consequently, the boy sees the mother as symbolizing the Other—the object of his desire—whereas the girl sees the mother as symbolizing the Same—her fate as an object of masculine desire and as a mother/helpmate. In short, this relationship is at the core of the cultural mythology of socially ordained heterosexuality and patriarchical hierarchy (for critique of the Oedipal trope, see Chapter 4, Sections 2 and 4, and Chapter 5, Section 3).

I want to emphasize that I am not asserting that the tropes I have sampled express Held's (or any other care theorist's) conception of the relationship between mothers and children. What I am contending is that these tropes encode a reserve of underlying cultural attitudes that block serious consideration of Held's proposal to use the mother-child relationship as a counterfiguration of social relations. I have rehearsed examples of mother-child symbolism in order to expose the extent of the need for cultural transformation to free up our moral and political imagination. The tropes I have sketched, along with numerous other complementary ones, transmit the attitudes of sentimentality and contempt attaching to mother-child relationships from generation to generation, immunize these attitudes against criticism, and protect them from change. It is futile to point out that neither sentimentality nor contempt is warranted or to urge people to recalibrate their attitudes to demonstrate due respect for mothers and children. As long as the symbols that normalize this sentimentality and contempt are preserved intact in the discursive substrate and remain integral to it, reason and exhortation will not succeed in displacing them. In my estimation, then, it is not feasible to adopt the mother-child relationship as a figuration of social relations unless feminists undertake the wholesale *re*figuration of the mother-child relationship.

3. Refiguring Mother-Child Relations

In addition to extricating care theory's counterfiguration of social relations from the sinister view of mother-child relationships that is conveyed by the tropes I have discussed, refiguring the mother-child relationship would be immensely advantageous to women, for it would free them from the cult of motherhood and spare those women who choose to have children some of the disesteem mothers now endure. Still, it is necessary to ask how best to proceed. Should the aim be to figure maternity in ways that are less demeaning to mothers and less threatening to children, or should the aim be to supplant maternal tropes with gender-indifferent ones?

An issue that immediately arises is whether differences between female and male reproductive biology preclude completely neutralizing the emotional import of the mother-father distinction. Plainly, fusion imagery calls to mind the fetus's embeddedness in the pregnant woman's body during gestation. Feminists are deeply divided as to whether such imagery can be salvaged. Indeed, there is no consensus among feminists with regard to the general questions of how much prominence to give to and what significance to attribute to women's reproductive biology. At one extreme, Simone de Beauvoir blasts the mystique of motherhood. Declaring that gestation and childbirth are merely natural processes, she holds that classifying childbearing as an achievement is an act of bad faith. To valorize it as the crowning glory of femininity is to enforce women's immanence and to collude in the subordination of women (Beauvoir 1989, 495–505, 522–525). At the other extreme, cultural feminists venerate women's childbearing capacity as the wellspring of interpersonal and ecological sensitivity and hence of life-affirming, pacific values. Held is not unsympathetic to this focus on women's reproductive biology. She strives not to belittle the moral sensibilities of women who do not bear children and of men (Held 1993, 83–84). Nevertheless, she maintains that gestation and childbearing afford birth mothers a special kind of moral experience and thus an opportunity for moral understanding that other people lack (Held 1993, 82–83; also see Bordo 1993, 94–95).

bell hooks stakes out a third position, a pragmatic one. Since men will avoid participating in childcare as long as it is labeled mothering and perceived as feminine, feminists should retreat from their celebration of prenatal bonding and accent the potency of postnatal ties (hooks 1984, 137–140). It is more urgent, in hooks's view, to persuade men to assume equal responsibility for raising children than it is to validate the marvels of women's reproductive biology. I would add, moreover, that it would be awfully nice if deemphasizing the prenatal period alleviated the crushing feelings of inadequacy suffered by many women who cannot conceive or bring a baby to term, and if in turn alleviating such feelings curtailed women's appetite for risky technological and pharmacological infertility treatments (see Chapter 2, Section 1). It would be nice, too, if adoptions were destigmatized. Both adopted children and adoptive parents would benefit.

Attracted as I am to hooks's pragmatism, however, I recognize that the entrenched, albeit constructed, meanings of childbearing cannot simply be jettisoned at will. Women experience the reproductive process through culturally furnished interpretations of gestation and birth, and their experience is imbued with these meanings. Thus, the project of conferring discursive precedence on the nurturance relationship and of affirming the preeminence of this relationship in our emotional lives must be viewed as a protracted, gradualist one. It is too much to expect that we can skip over intermediary adjustments and catapult straightaway into envisaging and instituting degendered, postpatriarchal family relations. Meanwhile, there are two strategies that are worth pursuing.

First, feminists need to highlight the extraordinary value of relations between women and children that do not involve birth mothers. Adoptive mothers, stepmothers, lesbian partners of mothers, nannies, and other childcare workers frequently form complex, loving, and lasting relationships with children, and they do so without being primed by pregnancy and childbirth or by genetic lineage. It is important, as well, to recognize the childcare donated by sisters, grandmothers, and aunts—women who have genetic connections to the children they help raise but who have not given birth to them. The dynamics of all of these relational bonds presuppose a generosity of spirit that is seldom acknowledged, and they enrich the caregiver's emotional capacities in ways that are not sufficiently understood, appreciated, or culturally represented.

Unfortunately, many women find the idea of honoring these relationships threatening. Women's ambivalence about their nonmaternal aspirations conspire with birth mothers' reluctance to relinquish their specialness in their child's eyes to spark resistance to properly valuing the nurturing other caregivers provide. Birth mothers are often jealous of the love that their children feel for hired childcare workers (Macdonald 1998).

The fairy-tale figure of the wicked stepmother encodes birth mothers' fear of being replaced in their children's affections, as well as children's fears of abandonment. Cultural ideology representing children as parents' private property reinforces these competitive and counterproductive maternal feelings and further impedes the project of recognizing the depth and desirability of nongestational attachments.[4] Likewise, the fraudulent image of the dysparental lesbian—the perverse anti-Mom—must be exploded if this counterfigurative project is to succeed (for related discussion, see Calhoun 1997, 204, 212; Young-Bruehl 1996, 427). Again, I do not pretend that symbolically recoding these relationships can be accomplished quickly. Nevertheless, I am convinced that getting the process under way is key, for the care ethic's recommendation of the mother-child paradigm will seem too bizarre to gain serious consideration until the discourse of mother-child relations shrinks the biological component of motherhood to credible proportions and dissipates the anxieties that excessively biologistic imagery aggravates.

Second, feminists need to generate and promulgate alternatives to traditional mother-child tropes. Bracha Lichtenberg Ettinger and Luce Irigaray are among the feminist psychoanalytic theorists who have contributed to this fledgling discourse. Ettinger adopts the Freudian strategy of elaborating genital-based tropes and develops a schematically uterine, nonscopic trope—the matrix. One meaning of the term *matrix* is "womb." Thus, her conception of the matrix is modeled on pregnancy and prenatal existence. However, it denies that the relationship between a pregnant woman and a fetus is one of nondifferentiation. Matrixial subjectivity, she claims, is "more-than-one and/or less-than-one . . . a network of subject and Other in transformation" (Ettinger 1992, 195). She emphasizes that this relational form of subjectivity involves a recognized "*unknown not-I*" and a shared space "for the co-emerging *I* and *not-I(s)* which are neither assimilated nor rejected" (Ettinger 1992, 200, 197). The unknown not-I can be a stranger, an unknown dimension of the self, or an unknown dimension of an acquaintance (Ettinger 1992, 200). The matrix, then, is comprised of ordered "contact spaces" in which mutual, but not identical, change occurs and occurs without domination and subordination (Ettinger 1992, 200).

What draws me to Ettinger's evocation of pregnancy and subsistence in utero is its privileging of touch and internal bodily sensation as sources of boundary awareness and identity formation (for related discussion, see Stern 1985, 45–61). Likewise, her imagery acknowledges the role of proprioception—the unconscious perception of movement and spatial orientation that arises from within the body—in sustaining body image, identity, and agency. Downplaying the visual, Ettinger bypasses the fusion-versus-separation polarity. The child need not be either totally engulfed or totally independent. The mother need not be either totally devoted or totally indifferent. The matrixial trope refigures the mother-child relationship as one of protodifferentiation between self and other through ongoing interchange. Reconciling distinctness and connection, Ettinger's imagery defuses anxieties about feminine power without forfeiting the gratifications of feminine plentitude.

Luce Irigaray offers another promising alternative to the specter of fusion—namely, a mother and a daughter playing a game of catch with images of one another (Irigaray 1981, 61–62). In this trope, as in Ettinger's, we find exchanges between differentiated individuals, but we do not find formalized, self-interest–driven contracts. Catch is a casual game with rudimentary, flexible rules that encourage players to tailor the game to suit themselves. Players are left to choose the type of ball, to select from a repertoire of tosses, to improvise throwing and catching styles, and so on. Lacking a system of score keeping, catch designates no winners or losers. People play catch for pleasure or for practice, not to strut their superior skill and vanquish an opponent. Perhaps most important, there are no rules limiting the number of people who can join a game of catch. Although a crowd of players would make the game too congested and too boring, one-on-one is not the sole option. As a result, it is easy to imagine moving from a dyadic mother-daughter game to a triangulated mother-daughter-partner game, and on to many different geometries of play. Irigaray's trope is not confined to the patriarchal family or to the postpatriarchal nuclear family. It seems well suited, then, to serve as a transitional trope. Indeed, since there is no reason to suppose that one version of the game should be favored over all the rest, the trope has the virtue of countenancing a wide array of childcare arrangements.

Ettinger's and Irigaray's images felicitously inaugurate the counterfiguration project that I am claiming is a precondition for entertaining Held's refiguration of social relations. Ettinger's matrix recognizes the impact of physical interaction in demarcating subjectivity and the role of visceral cues in sustaining a sense of self. Thus, it advances the feminist critique of sharp mind/body dualisms, of rationalistic, mentalistic accounts of identity, and of the devalued body. In addition, it corrects the commonplace error of regarding the pregnant woman and the fetus as a single biological system while preserving the closest imaginable ties between them. The tight, intricate structure of matrixes aptly symbolizes a form of intersubjectivity that does not collapse into subjective amalgamation. Thus, it is consonant with Held's suggestion that giving birth enriches moral insight into the value of newborn life.

Irigaray's image of a game of catch takes Ettinger's discursive initiative a step further. Detachable from maternity, Irigaray's trope can easily be appropriated by men and by women who care for children but who are not their biological mothers. Thus, it is consonant with the rationale behind Held's shift from the image of the mother-child relationship to the image of the mothering person–child relationship, and it facilitates moving on to the gender-neutral image of the caregiver-child relationship. In other words, it contributes to a discursive context that both expedites women's escape from sexist views of their proper role in childcare and undermines the heterosexist teleology of childrearing in the traditional nuclear family.

Although I am not sanguine about displacing the culturally entrenched trope of mother-child fusion, my prognosis is less pessimistic than Jessica Benjamin's. Benjamin repudiates Ettinger's rhetorical strategy of displacing the trope of fusion with a feminine anatomical representation of identity and culture. She maintains that neither reversing previous cultural abhorrence of women's anatomy through aestheticization nor seeking a nonphallic representation of intelligible utterance and gesture can succeed (Benjamin 1988, 124). Moreover, she claims that fusion imagery is beyond the reach of feminist critique and that the only solution is to bear in mind that it represents a fantasy, not a truth, about maternity (Benjamin 1994, 132, 134, 141, 145). Although I believe that Benjamin overlooks the virtues of feminist reclamations of female genital imagery (Meyers 1994, 86–91), I agree that it is inadvisable to rely exclusively on female genital imagery to refigure mother-child relationships. That is why, in this work I choose not to discuss one of Irigaray's well-known female genital tropes—that of two lips touching—and instead explore her little-noticed trope of the game of catch. Still, I share Benjamin's conviction that orthodox maternal tropes are firmly ensconced in culture and that they are internalized by individuals, and I readily concede that dislodging them will be a slow and arduous process. Nevertheless, what I think this shows is that the feminist project of cultural transformation is radical in the sense of requiring reconstruction of the foundations of culture, not that this project is futile. In the meantime, it is imperative to heed the distinction between fantasies of motherhood and realities. Women need to foreground that distinction when they think about becoming mothers themselves and when they think about childcare arrangements if they are mothers, and everyone needs to be aware of that distinction when interacting with their mothers.[5]

Important as reconstructing the iconography of childrearing is, ensuring that feminist counterfigurations become lodged in the popular imagination and supplant entrenched, retrograde imagery is no less urgent. To do their work, emancipatory figurations must shape common knowledge, and, to shape common knowledge, they must be integrated into the cognitive infrastructure that undergirds what people take to be reasonable belief and sensible expectation. Here I would venture that broadcasting feminist counterfigurations will have little effect unless this publicity is coordinated with changes in the customary distribution of everyday childcare tasks and also with legal changes that secure and condone alternative childrearing arrangements.[6] For example, men who defy gender stereotypes and are seen gladly taking care of children—changing stinky diapers, wiping snotty noses, calming cranky tempers, and taking family leave while mother financially supports the family—provide a hook for the image of a father playing catch with a daughter to latch onto. Likewise, moves to legalize all manner of domestic partnerships legitimate unorthodox constellations of parental caregiving. Since assimilable tropes capitalize on ordinary beliefs, and since ordinary beliefs are sustained by assimilated tropes, discursive transformation cannot succeed without institutional reform—that is, without changes in "appropriate" behavior (for reasons why institutional reform cannot succeed without discursive transformation, see Chapter 7, Section 4).

I find Irigaray's trope compelling partly because it can be adapted to represent a variety of salutary caregiver-child relationships. The desirability of preserving this openness to innovation is one reason why it would be inadvisable to privilege a single caregiver-child trope. It is imperative that feminists avoid duplicating the regimentation of gender codes and legislated family structures that dominant discourses now enforce. Moreover, it is undeniable, as Ettinger's trope shows, that no one trope can possibly suffice to capture all forms of salubrious caregiver-child interaction.

For people who are familiar with European medieval and Renaissance painting or who are immersed in the religious tradition that sponsored this art, mentioning caregiver-child relations may bring to mind the image of a babe in arms. People who are acquainted with recent trends in psychoanalytic theory may recall Ettinger's essay and picture a matrix that organizes unpredictable mutual influence, or they may recall Irigaray's essay and picture a mother and a daughter playing catch. But each of these images omits far more about caregiver-child relationships than it conveys. The process of childhood development is staggeringly dense and multi-tracked and notoriously circuitous.[7] Childhood experience encompasses exploration and pride, vulnerability and dread, mystery and wonder, trauma and fear, play and delight, secrets and shame, and much more besides. All of this children apprehend, yet by no means comprehend at the time. They rely on nurturant adults to challenge them, support them, and meet their ever-changing physical, emotional, and intellectual needs as they encounter and discover the world. Thus, the responsibilities of child-rearing are multifarious. Moreover, childhood has no conclusive outcome. At different stages of their lives, people recall previously forgotten childhood incidents, incorporate them into their autobiographical narratives, and reinterpret their past. Since images of the caregiver-child relationship reverberate in memory, there is no moment when this relationship definitively ends, no moment when the character of this relationship is finalized. It is hardly surprising, then, that the caregiver-child relationship has traditionally been symbolized by a wide variety of tropes nor that many feminists agree that alternative emancipatory imagery must also be eclectic.

4. The Inconclusiveness of Moral and Political Theorizing

Both to avoid excessive prescriptivity and to express the richness of caregiver-child relationships, feminists must create a sizable repertoire of post-patriarchal tropes. It might seem, however, that bringing so much imagery into play would defeat the project of analogizing social relations to the caregiver-child relationship. To still this worry, let me return to the comparison with social contract theory I introduced earlier.

The social contract is not a freestanding image either. Since a static image of a handshake gets one nowhere philosophically, social contract theory exploits background tropes, and different social contract theories rely on different collocations of background tropes. Are we at war, or are we in arcadia? Does bargaining precede the handshake? If so, how is bargaining conducted? Who are the contractors? Can any two people negotiate, or must they be alike in certain respects? Are there any women at the table? As we know from the history of philosophy, this constitutive imagery has a decisive impact on the view of justice that a theorist propounds. And we know, too, that which imagery is settled upon depends not only on actual social conditions and prevalent practices, but also on the theorist's normative presuppositions and aims. John Locke's individualist social contract theory and Jean-Jacques Rousseau's communitarian social contract theory cannot depict the state of nature that precedes the social contract in the same way.

Those who consider social contract theory a worthwhile approach to moral and political philosophy have no reason in principle to eschew caregiver-child theory. Indeed, it may well be because the image of the social contract is a rich figurative lode—amenable to both variation and idealization—that it has persisted for centuries as a framework for moral and political philosophy. There is no reason to think that the caregiver-child trope cannot be equally illuminating and enduring.

In general, one of the most effective means to perpetuate their own way of life that cultures have at their disposal is to make other ways of life seem weird, ridiculous, or abhorrent. We have seen that pronatalist cultures stigmatize nonmotherhood in these ways by representing this option in repellent, admonitory imagery (Chapter 2, Section 3). Likewise, rationalist, individualist moral/political cultures sideline alternative social visions by associating them with fearsome figurations. Sometimes these figurations accurately portray real disvalues. For example, modern liberal cultures identify totalitarianism with the knock on the door in the middle of the night and the windowless, subbasement torture chamber. But sometimes these figurations suppress social possibilities that deserve open-minded consideration on their merits. In so doing, they confound moral self-determination. To my mind, the dominance of social contract imagery and the correlative exclusion of mother-child imagery in social discourse is a case in point.

In proposing that we figure social relations on the model of the mother-child relationship, care theorists seek to reorder political priorities and to mute the harsh tenor of contemporary political debate. As I understand their objective, they are seeking to move beyond policies that respect personhood as such and to implement policies that value and sustain individuals as individuals. Instead of a society that rests content with providing equal opportunity and a perfunctory safety net, they envisage a society that undertakes to discern and to bring out the best in each individual. It can be a signal political advance to demolish repressive institutions or to eradicate practices that systematically sacrifice some members of society, and the ethic of care certainly does not deny that this is the case. This moral view maintains, however, that societies should not limit themselves to such narrow goals. Thus, care theorists invoke the trope of mother-child relations to spark our political imagination and to persuade us to embrace caring for every member of society as a political value. To the extent that contemporary Western cultures succeed in making people reflexively averse to this creditable viewpoint, it seems clear that these cultures are impairing their members' moral self-determination.

Analogizing social relations to mother-child relations, I have argued, is ambitious and propitious from the standpoint of the discursive renewal and the transformation of caregiver-child relations it presupposes. In addition, reconfiguring cultural representations of the mother-child relationship and culturally normative childcare practices would expand the scope of moral self-determination, for conscientious moral subjects would no longer be captives of a single system of imagery and the values it certifies. In my view, then, introducing mother-child imagery into political theory is also ambitious and propitious from the standpoint of the broad social change it augurs.

CHAPTER FOUR

The Family Romance: A Fin-de-Siècle Tragedy

A century ago in the midst of the political, artistic, and intellectual foment of fin-de-siècle Vienna, Sigmund Freud published "The Aetiology of Hysteria" (1896). This paper contains the shocking revelation that patients suffering from hysteria were sexually abused during childhood and the provocative explanatory hypothesis that the symptoms of hysteria are consequences of this abuse. Some scholars maintain that Freud never denied the high incidence of sexual abuse of children and was troubled by it throughout his life; others maintain that Freud's handling of this matter calls into question his personal and scientific integrity.[1] What is incontrovertible is that Freud soon repudiated the explanatory hypothesis put forward in "The Aetiology of Hysteria." In subsequent accounts of the genesis of neurosis, veridical recollections of early sexual abuse are replaced by recollections of incestuous childhood desires and fantasies of their consummation. Embellishing his initial account by interiorizing the substance of his patients' poignant testimony, Freud invented the elegant baroque conceit that became known as psychoanalysis.

On centennial, not to say millennial, cue, the issue of father-daughter incest has recently resurfaced with all the ferocity and vitriol that psychoanalysts associate with the return of the repressed. In comparison, the mother troubles I have been considering look mild. Culturally entrenched maternal imagery organizes social conformity: women become mothers, and most people embrace a social contract view of politics. Although self-determination is diminished, people's lives are not torn asunder. Institutions are not thrown into crisis. Both because paternal imagery is so electrifying in patriarchal cultures and because the rupturing function that these cultures allocate to fathers in psychic life carries connotations of violence, paternal imagery is capable of unleashing more personally and socially destructive forces. Thus, the revival of the dormant father-daughter incest controversy has unsettled contemporary family life, and it has reverberated through educational, recreational, and religious institutions. Adults who interact with children—teachers, school counselors, coaches, club sponsors, clergymembers—have scrambled to adopt protocols designed to protect themselves from charges of child abuse. Meanwhile, especially in the United States, large numbers of women are accusing their fathers of sexually abusing them when they were young,[2] and their supporters are engaged in pitched scholarly, media, and courtroom battles defending recovered memory against skeptics.

My aim in this chapter is to propose a way of interpreting the phenomenon of recovered memory that moves beyond the prevailing "Did it happen, or didn't it?" construal of the debate. Thus, I focus on figurations of female heterosexuality and the role of these figurations in autobiographical memory, in women's self-narratives, and in others' assessments of the credibility of these narratives. I begin by critically examining four prominent views of recovered memory, and I argue that none strikes the right balance between the epistemic opacity of the past and the obligation to respect women who claim to remember childhood sexual abuse after a long period of amnesia (Section 1). Turning to the role of culturally furnished figurations in autobiographical memory, I distinguish three versions of Freud's family romance—incestuous love, incestuous seduction, and sadistic incest—and I consider how these tropes are used to figure disparate adult outcomes for women—marriage and motherhood, on the one hand, and hysteria or multiple personality disorder (technically, dissociative disorder), on the other (Section 2). Focusing on the rhetoric of autobiographical memory in conjunction with the contribution of autobiographical memory to self-definition reorients the discussion of recovered memory (Section 3). Instead of stubbornly trying to answer the often unanswerable question "Which of these two people is telling the truth?" we can ask which psychological conditions the trope of sadistic incest aptly figures and whether this imagery is necessary or fruitful. In my view, both feminist therapists and advocates for victims of sexually abused girls have reason to develop alternatives to the family romance (Section 4). Moreover, feminist theories of the self need to be mindful of their figurative underpinnings. Some feminists have sought to reclaim women's experience of multiplicity and to defend the multiplicitous self. I argue, however, that linking the multiplicitous self to the trope of sadistic incest undercuts this reclamation project (Section 5). For purposes of psychotherapy, for purposes of justice to women, and for purposes of feminist theory, it is time to displace the family romance and to replace it with tropes that support feminist emancipatory aims.

1. The Controversy over Recovered Memory

That autobiographical reality is as much a matter of literary form as documentable content seems to be a truism among psychologists who study memory. Still, it does not follow that autobiographical reality is merely subjective. On the contrary, it is intersubjective in many and sundry ways. What does follow is that the personal past is not straightforwardly retrievable and also that the personal past is highly malleable. Of course, neither of these facts stops anyone from confidently representing her past—the minor details as well as the portentous watersheds and climactic events—to herself and others. This is by no means surprising, for however contestable, manipulable, and revisable memory may be, it plays a key role in personal identity. The continuity of one's memory sequence helps to sustain one's sense of ongoing individual selfhood, and one interprets one's experiences and choices and ascribes meaning to one's life in part by invoking memories.

In this context, it is obvious why recovered memories of childhood sexual abuse are both explosive and problematic. Likewise, it is predictable that accounts of the standing of these reports would proliferate. There are three principal accounts currently in contention. Jeffrey Masson (1992), Judith Herman (1992), and Lenore Terr (1994) are prominent among those who credit the memories. They believe that child victims commonly repress experiences of trauma, especially repeated trauma, and although Herman cautions against injudiciously using hypnosis or drugs to extract memories of abuse, she joins Masson and Terr in holding that there should be a presumption that patients' memories are veridical reports of actual incidents. Taking sharp issue with this view, Frederick Crews debunks recovered memories as suggestions implanted in vulnerable and pliant women by irresponsible, perhaps nefarious, psychotherapists and authors of self-help books (1994a, 1994b).

Ian Hacking proposes a more complex view of recovered memory. He does not deny that some patients are accurately reporting specific abuses, nor that therapists and self-help books can induce susceptible individuals to believe they were abused. However, he observes that these alternatives do not account for all of the cases. According to Hacking, intentional action is indeterminate, for there are many correct ways to describe a single act (Hacking 1995, 235). Moreover, as new descriptions become available, people can redescribe and reexperience past events (Hacking 1995, 241). Consider, for example, a "less flagrant" form of abuse that gave a child a "shady feeling of sexual discomfort" at the time (Hacking 1995, 247). She may not forget her feelings of peril and intimidation even though she is not familiar with the concept of child abuse. If at a later time she becomes acquainted with the concept of child abuse and the narrative possibilities this concept authorizes, she may fill in scenes that blame her distress on the other person's conduct (Hacking 1995, 256). Now she remembers being sexually abused as a child. Even conduct that was considered innocuous at the time can be interpreted in light of new concepts. Retroactively revising the past, such recasting accounts for additional cases of recovered memory (Hacking 1995, 249).

Plainly, it is a virtue of Hacking's view that it respects the testimony of women who are remembering childhood trauma. Yet, some will surely find his view promiscuously inclusive. His account of "semantic contagion"—how concepts circulate, form chains of association, and latch onto remembered experiences—entails that there is almost no woman alive today who could not reasonably profess to have been sexually abused in childhood (Hacking 1995, 247). That girls are victims of incest becomes a historically conditioned tautology. Yet, Hacking draws back from this conclusion. Insisting on preserving the distinction between true and false beliefs about one's past, he defends the value of lucid self-knowledge (Hacking 1995, 258–267).

The territory of memory is notoriously treacherous. Once we relinquish the untenable idea that remembering is like playing a tape one has recorded on an interior video camera (this is Hacking's simile), we are obliged to acknowledge that memory is full of holes. Moreover, it is often impossible to determine which features of an incident one registered at the time and which features one picked up in later conversations with other participants or from other reports. The miscellaneous materials of memory are cobbled into narratives that include selected materials while omitting others and that could be framed and organized in indefinitely many ways (Bruner 1994, 53). Rehearsal helps to preserve memories. Yet, people relate their experiences in stories fashioned for particular audiences, and these retellings may erode memory (Loftus and Kaufman 1992, 215–216, 219). It is amazingly easy to induce people to believe that they are remembering major events that never happened to them (Loftus 1993, 532–533). It is extremely difficult to persuade people that they are misremembering events if their recollections are vivid and detailed, form a coherent sequence, and maintain consistency of character (Ross and Buehler 1994, 227–229). Since verisimilitude secures memory as effectively as accuracy, dissolving the distinction between recalling an experience and believing an experience took place or imagining that it did is an ever-present danger. Although Hacking resists subjectivizing memory by appealing to shared, though contestable and modifiable, conventions of language use, it is not clear that he altogether avoids merging these phenomena.

The obligation to show respect for rememberers and their recollections coupled with the overwhelming evidence of the incompleteness, the variability, and indeed, the downright unreliability of memory is confounding. This baffling conjunction of a compelling moral imperative to respect others' self-narratives and the seemingly insuperable epistemic opacity of the past may make Freud's psychoanalytic solution seem attractive. According to Freud, recovered memories are reports of repressed childhood fantasies of seduction, and these fantasies are constituents of psychic reality. Psychic reality is the unconscious inner world where wishing is indistinguishable from doing a certain act or being subjected to a certain treatment and where the effects of wishing on personal well-being may be as profound as the effects of acting or undergoing. A girl's repressed fantasies of incest may lead to neurosis later in her life. Women who report childhood sexual abuse but whose parents and siblings adamantly and convincingly deny it are neither lying nor are they completely deluding themselves. They are reporting actual past experiences of a riveting fantasy, but they do not realize that they experienced a fantasy, not an incident, of molestation.

By positing psychic reality, Freud supplies real events for psychoanalytic interpretations to correspond to and a way out of the either-it-happened-or-it-didn't dilemma. Psychoanalytic theory holds that the deliverances of memory require quite a bit of professional decoding, for they may conflate fantasies with interpersonal incidents. Still, Freud's fantasy-packed psychic reality secures the basic truthfulness of women suffering from hysteria or multiple personality disord: and vindicates a qualified affirmation of the veridicality of their memories. Concomitantly, it upholds the veracity of their fathers and avoids besmirching their reputations.

Recovered memories of childhood sexual abuse generate a triadic antinomy of memory and morals. By consigning recovered memories to psychic reality, Freud obtains a neat correspondence between his patients' recollections of sexual molestation and their childhood experiences at the price of suppressing or, at least, sidelining the possibility that their fathers really raped or otherwise molested them. Moreover, he opens his clinical practices to the charge of suggestion, for psychic reality may be nothing more than a fabrication that the therapist persuades the impressionable patient to embrace. Masson, Herman, and Crews revert to a more commonsensical distinction between true and false memories but at the cost of indiscriminately countenancing or dismissing recovered memories. Masson and Herman merely pay lip service to what they seem to regard as the remote possibility that a father accused of incest is innocent. However, unqualified support for recovered memory claims neglects a substantial body of empirical data demonstrating the mercurial workings of memory, and it scorns out of hand the testimony of anyone who denies the truth of these accusations. In contrast, Crews's impatience with women who report recovered memories of childhood sexual abuse and his contempt for therapists who ally themselves with these women are undisguised. Crews's apostate antipathy for psychoanalysis blinds him to the real possibility that the long-run psychological impact of incest may assume a number of different forms. Hacking proffers a subtle account of memory that is faithful to related social practices. One advantage of his theory is that it does not preclude solidarity with women who allege that they were sexually abused, although Hacking distances himself from many women who make such allegations. It is troubling, however, that Hacking blurs the line between beliefs representing facts about the past and beliefs projecting present anxieties onto the past. Evidently, no account of memory and recovered memory is free of serious liabilities.

2. *Figurations of Sexuality and the Family: The Cultural Cache*

A second truism among psychologists who study autobiographical memory is that people generally rely on a cultural cache of stock concepts and interpretive schemas, often encoded in familiar figures of speech and mythic tales, to recount their past. Literary and artistic originality are rare, and most people appropriate culturally furnished figurations. It would be a mistake, though, to think of recollection as a two-stage process in which one starts with a bit of raw memory material and then articulates it via selected figurations. Rather, the figurations guide and shape recollection from the start. To some extent, people are captives of their culture's repertoire of figurations. It takes a conscious effort to become aware of and to criticize ubiquitous figurations, especially those that are integral to a cultural world view, and it takes a great deal of assiduous self-monitoring to begin to extricate one's thinking from this imagery. To understand recovered memory, then, we must consider which culturally entrenched figurations are fueling this phenomenon.

Figurations of gender, sexuality, and family relations are multifarious, pervasive, and captivating (Haste 1994; Gilman 1985; Kittay 1988; Rooney 1991; Lloyd 1993b; Meyers 1994). Among the most potent of these figurations is an age-old story popularly known as the *family romance*. According to Freud's influential adaptation of this tale, the Oedipus complex and its resolution explain the emergence of normal gender, that is, heterosexuality with the aim of procreation. For a girl, the Oedipus complex commences when she discovers that she lacks a penis, a deprivation that she takes for castration.[3] Angry with her mother for not endowing her with this supremely valuable organ, and repelled by her mother, who is castrated too, the girl falls in love with her father. Not only does her father have a penis, but also he can give her a penis substitute in the form of a baby. Eventually, the girl will detach her affection from her father and transfer it to a male peer, whom she will marry and have children with. Having made this transition, she achieves "femininity," and the curtain rings down.

But, of course, the family romance is a drama that is never out of production. The culmination of psychological development, the Oedipus complex is reenacted in every generation of every family with mother, father, and daughter or son as conscripted dramatis personae. Its plot embodies the meaning of the family as a site of procreative heterosexuality and as a transmitter of procreative heterosexuality. Its continuous run ceaselessly reaffirms that meaning (Silverman 1992, 35–51). Incest is, then, the reigning metaphor of the heterosexual mother (or father).

Although Freud regards the family romance as a childhood fantasy that becomes a prime component of psychic reality, I have classified it as a figuration. Here, I follow Elizabeth Abel, who likens psychoanalysis to fairy tales (Abel 1990, 191). Both genres situate prototypical characters in memorable stories that interpret experience and guide conduct, and both are widely disseminated. Using this view, we can understand the power of the family romance without becoming embroiled in sterile controversy over infantile sexuality and the fantasies it may or may not kindle. As long as this image of family relations is a cultural staple that is imparted to each new generation, it will be constitutive of the cognitive and emotional substrate of perception and memory, including self-perception and autobiographical memory.

In a discussion of Freud's theory of original fantasies, Jean Laplanche and J.-B. Pontalis characterize these fantasies in a way that further illuminates the view I am proposing. Laplanche and Pontalis claim that original fantasies take the form of skeletal, impersonal, present-tense scenarios, and they argue that this form facilitates psychological assimilation of these fantasies (Laplanche and Pontalis 1968, 13–14). The daughter's version of the family romance might be schematized as follows: A daughter falls in 84) 85 love with a father, and she becomes a wife and mother. This deceptively simple scenario resonates with the solemn grandeur of ancient Greek mythic tragedy, with the fatuous yet needling taunt of Freud's more recent portrayal of women's anatomical deficit and characterological shortcomings, and with commonplace tags like *daddy's girl* and pulsing pop songs in which women long for or pleasure with their daddies/lovers—all of this in the context of the unnerving cacophony of current news exposés of epidemic child abuse. Consolidating these cultural currents in a single emblematic narrative, the family romance is so culturally and psychically entrenched that it seems beyond the reach of critique and virtually impossible to uproot. The trope of father-daughter incest structures our conception of womanhood and hence our beliefs, expectations, and feelings about women.

Still, the family romance is not our sole source of imagery for gender and sexuality. Indeed, the family romance derives some of its power from its parasitic tie-in to other figurations in a vast cultural cache. Here I shall only adumbrate the dimensions of this cache by mentioning a few well-known images that are plainly relevant to recovered memory. Male heterosexuality is commonly personified as a predatory and voracious hunter or beast (W. Williams 1991, 20; Mann 1994, 29–30). Correlatively, women are commonly figured as sexual targets or prey, although they may also be figured as lascivious whores bent on leading upright men astray (Haste 1994, 172–173; MacKinnon 1982, 530; Bartky 1990, 73–74). Eroticized images of prepubescent girls often depict these minors as seductive gamines or waifs. One needn't seek out the sleazy depredations of child pornography or the lewd institution of the juvenile beauty pageant to encounter such images. A visit to an art museum, where one can see photographs by Charles Dodgson or paintings by Balthus, will suffice (for discussion of nineteenth-century literary treatments of this theme, see Gilman 1985, 39–58). Likewise, for aesthetically sophisticated depictions of the slightly more mature, but still girlish nymphet, revisiting Vladimir Nabokov's *Lolita* or its movie spinoffs suffices. The oscillation between figurations representing women and girls as innocent and ones representing them as depraved and between figurations representing men as violent and ones representing them as honorable sets the stage for what we might think of as unauthorized productions of the family romance.

I have sketched the scenario for happy wives and fulfilled mothers. But what about other women? Freud supplies a number of plots with different denouements, including the lesbian, the female professional, and the hysteric. How is the hysteric, the precursor of the multiple personality, portrayed? Here is a synopsis of Freud's nineteenth-century staging of the family romance with that plot twist interpolated: A father seduces a daughter, and she represses this shameful experience and develops hysteria. Now consider the twentieth-century update of this tragic scenario: A father forces sex upon a daughter, and she dissociates and develops multiple personality disorder. A rather whimsical tenor offsets the sordidness of the fin-de-siècle Viennese figuration of hysteria—a father romancing a daughter.[4] In the United States today, however, the figuration of multiple personality disorder, which presages recovered memory, is obscene and stark—a father savagely violating and wantonly exploiting a daughter. Unambiguous sadism supplants ambiguous romance.

3. Figuring One's Life

In many cases, memories of childhood sexual abuse raise no more doubt than any other memory. Either the individual has always remembered these assaults (that is, the memories have never been less retrievable than other memories), or credible corroboration of a recovered memory is forthcoming.[5] However, there are also many bewildering cases in which a recovered memory is met with resolute denial. The woman making the allegations seems sincere and deeply wounded, while the man denying the charges seems honest and loving. If there is no reason to believe that the woman has fallen into the clutches of an overzealous therapist, and if there is no feasible way to obtain relevant evidence about the past, it is impossible to decide between the irreconcilably opposed positions. These impasses, which pit the obligation to respect persons in the present against the epistemic opacity of the past, are best approached by placing auto-biographical rhetoric in the context of the functions of autobiographical memory.

Memory can resemble a radio announcer's blow-by-blow description of a sporting event: I said, "——," you said, "——," I said, "——," and so on. Sometimes this sort of bare word-for-word recall is precisely what is needed—say, to settle a dispute about the terms of an agreement. But obviously this kind of account leaves out important facts about how one perceived the interaction at the time. Thus, memory often introduces elements of manner and subjectivity: I said, "——," you acidly joked, "——," I blanched and retorted, "——," and so on. This sort of recollection might be germane, for example, to a determination of provocation. Such memory is informationally packed and motivationally intelligible. But except in the immediate aftermath of an incident (and not always then), people are seldom able to recall such minute detail. They are left with summaries: We fought bitterly over such-and-such. Or maybe just: We quarreled. Thin though these synoptic memories may seem by comparison with narratives that flesh out complex incidents, they suffice for many purposes, such as explaining the awkwardness of an encounter or seeing the need to initiate a rapprochement. Not only is the content of memories of particular actions, responses, or exchanges restricted by the limits of human retentive and retrieval capacities, but it is also edited and reedited depending on how the memory is being used to conduct social relationships or to make sense of one's life.

The case of life stories is parallel. People remember their lives by telling stories that excerpt key episodes and string these episodes together according to themes, such as traits of character, values, aims, norms, exigencies, and so forth. These stories are varied to suit different audiences and different purposes. A politician would hardly tell the same life story to her lesbian partner, to the voters, and to her five-year-old grandchild. Moreover, these narratives can be distilled and condensed. One's story of one's scientific quest might be captured in an image of oneself as an astronaut, or one's story of one's erotic escapades might be captured in an image of oneself as a Don Juan. When autobiographical narratives are encoded in self-figurations, memory's contribution to self-definition becomes salient.

Self-definition—synthesizing one's understanding of one's capabilities and one's value commitments into an aspirational self-portrait—mediates between self-knowledge and self-determination. Sometimes one takes a retrospective view and searches one's past in order to better grasp what sort of person one is, to anticipate one's future prospects, and to figure out how to lead as rewarding a life as one can. The pleasures of reminiscence notwithstanding, memory may be principally an instrumental good. Bonnie Smith's recounting of a Parisian concierge's autobiographical history of modern France suggests that the desire for and prospect of achieving some minimal degree of self-determination may be necessary for memory. Near the end of her chronicle, Smith comments: "It now became clear that during the past few weeks Mme Lucie had reached the end of memory. In the depths of old age, present and future prospects had disappeared from her perspective on life, so she lost sight of the past" (Smith 1985, 150).

In the process of self-definition, the distinction between memory and self-description can dissolve, for self-figuration easily elides the present and the past. In summing up one's life in a trope, one simultaneously represents one's past experience and one's present condition. This may seem unexceptionable since most people believe that they are largely, if not wholly, products of their past experience. However, the trope of summing up misleadingly suggests that memory works by digesting a superfluity of detail and extracting a trope. Remembered experience constrains autobiographical figuration, but the relation between remembered experience and figuration is not unidirectional. As we have seen, people seldom derive narrative forms and imagery from their experience. They typically adopt ready-made plot templates and tropes of life trajectories or personality types, and they remember their experience as these culturally furnished literary devices ordain. Thus, a self-definitional trope one embraces in the present is constitutive of one's recollected past: It provides thematic threads for life stories; it highlights certain incidents and obscures others; and it prompts one to impute certain attitudes and intentions to oneself and others and to dismiss other interpretations as implausible.[6] The past inherits the present.

Still, figurative self-definition can seem paradoxical, for a figuration can aptly symbolize one's present and can provide an advantageous springboard into the future without accurately representing one's past. A timid scientist whose research has been rather pedestrian might accent an emerging self-confidence and perhaps improve her chances of doing more innovative work in the future by figuring herself as an adventurous explorer. But because people typically assume that the past determines the present—"the child is the father of the man" is among modern Western culture's highly favored plot templates—and because they see memory as a guarantor of personal identity, they are disposed to see continuity between their past and their present. This disposition poses a danger that self-figuration will lead people to falsify the past.

The danger becomes acute when an apt figuration of oneself in the present has not been derived from one's past but has instead been appropriated from a cultural cache. The trope of the adventurous explorer may color the scientist's memory in rosy hues. Downplaying the disappointing results of her research program while underscoring the boldness of the (indefensible) hypothesis she proposed, she may remember her professional persona as less mousy and more forceful. Slightly exaggerating the extent to which her present self-confidence is latent in her past may be harmless. But if her self-figuration persuades her to remember the lackluster work she has done as a trove of cutting-edge discoveries and to convert decisive refutations of her work into plaudits, her memories of her professional accomplishments run squarely afoul of the facts. She is falsifying the past and deceiving herself.

Trouble arises when people misapprehend and misuse the rhetoric of self-definition. They may mistake figurations for literal truths, and they may proceed to literalize these images by filling in mundane details that personalize them and expand them into autobiographical narratives.[7] Whereas self-figuration is a way of answering the question "What does it mean to be this way, to have these needs, to lack (or have) these skills, to experience these feelings?" literalization transmutes a self-figuration into an answer to the question "What caused me to be this way?" Since memory plays a pivotal role in self-definition, and since self-figuration structures memory, keeping these questions disentangled is no mean task.

The temptation to literalize self-figurative discourse is almost irresistible when the figurations are images of childhood scenes. Indeed, it seems that Freud surrendered to this siren call. His theory of psychic reality is a sophisticated compromise between the therapeutic value of figurative discourse and the allure of literal discourse. According to Freud, a girl's infantile desire pairs off with an iconic tableau—a father seducing a daughter. By individualizing the features of the daughter and the father to match her own and those of her father, and by locating the action in a familiar setting, the girl spins a personalized fantasy of incest that will prove devilishly difficult to distinguish from a childhood incestuous assault. In contrast, Julia Kristeva perspicaciously characterizes psychoanalysis as "a scene of metaphor production" (Kristeva 1987, 276). Psychoanalytic interpretations are animated mainly by imagination, and their primary medium is figurative language. For Kristeva, memory is incidental to the talking cure, and nothing is gained by recasting self-figurations as life stories.

Plainly, feminists cannot endorse a conception of self-definition or a psychotherapeutic method that altogether excludes memory. Such an approach would distract women from identifying the social causes of their suffering and induce them to personalize the political. Whether a woman's problems stem from discrimination at work or from childhood sexual abuse, protesting unfair or persecutorial practices presupposes recognizing them, and recognizing them presupposes remembering being harmed by them. If victims of wrongful practices turn inward and figure their experiences in an upbeat way that enables them to feel better instead of tracing their suffering to its source, they will never challenge oppressive institutions or call malign individuals to account. Feminist analysis and activism cannot dispense with memory.

Still, it is not always possible to trace one's problems to their cause(s). The aetiologies of many of one's traits, desires, feelings, and the like are sketchy and speculative at best. In many cases of recovered memory, there is no way to reach a well-supported judgment about the accuracy of one's memories. In such cases, I believe, the best course is to regard the sadistic incest scenario as a figurative window onto one's present and to remain agnostic about its relation to one's past. Where the past is epistemically opaque and the consequences of misremembering are likely to be horrible, it is advisable to separate self-definition from memory.

Psychological conditions that a sadistic incest scenario could aptly figure readily come to mind. They include feeling damaged where one is most vulnerable and least mendable; suffering from persistent, unsoothable anxiety; living in fear of spontaneity that might reveal one's terrible deficiencies; and feeling aggrieved by a vague, unrectifiable wrong. All of these complaints are amenable to this figuration, and, to judge by my experience, all of them are appallingly widespread among contemporary women. If it is true that people tend to adopt culturally furnished figurations and elaborate these figurations into autobiographical narratives, it is understandable that some fathers are perplexed and injured by their daughters' allegations of sexual abuse.[8] Likewise, it is understandable that many of the women making these charges are unshakable in their conviction that they were sexually assaulted. After all, the sadistic incest scenario does aptly figure their present state of mind, and the narrative analogue of figurative aptness is factual accuracy. Moreover, since shifting from the self-definitional figurative mode to the autobiographical narrative mode produces closure and relieves the terrible anguish attendant upon agnosticism about childhood trauma, the benefits of believing in a literalized sadistic incest scenario may overpower an individual's qualms about its credibility. Nevertheless, I would submit that gaining a subtle and complex understanding of the meaning of one's psychic makeup is both emotionally satisfying and helpful in bringing about felicific change (for discussion of how psychoanalysis harnesses the transformative power of metaphor, see Kristeva 1987, 13–16; Cavell 1993, 96–97). When identifying the causal antecedents of one's suffering is not possible, figuring one's life is the key to figuring out one's life.

4. *The Family Romance and Feminist Politics:*
Cultural Critique and Social Change

Apart from the light the sadistic incest scenario may or may not shed on a particular individual's past, there are several perspectives from which feminists must evaluate this trope. One is the prospective aim of self-definition. It is necessary to ask not only whether a self-figuration aptly symbolizes one's present condition but also whether it is conducive to a more rewarding life. Does the sadistic incest scenario now in currency help women to overcome constraints and to lead satisfying lives, or, like its predecessor, the trope of castration and penis envy, does it stifle women's potential and divert them into a cramped, subordinate social niche? Since the clinical evidence that is now available is spotty and contradictory, it would be premature to hazard an answer to these questions.

From another angle, however, assessing the merits of the sadistic incest scenario need not await well-wrought, longitudinal studies. I have furnished no criterion for distinguishing literalized self-figurations from ordinary autobiographical narratives in controversial cases, nor, as my recommendation for agnosticism implies, do I expect one to materialize. Certainly, an apparently honest and loving father's vigorous protestations of innocence do not suffice to pick out literalized self-figurations. Those who are principally concerned with issues of legal and moral responsibility for child abuse might consider this lacuna fatal to my account. However, I would argue that on the contrary my view has the virtue of pinpointing the menace of the family romance while at the same time showing why this menace need not be tolerated. What is most deplorable about the sadistic incest scenario is the grave disservice it does to women who are not entirely certain about their memories of abuse and to incest victims, both those who are certain about their abuse and those who are not.

For women who have recovered memories of incest but who also have reason to question whether these memories are accurate, the cultural circulation of this trope together with its widespread use to symbolize various sorts of dissatisfaction, frustration, and dislocation virtually guarantees that their doubts will never be satisfactorily resolved. Since nothing internal to these memories distinguishes them from literalizations of self-figurations, many of these individuals are doomed to a tormenting state of autobiographical limbo. However, if this trope were taken out of circulation, there would be no more reason to doubt memories of childhood sexual abuse than there is to doubt memories of affectionate paternal nurturance. Thus, the modification of the figurative repertoire that I am proposing would redound to the benefit of women in psychotherapy and their therapists. They would have less difficulty determining whether the problem needing treatment was childhood incest, and better diagnosis would presumably speed recovery. For the sake of women who are confused and distraught by recovered memories, then, I would urge feminists to repudiate the family romance.

In addition and even more sobering than my concerns about the autobiographical perplexity into which the sadistic incest scenario throws so many women, the ubiquity of the sadistic incest scenario impeaches the testimony of individuals whose fathers have sexually assaulted them. The fact that it is always possible that a woman has seized upon this figuration and literalized it provides a ready and credible defense for the most scurrilous fathers. There is a startling parallel between defense strategies in sexual abuse trials that involve recovered memories and defense strategies in acquaintance rape trials. In acquaintance rape cases, defense lawyers often play on familiar temptress and tease imagery that illicitly implants doubts about the victim's credibility in the minds of jury members, thereby strengthening the defendant's claim that his accuser consented to have sex. Likewise, in childhood sexual abuse cases, the sadistic incest scenario predisposes juries to accept defense attorneys' imputations of suggestibility to the woman who has preferred charges. By helping to raise doubts about the reliability of her memory, this figuration adds credence to the defendant's claim that "nothing happened." In other words, to countenance the cultural prevalence of the sadistic incest scenario is to perpetuate a major obstacle to prosecuting real villains. Since other figurations could be devised to symbolize the miseries and sorrows unrelated to childhood sexual abuse that the sadistic incest scenario is sometimes used to represent, feminists have every reason to oppose it and to champion alternative figurations. For the sake of the untold numbers of real incest victims, then, I would urge feminist therapists and theorists to marshal their critical powers to dispose of the family romance once and for all and to dedicate their imaginative powers to crafting counterfigurations that better serve the interests of women.

It would be a mistake, though, for feminists to delete the family romance scenario from the cultural repertoire without inserting alternative representations of childhood sexual abuse. To eliminate the former without introducing compensatory imagery would be to silence many women who have been sexually abused when young by depriving them of a culturally authoritative discourse through which they can give voice to their injuries. In effect, it would be to reinstate the mass denial of this evil that preceded the ascendancy of the sadistic incest trope.[9] The trick is to disentangle figurations of childhood sexual abuse from figurations of abuse-free psycho-sexual development and also to figure childhood sexual abuse so as to include the full range of common perpetrators—uncles, older brothers and their peers, step-fathers and other sexual partners of the mother, teachers and other adults who work closely with children, as well as fathers. Unless the stock of cultural representations is weeded and re-seeded in this way, individual women who are now autobiographically disenfranchised will remain unsure of their own pasts, and women who are sure of their past abuse will remain unable to get justice.

Nothing I have said blunts feminist critiques of gender and the family that take aim at child abuse in the home, nor does my view of recovered memory stymie feminist initiatives that seek to reform the criminal law in ways that make it more likely that child abusers will be convicted and punished. It is indisputable that incestuous child abuse is sufficiently prevalent to justify concerted feminist opposition.[10] Indeed, the mounting evidence that such abuse commonly precedes enrollment in welfare programs and that it thwarts recipients' efforts to obtain and keep jobs heightens the urgency of these feminist goals (DeParle 1999). Plainly, childhood sexual abuse is inflicting lifelong economic hardship on many women, and it is preventing them from asserting control over their future prospects. It is critical, therefore, that girls be protected from this cruelty.

Since displacing the family romance would create a cultural climate in which victims' claims would be less suspect, my view complements these other feminist approaches. The fin-de-siècle outbreak of multiple personality disorder and recovered memories of incestuous abuse has subsided. Yet, as long as the family romance remains the governing plot template for women's understanding of the emergence of their gender identity, there is every reason to expect similar outbreaks in future and to assume that they will revive the same epistemological conundrums that I have been examining. In the interim between these headline-grabbing flare-ups, innumerable women may suffer in silence. If women's memories are to speak credibly, the family romance and its pathological variants must be retired from repertory. Once this drama is out of production, there will cease to be any respectable excuse for distrusting women who accuse their fathers of sexually abusing them.

5. The Family Romance and Feminist Reclamation: Obstacles and Prospects

I would like to conclude by reflecting on the implications of the foregoing view of recovered memory for the larger project of feminist theory. Reclaiming women's experience has been an important dimension of this project. So far, it seems to me that feminists have had their greatest success in reclaiming women's experience of motherhood. Lately, however, feminist reclamation efforts have moved in an intriguing new direction, namely, women's experience of multiplicity. I would like to offer some observations regarding the impact that the tropes I have been discussing have on this undertaking. Before I do, however, let me stress that my conjectures should not be blown out of proportion. I am not claiming that culturally entrenched figurations of multiplicity exhaust the obstacles impeding feminist reclamation, but I do think these figurations are obstacles that should not be underestimated.

To put the view I want to advance in context, it is worth briefly reviewing the history of the feminist bid to reclaim motherhood. Central to the overall critique developed at the beginning of second-wave feminism was a critique of motherhood. The economic disadvantages were documented; the missed opportunities for personal fulfillment were recorded; the undercurrent of social contempt for motherhood was exposed. This critique alienated many women who already were mothers or who wanted to become mothers. Yet, it is indisputable that it fastened on real and serious problems. Subsequently, feminists sought to address the needs of mothers and to increase their options by demanding concrete changes like family leave, affordable, high-quality daycare, flex-time work schedules, and so

forth. A change in feminist rhetoric accompanied these policy demands—
a change that was not limited to toning down the critique. More significantly, motherhood was reconceived and revalued partly through feminist
counterfigurations.

Freud's family romance looks like it has a happy ending—girls grow up
to be mothers. But if maternity means pursuing a penis equivalent to compensate for an irremediable anatomical lack, maternity can hardly be cause
for feminist rejoicing. For motherhood to be reclaimed, it must be refigured in ways that express auspicious meanings, like gladly caring for a pre-
cious child. To the extent that Freud's family romance clings to the activity of mothering, motherhood eludes feminist reclamation. That, I would
venture, explains why so many feminist psychoanalysts have devoted so
much attention to creating counterfigurations of motherhood (Chodorow
1978; Kristeva 1987, 234–263; for commentary on this work, see Chapters
2–3 in this volume and Meyers 1994, 62–91).[11] They are seeking to displace established figurations of maternity that distort its meaning and belittle the contributions of mothers. They are seeking to figure maternity in
a way that promotes women's emancipatory aims.

Turning now to the project of reclaiming multiplicity, I think it is possible to discern a similar pattern. No feminist account of the self would be
complete without an account of oppositional agency and, specifically, an
account of how feminist critique can emerge and how feminist initiatives
can be mounted. Many feminist theorists have pointed out that a complex,
nontransparent self is needed to undergird an account of feminist agency.
A number of feminists who are sympathetic to postmodernism have proposed to understand the complex, nontransparent self as a multiplicitous
or plural self.

Maria Lugones's influential work illustrates the turn to multiplicity. Lugones maintains that she is constructed differently in different social
worlds—in the Anglo world, she is serious; in the Latino/Latina world,
she is playful (Lugones 1987, 9). For Lugones, this is not a case of being a
playful person who is inhibited in some social milieux but not in others
(Lugones 1987, 14). Rather, she insists that she is a different person in
each social context (albeit a person who remembers what it is like to be the
other person), and she concludes that she is a multiplicitous self (Lugones
1987, 14).

What is at stake in this line of thought becomes clear in Naomi Scheman's account of the self. After explicating the evils consequent upon
fetishizing a unified self, Scheman embraces the multiplicitous self (Sche-

man 1993, 96–105). But plainly a multiplicitous self is in danger of succumbing to terrifying and paralyzing fragmentation. Scheman concedes this liability: "The most striking and clear-cut cases of internal multiplicity are cases of multiple personality, a pathological condition typically caused by severe childhood abuse" (Scheman 1993, 102). Multiple personality disorder is a defense against devastating child abuse, often including incestuous sexual assault. By creating a "bad" alter who deserves the brutality heaped upon her, a child can make sense of her suffering and avoid condemning an adult whom she needs to trust and whose love she needs (Herman 1992, 103–107). Her need to protect herself from knowledge of the vicious harm she has endured may eventually bring about a proliferation of alters, that is, multiple personality disorder.

For women, the multiplicitous self is associatively linked to multiple personality disorder and incestuous childhood sexual assault. In other words, a dysfunctional condition brought on by unforgivable, pseudo-caregiving behavior figures multiplicity. It is no wonder, then, that the road to reclaiming multiplicity has proven nearly impassable—it is booby-trapped. No one wants to embrace pathology and victimization, and there is an alternative course that is by no means unattractive. Arguably, working to eradicate child abuse—to reform family relations and create a family environment in which dissociation would not be psychologically necessary—makes more sense than identifying with multiplicity. More tellingly, feminists cannot maintain that culturally entrenched figurations of gender generally have a profound effect on thought and yet theorize as if they were exempt from this insidious influence. Accordingly, there is reason for feminists to proceed cautiously in conceptualizing multiplicity since the trope of incest-driven alter formation is presumably shaping this theorizing.

Incest is a shattering experience that often leads to a shattered condition. As Scheman points out, therapists seek to repair this damage by persuading different alters to communicate with one another and to agree to some cooperative arrangements (Scheman 1993, 103). Unfortunately, the alters of multiple personality disorder are a fractious throng, and they mightily resist collaboration.

This description of multiple personality disorder is strikingly reminiscent of some well-known philosophical accounts of the state of nature, and it brings to mind feminist critiques of social contract theory. Feminists have argued that the contractarian conception of the individual as an independent, self-interested atom denies interdependency and the need for care and also that modeling justice on a bargain reached by wary rivals yields an impoverished vision of social relations (Baier 1987; Held 1987; Kittay 1999; for further discussion, see Chapter 3). Feminists must reject conceptions of the self that repeat the mistakes they have diagnosed in social contract theory. Conceiving the self as an internal population of self-interested, mutually competitive, unitary individuals would sabotage feminist agency, for feminist values and demands cannot be construed as those that no internal self would veto. Since living in a society structured by male dominance ensures that most women have internalized traditional feminine norms, the multiplicitous model of the self that multiple personality disorder figures entails that most women have an internal self that will refuse to endorse emancipatory values and demands. Women may have other internal selves that support feminist aims, but these selves need not prevail in the negotiation process.

I am not arguing for jettisoning the multiplicitous self.[12] Nor am I accusing Scheman of lapsing into theorizing the self as an internal population of possessive individualists. Indeed, her text guards against this very trap by tendering a diverse array of figurations of multiplicity (Scheman 1993, 100–103).[13] This leads me to believe that Scheman would agree that feminists need to vigilantly resist some of the implications of figuratively linking multiplicity to multiple personality disorder.[14]

My point is that reclamation requires reconception, as well as revaluation. Reconceiving the multiplicitous self requires figuring it in a more felicitous way, for multiplicity will remain in the grip of the picture of an internal mob of warring alters and the connotations of pathology and victimization that this picture conjures up unless it is refigured. It would be naive to suppose that the figurative connection between multiplicity and incest in Western culture can be severed by counterfigurative fiat. Indeed, this point should be underscored. Although Freud articulated the family romance in a particularly compelling way, and popularizations of psychoanalysis subsequently broadcast this figuration far and wide, various versions of this figuration have been in circulation virtually throughout recorded Western history. The family romance is, then, deeply embedded in Western culture, and it is durable. It would be wrong to try to suppress this figurative history, for to do so would be to betray women who have been subjected to unspeakable abuse. However difficult it will be to supplant it, though, it is plainly a task that feminists must undertake (Meyers 1992, 151–158). Meanwhile, it would be self-defeating for feminists to let multiplicity be absorbed by the trope of incest.

THE FAMILY ROMANCE

Happily, the counterfiguration project I am advocating is already under way. As I mentioned a moment ago, Scheman cites African, African-American, Latina, and lesbian figurations of multiplicity. I would also like to commend Ruth Leys's psychoanalytic counterfiguration to readers' attention. Ironically dubbing multiplicity "the scandal of dedifferentiation," Leys refigures multiplicity as primordial mimetic identification with the mother (Leys 1992,189, 201–203).[15] I urge feminists to build on this groundbreaking counterfigurative work. In conjunction with counterfigurations of motherhood and the mother-child relationship (see Chapter 2, Section 4; Chapter 3, Section 3), counterfigurations of multiplicity give voice to and redeem a domain of women's experience that culturally entrenched imagery misrepresents and vilifies. Thus, I close this chapter by opening another inquiry—an inquiry that I believe holds promise for preventing this fin de siècle from turning into a dead end for feminism.

CHAPTER FIVE

Lure and Allure: Mirrors, Fugitive Agency, and Exiled Sexuality

There are no ugly women, only lazy ones.
—Helena Rubenstein, quoted in Bartky, *Femininity and Domination*

The Clairol home treatment . . . has been a kind of purging for me, a tearing out
of my old life so that I might look in the mirror and see a new person, find a new
life, a way to be in the world that worked this time.
—Lynne Taetzsch, "Fighting Natural"

My mirror is the cemetery of smiles.
—Tada Chimako, "Mirror"

Starting from an early age, I had an unusually congenial acquaintance
with mirrors and a happy relationship with my body. All of this good fortune came to me in ballet studios.[1] Although many people seem to think
of ballerinas as epitomizing fluffy femininity, theirs is in fact a highly unorthodox femininity. In studios, they wear their hair pulled back tightly in
a sleek bun, and they dress simply in leotards and tights. The regulation
hairdo and costume are not designed to flatter. They are designed to expose every detail of the body's alignment and movement and to reveal
every imperfection. Mirrors panel the walls of ballet studios. Yet, for me
at least, the studio was never a place of narcissistic excess or anorexia. It
was a place of striving and discipline, a place of challenging but rewarding
work.[2] Of course, ballerinas care about how they look. I did, but I cared because I wanted to learn to perform in a way that would be worthy of an au-

dience. That meant dancing well, not admiring myself (or hating myself) in the mirror.

A ballerina cannot dance well by watching herself trying to dance well. If you have ever seen a ballet performance, you know that the dancers do not gape at the audience from the stage as if a mirror were before them. Head movement and the direction of the ballerina's glance are part of the choreography. In class, ballerinas check their placement once in a while and catch fleeting glimpses of themselves in the mirror as they dance. In rehearsal, they may pause and use the mirror to work on a difficult passage. Mostly, though, they rely on visceral cues. They aspire to move in beautiful patterns and to know when they are succeeding, not by looking in the mirror, but by feeling it in every sinew and nerve ending and in the flow of the movement. They aspire to dwell in the beauty of the dance, not to see themselves being beautiful.

My sensible relation to mirrors came to an abrupt and regrettable end with the onset of adolescence. Because my goals shifted from ballet to academics, I ceased to frequent the healthy mirror environment of the ballet studio. This void left me vulnerable to peer pressure and feminine norms, which promptly wrecked my alliance with my mirror image. Soon, I was as preoccupied with my looks and as distraught by what I saw in my looking glass as every other girl in my circle. Still, my memory of studying ballet has remained a beacon, and this chapter seeks to articulate the meaning of that flame—to decipher the codes of feminine narcissism and to rethink women's relationship to mirrors.

Although Narcissus was not a woman, narcissism is commonly considered a feminine vice. I trace this switch in Western cultural constructions of gender through three kinds of texts: the ancient myth of Narcissus together with versions by Ovid and an unknown medieval poet (Section 1), European and American paintings of women with mirrors (Section 2), and Freud's psychoanalytic resuscitation of narcissism as a primitive psychic need (Section 3). In these discourses, the rigidification of heterosexist norms goes hand in hand with the reassignment of narcissism to women. Pernicious as well is the particular narcissistic economy that cultural norms impose on women. Not only does this economy obstruct women's self-determination, but, perversely, it also undermines their narcissistic satisfaction. The stereotype of the narcissistic woman and the ubiquitous pictorial tropes and narratives that keep it alive encode a no-win feminine psychodynamic of eroticized estrangement from self—a subjectivity of self-doubt, perplexity, and frustration that defeats authentic narcissistic agency (Section 4). Challenging this lethal strand of misogyny, a number of feminist artists appropriate, interrogate, and reconstruct woman-with-mirror imagery. Sampling this work, I explore provocative and insightful woman-with-mirror imagery by Claude Cahun, Mary Cassatt, Orlan, Sam Taylor-Wood, and Carrie Mae Weems (Section 5). In my view, these artists' self-visionary imagery distills the key principles of an emancipated narcissism for women (Section 6).

Self-esteem, including appreciative regard for one's own appearance, is healthy. Indeed, such narcissistic satisfaction may be necessary to avoid self-effacement, desexualization, and craven mimicry of faddish beauty ideals. Yet, to ascribe narcissism to women is to sneer at them, to accuse them of overweening self-absorption and obsession with ridiculous beauty routines. Since contemporary gender stereotyping casts this aspersion indiscriminately on all women, reconceptualizing and reclaiming women's narcissism in feminist terms is long overdue.

1. Narcissus *and* Narcissa: *A Founding Tale and Its Repressed Double*

Everyone knows about Narcissus and his namesake, narcissism. However, many people make the mistake of assuming that Narcissus fell in love with himself, although the myth recounts a more complex psychosexual trajectory. Moreover, the line of descent between Narcissus's story and the vice that bears his name is convoluted, to say the least. I shall trace this lineage in some detail because it lays bare a feature of contemporary gender ideology that many women find disabling.

Let us begin by recalling the Greek myth (Graves 1960, 286–288). Shortly after Narcissus's birth, it is prophesied that he will live a long life provided that he never knows himself. A beautiful child, Narcissus grows up to be an equally beautiful youth. Suitors of both sexes fall in love with him because of his good looks and vie for his affection. Awash in others' admiration, Narcissus becomes so proud of his own beauty that he callously rejects one and all.

The nymph Echo joins this retinue of disappointed lovers. Echo has no voice of her own because Hera condemned her to repeat what she has last heard others say to punish her for using her voice in a conspiracy against the goddess. Still, luck gives Echo a chance to declare her love. Narcissus is separated from his companions while hunting for stags in a dense forest. When he realizes he has lost his party, he shouts, "Is anyone here?"

Echo, who has been tracking her dreamboat, replies, "Here!" and a duet of doubled lines ensues. Echo's last lyric is a plaintive entreaty, "Lie with me!" But, predictably, when she and Narcissus meet, he spurns her, as he has all the others. Now Echo's plight worsens. Tormented by unrequited love, her body fades away. All that remains is her mimetic voice.

Fortune treats another of Narcissus's admirers, Ameinius, even worse than Echo, for love drives him to suicide. In meeting this unhappy end, however, Ameinius retains a modicum of initiative and seals Narcissus's fate along with his own. What transpires depends on a malevolent gift, a weapon. Narcissus sends Ameinius a sword, which Ameinius soon uses to do away with himself. Unreciprocated love kills Ameinius, but it does not reduce him to abject desolation. He beseeches the gods to avenge his death as he falls upon the blade Narcissus gave him. Hearing his plea and displaying an Olympian flair for poetic justice, Artemis sentences Narcissus to die of the same misery he so cavalierly inflicts on others — unrequited love.

On another outing, Narcissus comes upon a clear and placid spring where he stops to drink. Espying his beautiful image in the water, he falls head-over-heels in love. He reaches out to embrace the beautiful youth who captivates him, but eventually he recognizes himself. Although he now knows it is his own reflection that he sees in the pool, he remains enthralled, unable to tear himself away. Knowing that he loves a phantom, he is consumed by grief. Yet, knowing also that this phantom will reappear whenever he looks into the water, he rejoices in its faithfulness, even as he suffers from its ephemerality. Echo sees the misfortune that has befallen Narcissus, and she pities him. But there is nothing she can do to save him. She can only repeat his despairing lament, "Alas! Alas!" as well as his last defeated words, "Ah, youth, beloved in vain, farewell!" At that, Narcissus follows Ameinius's lead, takes up a dagger, and dies by his own hand. From the blood-soaked ground where his body lies, a narcissus flower springs up. (The plant is said to be effective as a medication for ear problems, wounds, and frostbite.)

I have sketched Robert Graves's rendition of this myth, but there are others. Ovid embellishes the tale with an extended monologue in which Narcissus bemoans his frustration at not being able to touch or hear his beloved and stammers his mystification that his beloved refuses to surface and meet him (Ovid 1955, 85–86). Also, Ovid's ending differs from Graves's. Narcissus does not kill himself. Consumed by love, he loses his looks, grows emaciated, and perishes (Ovid 1955, 87). Like

Self-obsession can read the female body to waste

Echo's, Narcissus's body vanishes. All that remains in its place is a blossoming narcissus.

Ovid accents the fascinating questions about body image, subjectivity, and specularity that Narcissus's perceptually naive passion for his reflected image raises. Noteworthy, too, is Ovid's feminization of Narcissus. Unlike Graves's rendition in which Narcissus reaches an irresolvable *crise d'amour* but retains his capacity to act decisively, Ovid's telling lets Narcissus—like the fragile, albeit lovely, botanical species that bears his name—wither and die. Graves's Narcissus meets a manly death, taking control and wielding a warrior's weapon. Ovid's Narcissus becomes a passive victim of his ill-starred love. From the standpoint of norms of masculinity, this is an ignoble, womanish death. Indeed, it is plainly reminiscent of Echo's disembodiment. I emphasize this congruence because Ovid's death scene adumbrates the recoding of narcissism as a feminine attribute. Arguably, it adumbrates the recoding of Narcissus's bisexuality as culpably effeminate, as well.

Medieval poets revived Ovid's version of the Narcissus myth and recycled it as a cautionary tale for courtly lovers. In his study of *Narcisus*, a twelfth-century poem penned by an unknown Norman-French author, Frederick Goldin both analyzes the psychic underpinnings of the myth and distills the moral of the story for the medieval knight (Goldin 1967, 22–52). In transposing the myth into the human social world and exploring the pedagogical powers of love, the medieval poet supplies the mediating symbolism that finalizes the curious reversal from Narcissus's maleness to the femaleness of the vice of narcissism.

In brief, what happens in *Narcisus* is that the beautiful young man spurns a maiden, Dané, who prays that he will suffer, as she does, the agonies of unrequited love (Goldin 1967, 23). The male suitor, Ameinius, is banished from the twelfth-century account, which locates the story in an unequivocally heterosexual social universe. In the medieval lyric, a narrative symmetry between Dané's and Narcisus's psychological development —the emergence of their subjectivities through the experience of love and love's terrible tribulations—replaces the ancients' aural trope of doubling, Echo (Goldin 1967, 24). Departing again from ancient mythology, the medieval poet adds an episode in which Narcisus learns his lesson before he dies. Not only does he realize his folly in falling in love with a mere image, not to mention an image of himself, he also realizes that loving Dané would extricate him from his morbid impasse. Thus, he reproaches himself for his cruelty and prays that she will come to the spring (Goldin 1967,

38–39). His wish is granted. But, his strength severely depleted, Narcisus is overcome by anguish, and he succumbs to a fainting fit. Resurrecting but repositioning the original myth's motif of lost voice, the medieval poet deprives Narcisus of his ability to speak. Mutely gesturing at the pool where his beautiful image lured him into an impossible love, he manages to convey to Dané what distracted him from her charms and why he was indifferent to her overtures (Goldin 1967, 40). Grateful for his remorseful confession of error, Dané regrets her vengeful entreaty that Narcisus be made to endure the misery of unrequited love, and the reconciled pair die together (Goldin 1967, 40). Although the lovers do not live to consummate their bond, Narcisus understands—and readers are advised—that it is necessary "to find a living person with all the beauty and perfection of the image" and to devote oneself to that person (Goldin 1967, 40). Unrequited love is death. Only the love of a living woman can requite a man's love.

Schematically, the medieval poem moves from identifying beauty with manhood in the figure of Narcisus and picturing love as Narcisus's rapt gaze at his reflected image to displacing the value of beauty onto a woman and redefining love as heterosexual congress. The glassy surface of the water discloses to Narcisus a vision of perfection—his beautiful visage or, metaphorically, his ideal self (Goldin 1967, 37). But it is merely an alluring image that the water returns. It paralyzes the beholder who does not see through its deceptive resemblance to a real person. To break the circle of delusional self-absorption, a man must project his vision of self-perfection onto a woman—in medieval parlance, a lady—who thereafter serves as the mirror of his beauty, or, in other words, as the image of his ideal self. His self-ideal is preserved and symbolized. But by loving a flesh-and-blood woman, he can go on living, for his love can be returned.

The medieval lyric makes it clear why narcissism is not culturally ascribed to men. For a man, the price of narcissism is emasculation, which the poem represents as Narcisus's losing his voice and, finally, dying. There is also a heterosexist subtext in the medieval rendering of Narcisus's demise. Amors, the power of love, destroys Narcisus because he "annihilates procreative love," that is, reproductive heterosexuality (Goldin 1967, 42). A man must love an ideal, ultimately unattainable woman, and he must perform great deeds to win her affection. He must become an accomplished knight and a courtly lover. Still, it is not obvious why narcissism is culturally ascribed to women. Since neither the ancient myth nor the medieval poem ever raises doubts about the genuineness of Echo's or

Dané's love for Narcissus/Narcisus, and since neither woman is accused of excessive self-regard, it is necessary to ask how women gained their stereotypical reputation for narcissism.

The sequence of events in the twelfth-century narrative subtly effects the symbolic transfer of narcissism from Narcissus (or Narcisus) to Woman. If Man's self-ideal can only be represented as a vision of beauty, and if the Lady's role is to be a substitute for the reflective surface that gives Man his first glimpse of his self-ideal, the Lady must embody Man's self-ideal by being beautiful.[4] Surely, one need not be a committed Platonist, as so many thinkers of the twelfth-century were, to know that no actual woman's natural physical endowment is flawless. Thus, imperfect as they are, yet assigned the task of representing perfection through their appearance, women are obliged to dedicate themselves to self-beautification. To meet men's psychic needs—to free men from the icy specular sepulcher of self-love—women must take up the mirror and become narcissistic.[5]

Now, it might seem that the ancient Greek tale gives women a stake in this dynamic. Unlike his medieval descendant, Narcissus is not monosexual. Perhaps it is accidental that his genitalia are male. Perhaps there could just as well be a myth of Narcissa. Indeed, the ancient version of the story can easily accommodate this hypothetical sex change. Although it initially seems a little implausible that a woman would love her own looks so much that she would be bewitched by her reflection, wither away, and die, it is necessary to bear in mind that when Narcissa first spots her image in the perfidious pond, she has no previous knowledge of what she looks like and therefore cannot yet know that she is seeing her own image.[6] Maybe women would be more appreciative of their appearance if they could be tricked into thinking they were viewing someone else's reflection.

What, though, if we attempt to transcend Narcissus's tragedy by inserting Narcissa into the medieval finale? Suppose that Narcissa learns that she can be released from her emotional frustration and her bondage to her exquisite image by projecting her specular ideal onto a man who will henceforth dedicate himself to cultivating his appearance in order to embody her ideal as fully as a mere male mortal possibly can. At this point, I suspect most readers' cognitive and emotional gears are starting to grind and clank. The idea of a masculine life consumed by the narcissistic project of appearance enhancement is at odds with everything masculinity conventionally connotes. Likewise, casting the Lady's counterpart, the Knight, as the dutiful servant of Woman's imperious psychic needs seems like a bit of self-refuting nonsense. Common sense tells us that narcissistic self-objectification is not a salient dimension of a credibly masculine psychic economy.

I think that the anonymous twelfth-century author of *Narcisus* elegantly captures a gender asymmetry that lingers and plagues us to this day. The myth of Narcissa is a silly comedy, if not a preposterous one, because the myth of Narcissus is a moving tragedy that capitalizes on the logic of culturally entrenched gender imperatives. The weakness of the poem lies in its philosophy of love. In my view, its author does not understand love well enough to recommend a good remedy for Narcisus's desperate predicament. In particular, he fails to grasp the significance of a highly illuminating twist of the ancient Greek plot. Recall that Echo, who speaks only fragments of Narcissus's prior utterances, is desolate as she witnesses her beloved's lovelorn suffering. Recall, too, that she is powerless to prevent his suffering from culminating in suicide. To be loved by a woman who has no voice of her own is to be loved by an individual whose capacity to deliberate and act is gravely impaired. Narcissus's dying while Echo helplessly looks on dramatizes the insight that a love constituted by one partner's dumb mirroring of the other is a love at risk. Alas, this ancient wisdom has escaped its heirs. Specular imagery of women is pervasive in the history of Western art, and it dominates modern psychological accounts of subjectivity and interpersonal relationships.

2. Narcissus *(a Translation): The Visual Culture of Feminine Narcissism*

The ancient Greeks and Romans were in some respects less rigid about gender and sexuality, but it is jarring to many twenty-first–century sensibilities that a male, Narcissus, personifies beauty in all versions of this tale. The Narcissus myth's low profile in European and American art from the Middle Ages to the present may have contributed to these attitudes. Paintings of female incarnations of beauty abound, as do paintings of male incarnations of virility. But paintings of the fair Narcissus gazing at his reflection are scarce. In a relatively unknown work, Caravaggio essays this subject: Narcissus hovers breathlessly above his watery double, gazing longingly and tenderly upon it.[7] In contrast, Salvador Dali deemphasizes Narcissus's beauty and spotlights his rebirth. Narcissus crouches in the shallows of the pond, his golden body reduced to smooth outlines, his face invisible, while beside him an elongated, gray hand holds aloft a white egg from which a narcissus sprouts.[8] Other pictorial treatments of this myth are far less well known.

This dearth is surprising because Western artists (and their patrons) seem to have an insatiable appetite for mythological themes and because the Narcissus tableau would seem to present a tantalizing subject for painting.[9] Nevertheless, it is altogether in keeping with the wider suppression of man-with-mirror imagery in European and American art. Although this aesthetic tradition supplies few images of men looking at themselves in mirrors, the extant examples pinpoint instructive differences between these artworks and those that feature women. Apart from the rare depictions of Narcissus I have mentioned, one finds pictures of male artists using mirrors to paint their self-portraits[10] and, less frequently, pictures in which the virtue of prudence is rendered as a man gaining self-knowledge by contemplating his specular self.[11] Men are never shown at their toilette preening before the silvered glass, let alone studying their looks and laboring to improve them. At least, I have not been able to locate such an image.

This hole in the history of Western art stands in stark contrast to the profusion of woman-with-mirror imagery produced during the same historical periods. Indeed, it is virtually unimaginable that imagery conjoining women and mirrors could be culturally and psychologically foreclosed in the same way that comparable imagery of men and mirrors is. Except in paintings depicting a virtue or an artist at work, man-with-mirror imagery is perceived as effeminate, if not homosexual, whereas paintings depicting the vice of vanity are perceived as archetypal images of femininity. Still, to appreciate the complexity of the gender issues that woman-with-mirror artworks raise, it is important to inventory the full range of these representations.

No female figure is more pictorially identified with the mirror than Venus, the sexpot prototype. Goddess of love—especially sexual love—her prime attribute is beauty (Pomeroy 1995, 6). By bourgeois standards, her character leaves everything to be desired. She is frivolous and deceitful; she indulges in adulterous liaisons (Pomeroy 1995, 6). Yet, her bimbo reputation only enhances her allure. Although associated with fertility, Venus is no mother figure. Her femininity is that of the passionate, sensual lover par excellence, the femininity of sex appeal. Fittingly, a cadre of "harlot-priestesses" presides over her cult, and the prostitutes of Rome worship at her temple (B. Walker 1983, 1043; Pomeroy 1995, 7).

Renaissance "portraits" of Venus in conference with her mirror are circumspect. Their approval is evident but qualified. Invariably, Venus's impish son, Cupid, proffers a looking glass, and she does not resist this invi-

FIGURE 5.1 *Venus with a Mirror*, Titian, c. 1555,
National Gallery of Art, Washington, D.C.

tation to narcissistic dalliance. However, the mirror is not kind to Venus in two major works of this genre. Complacent—and justly so—as Venus seems to onlookers, her mirror image is not commensurate with the gorgeous and poised "real" figure the artist describes.

In Titian's rendition, *Venus with a Mirror* (Figure 5.1),[12] the goddess modestly draws a luxurious cloak around her lower torso and raises a hand to cover her bosom. As an eager putto advances from the background with a laurel wreath to crown her pearl-entwined coiffure, Venus looks intently, but serenely, into her mirror. We see only a fragment of her reflection, for the angle at which Cupid holds the mirror makes it look as if Venus's reflection is peering out from a hiding place. But what we see of her reflection is unexpected—a furrowed brow and a frightened eye that bear no resemblance to the expression on the face they supposedly reflect. The mirror seems to show her how she feels or how she should feel, not how she looks.

In Velazquez's version, *The Toilet of Venus* or, as it is better known, *The Rockeby Venus* (Figure 5.2),[13] an alabaster-complected, curvaceous nude lies langorously on a gauzy coverlet, her back to her beholders. We see Venus's neatly coiffed head, but we are vouchsafed only a sliver of her facial profile. Nevertheless, the contours of the face that we glimpse are delicate and refined, which makes the rather coarse visage staring back at us from the smoky mirror all the more startling. It is as if a pudding-faced, frizzy-haired servant girl has taken possession of a high-class courtesan's mirror and is brazenly inspecting her employer's company from that privileged vantage point.

In contrast, one of Rubens's tributes to Venus, *Venus before the Mirror* (Figure 5.3),[14] presents an unalloyed celebration of her corporeality and allows her to enjoy her self-regarding interlude without recrimination. While Cupid and a black servant direct their attention to her adorable face, Venus gazes impassively at her stunning image in a bright, beveled glass. Unlike Titian and Velazquez, Rubens gives Venus a flattering mirror. If anything, Venus's mirror image looks more magnificent, more assured than her "real" face in his picture. To be sure, all three of these paintings worship at the altar of female pulchritude. Still, feminine narcissism is rewarded only in the Rubens.

There is reason to be cautious about interpreting these mirror images. Renaissance mirrors were far less clear than today's unforgiving glasses. Still, I would urge that they were reasonably accurate, and, besides, painters can insert any image they want within the frame of the glass. Although primitive optics and crude manufacturing must be adduced to ac-

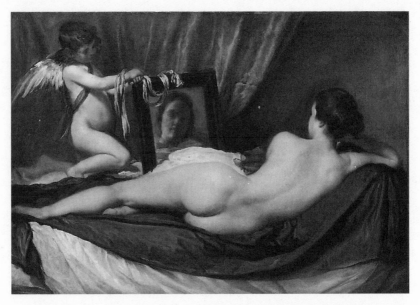

FIGURE 5.2 *The Toilet of Venus (The Rockeby Venus)*, Diego Velazquez, 1647–1651, National Gallery, London.

count for blurriness and darkness in mirrors of this period, they cannot account for the substantive discrepancies between Titian's and Velazquez's Venuses and their respective reflected images. Refractive distortions stretch, compress, and bend images. Since mirrors neither reinvent facial expressions nor conjure up absent faces,[15] the mirrors in these works must be viewed as pictorial devices through which each artist articulates a distinctive view of his subject. If this is so, Titian's Venus betrays the anxiety that haunts a narcissistic economy: "Am I really perfect?" "How long will it last?" Velazquez's Venus reveals a preoccupation with being seen that belies her studied nonchalance and intrudes upon her narcissistic communion: "Are others seeing me the way I want them to?" "Are they still enthralled?" Narcissism, these painters suggest, is not a self-contained, self-sustaining form of selfhood.

It is possible that Rubens sees this difficulty, too, but represents it more obliquely. Although he depicts no conflict between Venus and her mirror image, his scene includes an underling Other whose reassuring gaze may insulate and buoy Venus's narcissistic gaze. As I read this painting, the slight magnification of Venus's beauty that her mirror bestows is an effect of this servant's scopic ministrations, not to mention her day-in-day-out,

FIGURE 5.3 *Venus before the Mirror*, Peter Paul Rubens, 1616,
Collections of the Prince of Lichtenstein, Vaduz Castle, Lichtenstein.

ego-boosting assistance with hygiene and self-display. By itself, unrivaled beauty—nonpareil sexiness—cannot support narcissistic contentment.

Even idealizing woman-with-mirror imagery has an edge, it seems. But plenty of woman-with-mirror imagery is overtly derogatory. Many paintings describe a woman's obsession with or undue satisfaction with her mirror image and use it as a pretext to moralize about the vice of vanity. Moreover, Christianity brings the themes of vanity—overinvestment in one's outward appearance—and vanitas—the futility and foolishness of pursuing worldly goods in the face of the inevitability of death—into close proximity.[16] Excessive concern with or inflated pride in one's appearance interferes with religious observance. Moreover, inasmuch as beauty incites nonprocreative eroticism, it belongs among the transient, worldly pleasures that are best shunned in the quest for eternal salvation.

By and large, woman-with-mirror vanitas imagery is awfully ham-fisted. In some early works, a skull appears in the woman's mirror, or the Grim Reaper stalks her while she stands mesmerized before her reflected image.[17] The most enviable appearance, these paintings allege, merely masks the inner corruption that is steadily propelling the vain woman toward a death devoid of salvation. Unlike in Dali's *The Metamorphosis of Narcissus*, there is no redemption in these paintings. Narcissism is fatal. Nothing of value comes of the life or death of a narcissistic woman. Beauty is an illusory value, a distraction from piety.[18] This is the censorious teaching of Georges de La Tour's memento mori depictions of Mary Magdalen. In *The Penitent Magdalen*,[19] for example, Mary Magdalen is shown renouncing her compact with the mirror. Seated with a skull resting in her lap and her hands folded upon the skull, she gazes at a blackened mirror that reflects only a candlestick holding a short, burning candle. Whether the soon-to-expire flame represents the fleetingness of life, or the glow it casts on Mary represents her successful atonement and spiritual grace, it is clear from the discarded jewelry strewn next to the mirror and below at Mary's feet that she has eluded the clutches of vanity and sent Satan packing.

Let me add that this dreary theme did not vanish with the advent of modern painting. Although redemption has no place in Ivan Albright's morbid world view, his skepticism does not deter him from taking a jab at feminine narcissism in *Into the World There Came a Soul Called Ida*.[20] Her dressing table littered with all the paraphernalia of classic vanitas still lifes—fragile flowers, filthy lucre, a burning cigarette (instead of a candle!)—Ida is seated on a rickety wicker chair. Shreds of a handwritten note—her lover's exit?—are scattered beneath her chair. She wears only undergarments, an open blouse, and black pumps. Her face is puffy, and her bruise-toned flesh bulges out of her tight slip and shoes. Still, her eyelashes are curled and mascaraed, her cheeks and lips are rouged, and she raises a hand mirror and powders her bosom. Although her appearance is well beyond repair or camouflage, Ida does not abandon her self-beautifying routine, and she keeps faith with her cruel mirror. Feminine narcissism is both a trope and a tropism—an ingrained behavioral sequence—in Albright's painting.

The predominant tenor of European and American woman-with-mirror imagery is bleak. Narcissism is fraught with perils; vanity is a sin; beauty is no substitute for piety. But there are a few pictures that use woman-with-mirror imagery as a vehicle for depicting a virtue. I have already noted that one form of culturally condoned man-with-mirror imagery represents the virtue of prudence. Peering into a mirror is a metaphor for introspection and the acquisition of self-knowledge, a prerequisite for prudence. Happily, masculine imagery does not monopolize this virtue; a number of artists opt for woman-with-mirror imagery to represent it.[21] But because of the inscrutability of pictorial imagery and the widespread use of woman-with-mirror imagery for a host of other purposes, it is not always obvious whether a work's subject is a virtue or a vice. Since the female figures in allegories of prudence and vanity are often equally comely, and since the mirror's verdict in an allegory of prudence can be as harsh as its verdict in an allegory of vanity, allegories of prudence that would otherwise be difficult to distinguish from allegories of vanity sometimes declare their intended subject by including the serpent of wisdom among the female figure's attributes (Miller 1998, 172). In contrast, painters never developed an ancillary iconography to identify feminine personifications of vanity. Evidently, artists rely on misogynist gender stereotyping to make the meaning of the combination of a mirror and a woman (she need not be avidly interested in her image, nor need she be pretty) transparent. More explicit pictorial labeling of this device for depicting vanity is not needed.

Jonathan Miller claims that mirror imagery falls into two categories: (1) "ethically neutral, nonjudgemental [sic] representations" in which the mirror is merely a "household appliance" and (2) "moralising tableaux" in which a virtue or vice is personified (Miller 1998, 142). I agree that some of these works have a definite moral agenda, but I disagree that any of these works is normatively neutral. As instances of the "neutral" representations, Miller cites pictures of mundane domestic scenes, for example, women washing, putting on makeup, or dressing to go out, and commercial scenes, for example, women being fitted for new dresses or trying on hats in a shop.[22] These works desacralize and deflate the pretensions of the woman-with-mirror imagery I have discussed so far; however, it does not follow that they are not individually and collectively normative, for the scope of the normative is considerably broader than that of the moral.

Without comment, the pictures Miller deems neutral reiterate in the medium of paint what many middle-class women of the period were in fact doing. Under the circumstances, that none of these pictures critiques these routines or suggests that there ought to be more to these women's lives is advocacy enough. To encourage people to keep doing what they are already doing, it is not necessary to glorify their practices. In the absence of strong condemnation of their behavior or potent incentives to do otherwise, inertial propensities coupled with a lack of socially acceptable alternatives suffice to perpetuate the status quo and consolidate allegiance to it. It is also worth considering how women might respond to these pictures today. To an overburdened, stressed-out working mother, these scenes of unhurried personal care and leisurely shopping might well assume a nostalgic aura and remind her of lost values, such as privacy, solitude, and tranquility. Consequently, these depictions of unrealistically calm feminine lives may be perceived as arguing for women to shed their hectic double day of work and home life and return to the domestic sphere.

Whether we focus on their reception at the time they were made or their reception now, it is clear that these ostensibly neutral, seemingly benign images carry normative weight. It is important, then, to notice what that normative content is. These woman-with-mirror images depict the norm of feminine narcissism along with everyday pleasures and values. By associating the pernicious norm of feminine narcissism with these genuine pleasures and values, they contribute to the cultural climate that locks that norm in place.

It might be thought that contemporary cinema shatters the representational bond between woman-with-mirror imagery and narcissism, for scenes showing a man grooming before a mirror are not uncommon. I doubt, however, that the gender barrier between man-with-mirror imagery and the theme of narcissism has been breached. If a male character is neither gay nor a target of ridicule, his checking and adjusting his hair, his costume, and his countenance functions in the plot as a preparation to take on whatever momentous challenge the script has waiting for him. The hero is about to seduce a woman, to make a crucial speech, to wow a prospective employer, or to vanquish some formidable foe. For "real" men, primping and self-admiration are never ends-in-themselves. They are means of using one's looks to bolster one's confidence and achieve one's goals. Masculine norms still dictate that a man's identity derive from who he is and what he does, not how he looks.

Feminine norms dictate the opposite. Women are supposed to depend on their mirrors to know who they are. From this standpoint, woman-with-mirror figurations of prudence do not read as metaphors for introspection. They read as admonitions to look and learn. Indeed, Christian doctrines of eternal life aside, vanity and prudence are not in tension for women as long as feminine narcissism is the norm. For women, to know oneself is to know one's appearance and the worth of that appearance in the parallel economy of heterosexual partnership. How apt that the French call a woman's boudoir mirror her *psyché*![23]

If a woman's identity is the image she finds in her mirror, cultivating her appearance must be central to her agency. Just as the cultivation of character and capabilities is an approved form of masculine self-definition, so self-beautification is an approved form of feminine self-definition. But whereas men augment their self-determination in this way, it is far from clear that what I shall term women's psychic/*psyché* economy is compatible with women's self-determination. Indeed, I shall argue that, although it makes women more alluring commodities on the principal erotic attraction exchange—the heterosexual market—it confounds authentic agency. Freud's psychoanalytic update of the Narcissus myth extends the imprimatur of "scientific" psychology to the norm of feminine narcissism and concedes its disabling consequences for women's agency.

3. Narcissus Meets Oedipus *(the Sequel): Psychoanalysis, Agency, and Heterosexism*

The modern mythology of psychoanalytic theory reformulates the psychodynamics of doubling and keeps a narrative of narcissism in circulation.[24] Freud's retelling of the Narcissus fable should not be overlooked, for it replaces self-righteous condemnation of women's vanity with a pseudoscientific account of the psychological consequences of women's "inferior" anatomy; it certifies the psychic/*psyché* economy as the governing principle of "normal" women's lives; and it codifies the heterosexist moral of the tale.[25] Since Jacques Lacan names a key stage of identity formation the *mirror stage*, his psychoanalytic theory might seem most germane to my discussion. However, because Lacan's version of psychoanalysis has never been popularized to the extent that Freud's has, and because Lacan's remarks about homosexuality are so brief and cryptic, I shall focus on Freud's more culturally influential reframing of the Narcissus myth. Reviewing his psychoanalytic account of narcissism underscores how this theme endures in the gender and sexuality ideology of our own epoch.

For Freud, infants are born into an undifferentiated state—they do not distinguish between themselves and their environment. Neither other people nor physical objects are recognized as distinct entities. This original condition is called "primary narcissism," for one cannot respond to anyone else if one does not realize that there is anything more to the universe than one's own feelings and needs. One is self-absorbed—concerned only with oneself—by default. As Freud memorably puts it, we all once fancied ourselves " 'His [*sic*] majesty, the baby' " (Freud 1990, 194).

But soon the infant experiences disappointment and frustration—hunger is prolonged before feeding, crying fails to bring instant cuddling, and so on. These troubles prompt the individual's emergence from the narcissistic cocoon. Obliged by deprivation to recognize the existence of independent individuals and things, the infant gradually develops an awareness of its own physical boundaries along with a sense of a distinct subjectivity.

Time passes. The anal stage displaces the oral stage, and then the phallic stage begins. Narcissism does not disappear. But it is now tempered by the reality principle, and it is focused on an individuated subject. Let's pick up the story at the phallic stage—the climactic moment when Narcissus meets Oedipus.

The Oedipus complex is all about narcissistic wounds, and, as in the myth of Narcissus, sight plays a prominent part. Indeed, children enter the Oedipus complex by seeing the difference between anatomical completeness and anatomical defect. In particular, they see people with penises and people without penises, that is, they see presence and absence, and they see their own bodies as whole or lacking. This scopic discovery plunges them into the trauma of the castration complex—for boys, anxiety about keeping what they've got; for girls, shame about their missing part. The castration complex sparks the development of sexual orientation and gendered personalities.

The boy who loves his mother and wants to kill his father confronts the incest taboo. Having learned that some people do not have penises, he fears that his father will castrate him if he persists in wooing his mother. Deterred by the prospect of the ultimate narcissistic wound, the boy identifies with his father's masculinity and gives up his amorous attachment to his mother. When he reaches the genital stage (puberty) much later, he will seek another woman as a sexual partner. In contrast, the girl enters the Oedipus complex by discovering that she already lacks a penis—that she is already castrated. Angry at her mother both for not having a penis and for not giving her one, she redirects her erotic interest to her father. Of course, that object choice is incestuous, too. So, at the genital stage, love for a male from another family will supplant it.

What becomes of Narcissus? Because of their sheer terror in the face of the castration threat, boys are highly motivated to prevail over the Oedipus complex. As a result, they decisively repress their love for their mothers and find outlets for this repudiated affect in sublimation. They develop strong superegos (consciences). They seek achievement through work— the arts, politics, science, and so forth. In love, they are giving. They experience what Freud calls "attachment" or "anaclitic" love—loving, as children do, the person who cares for them and on whom they depend. Men's principal need is to love another, and they idealize the beloved other, whoever she may be (Freud 1990, 192). Freud terms the result "sexual overvaluation," and he maintains that the man's ego is thereby impoverished (Freud 1990, 192). Thus, he absolves heterosexual men of the sin of vanity and endows them with socially responsible desire and agency.

In contrast, the Freudian tale assigns narcissism a leading role in women's lives. Unlike "normal" men, "normal" women love only themselves and desire to be loved by men, not to love them (Freud 1990, 192–193). Since females are castrated by nature, girls have little incentive to move beyond the Oedipus complex. Not only are their superegos weak, making them morally unreliable, but also they have difficulty with sublimation and less ability to gain fulfillment through socially useful projects (Freud 1990, 357, 361–362). Encumbered by their genital defect and the blow it delivers to their egos, they contrive an exaggerated, compensatory narcissistic economy (Freud 1990, 360). Busy with self-adornment and self-display, they relish compliments and tokens of affection. When women's narcissistic defenses are working well, they resemble children in the throes of untrammeled narcissism and exhibit a charming "self-contentment and inaccessibility" (Freud 1990, 193).

In general, women only experience attachment love (also known as "complete object-love"!) for their children. But even here the roots of feminine love confirm women's unquenchable narcissism. Because mothers perceive their children as separated parts of their own body, and because a penis-bearing male child symbolically heals their narcissistic wound, they may be able to extend their self-love fully to a child (Freud 1990, 193, 356, 361). Indeed, the only way a woman can truly love a man is by infantilizing him (Freud 1990, 361). When an adult male assumes the position of a woman's son, her narcissistic affect can be converted into attachment love for him, too.

Freud's contention that people are fundamentally bisexual has won him a reputation for fair-minded views about homosexuality. To some extent, this reputation is deserved, for Freud denies that homosexuality is pathological. Unfortunately, he also regards it as deviant. His biologistic supposition that the Darwinian survival-of-the-species imperative entails that "normal" development must eventuate in procreative heterosexuality prejudices his account.

Freud's views about gay sexuality suggest that, like women, these men are drowning in Narcissus's transfixing puddle. Because of their disturbed libidinal development, the model for their choice of love objects is "not their mother but their own selves" (Freud 1990, 191–192). Never having surpassed a pre-Oedipal narcissistic economy, these individuals "are plainly seeking *themselves* as love object, and are exhibiting a type of object-choice which must be termed 'narcissistic'" (Freud 1990, 191–192). Their modus operandi is to "find a young man who resembles themselves and whom *they* may love as their mother loved *them*" (Freud 1990, 94, n.1). Freud's remarks are cryptic. But what is clear is that gynophobia causes men to be attracted to men, whereas the nature of their love is feminine. Although gays may outwardly appear masculine, they are emotional and erotic women—that is, narcissists. Worse, it is doubtful that gay narcissistic love could evolve into attachment love as a mother's love for her son can, for the gay man's beloved is his double, not his complement.

Predictably, Freud assimilates lesbian sexuality and love to that of the heterosexual man. Lesbians suffer from "masculinity complexes" (Freud 1990, 357). Instead of surrendering to the "wave of passivity," which is the "normal" response to the feminine castration complex, future lesbians retreat to their innate masculinity—that is, their pre-Oedipal, active, clitoral sexuality (Freud 1990, 357). In Freud's case study of a young woman's lesbianism, he highlights her masculine character traits. In her relations with the older woman she fastens on, the lesbian is emotionally masculine: She idealizes her beloved, renounces her own narcissism, and prefers loving over being loved (Freud 1990, 249). Like many men who become enamored with women of "ill repute," she entertains fantasies of rescuing her beloved from her disgrace (Freud 1990, 256). Motherhood holds no interest for her (Freud 1990, 264).

This account parallels Freud's account of masculine heterosexuality to some extent. "Normal" boys take measures to avoid castration. Similarly, the lesbian denies her socially ascribed mutilation and impudently contrives to preserve a sense of intact selfhood. The difference, of course, is that boys really have penises to protect, and girls really do not. Lesbians mobilize residual narcissistic propensities to sustain an illusion. Thus, the agency fueled by a masculinity complex is not true agency. It stems from regression to a pre-Oedipal active eroticism, not from demolishing the Oedipus complex and sublimating incestuous affect and castration anxiety. Whether they are lesbians or heterosexuals, then, women are agentically disenfranchised. If they escape the confines of self-beautification and mothering, they merely mimic the activities of men. Self-determination eludes them.

When medieval poets appropriated the story of Narcissus, they purged the homoerotic subplots and shifted the liabilities of narcissism onto women. Subsequent representations of narcissism in European and American painting did nothing to dispel these simplifications of the ancient myth or to refute the heterosexism and misogyny that underwrite them. Much contemporary popular culture remains well within that tradition. Psychoanalytic narratives naturalize these cultural undercurrents and embed them in comprehensive and authoritative stories of our lives.[26] That feminine subjectivity and agency are governed by a disabling psychic/*psyché* economy is culturally reaffirmed. Modern heterosexual men, like the courtiers and knights of old, are the only authentic lovers and agents.

4. Narcissa *(a Pitch for an Adaptation)*: The Need for Feminist *Reconstruction of Narcissistic Identity and Agency*

Among post-Freudian, "postfeminist" women, the belief that women are already free has taken hold, and feminist concerns about women's agency are dismissed as paranoid victimology. Many young women affirm "looking good" and the effort that goes into it as what they truly want, and they deny being manipulated or controlled. Customers of cosmetic surgeons commonly testify to their self-determination. "I did it for me," they aver, not to satisfy a male partner or to attract one (Davis 1995, 127). For these women, appearance is a nonissue at the personal level, and it is equally irrelevant at the political level. Is it true, then, that these women have achieved a self-sustaining narcissism—a narcissism that is not fueled by manufactured insecurity and that does not depend on accolades to thrive? Have they found themselves and an aesthetic that is truly their own?

One of their partisans among theorists hastens to assure us that what seem to be self-beautification projects are "not about beauty, but about identity. . . . a way to renegotiate identity through [one's] body" (Davis 1995, 163). Another writes, "Pride in one's appearance, earned by time and attention devoted to it, is a way of positively identifying the self with one's body, . . . an antidote to the historical traditions and contemporary tendencies that alienate women from their bodies" (Furman 1997, 63; but for a more modulated view, see Furman 1999, 15). I agree that women exercise what I shall refer to as narcissistic agency, and I also agree that identity is pivotal to this form of agency. But I am convinced that neither of these insights obviates feminist critique. In my view, it is necessary to ask whether this form of narcissistic agency stems from women's authentic desires, values, and goals, and whether the decisions many women are now making can be perspicuously classified as acts of self-determination.

Turning to the latter question first, I believe there is much to be learned from the work of Sandra Bartky and Susan Bordo (also see Morgan 1996, 223–334). Although neither Bartky nor Bordo regards women as mere dupes of what Bartky dubs the "fashion beauty complex," both emphasize that women are making choices in the context of consumer capitalism and that economic growth and prosperity require expanding markets. This being the case, the manufacturers of beauty merchandise and the purveyors of beauty services have a survival stake in persuading women that they need their products. The aspirational aspect of gender stereotypes—they define what women and men should be, not how they are—provides a platform for consumer capitalism, and this fact is not lost on the businesses that profit from selling the latest fashions, this season's shades of makeup, youth-prolonging skin creams, diet drugs, cosmetic surgical procedures, and so forth. Their marketing strategies are heavily implicated in arousing the specific desires that move women to make self-beautification purchases (Bartky 1990, 39; Bordo 1997, 43). Although there are branches of the appearance industry that cater to a male clientele, we shall see that the result is not equality of narcissistic malfunction.

Bartky and Bordo point to two surefire techniques for creating consumer demand. One tactic plays on women's insecurity by insinuating that they are inadequate unless they wear X, use Y, or undergo Z. But since demand for X, Y, and Z would flag if taking this advice got rid of the perceived defect, the logic of selling dictates that customers' insecurities be perpetuated. Thus, appearance industry advertising (ably assisted by allies in the entertainment industry) seeks to establish such high standards of attractiveness that no one ever completely fulfills them (Bartky 1990, 40). Decreeing standards with built-in escalator clauses—"You can't be too rich or too thin"—ensures that the goals consumers aspire to always remain beyond reach. So does periodically reversing the standards—flat chests and bodacious bosoms, long wavy tresses and scalp-skimming waif cuts, fleshiness and muscle tone have all been glamorized. There is no end to what one needs to buy to keep up with shifting trends and to fend off the specter of ugliness. Is it any wonder that most self-help books for women that aren't full of beauty and dieting tips are devoted to beating depression?

A second marketing technique assures people that they are "'empowered' only and always through fantasies of what [they] *could* be" (Bordo 1997, 51). The fantasy factor is a carry-over from the first strategy—the goals that are proposed are not realistic prospects. People are encouraged to yearn for and strive after "ideals" that are ultimately unattainable. What is added here is the assurance that pursuing them is the essence of individualism and free agency:

"Just Do It!"
"Think Different!"
"Be All You Can Be!"
"Live without Limits!"

To express your unique self and to be an independent agent, proclaim these advertising slogans, buy X (Bordo 1997, 32–33). Purchasing power plus enterprising shopping equals self-determination.

In this economic environment, the claim that women's narcissistic agency is authentic should spark suspicion and further investigation. If anxiety about their alleged flaws or faith in a product as an emblem of agency propels many of women's self-beautification decisions, they are often opting for products and services on the basis of a false promise of benefits that will not be delivered. It is impossible to purchase self-determination, and increased confidence in one's appearance will be short-lived, at best. Thus, there is reason to think that many women's narcissistic agency is compromised.

Still, it is not altogether clear why self-determination is eluding them. Selecting a marketed product does not automatically disqualify one's autonomy. If it did, autonomy would be virtually impossible outside a subsistence economy. It is important to bear in mind, as well, that many women are highly skilled users of beauty products and expert in putting together smart outfits.[27] They are not automatons, whether in the marketplace or before their mirrors. In addition, narcissistic needs are compelling, for attractiveness and feeling attractive are needed to enjoy one's sexuality fully. Then, too, beauty is a bona fide value. Indeed, I think that women as a group deserve our gratitude for the untold beauty they have brought into the world. So why doubt that their self-beautification decisions enact authentic desires, values, and goals?

There will always be businesses tantalizing us with all sorts of self-improvement products. There is nothing wrong with striving to be attractive. But, as Bartky observes, "guilt, shame, and obsessional states of consciousness" are the price many women pay for trying to satisfy their narcissistic needs (Bartky 1990, 42). Since they can never succeed in satisfying them in the present social and economic context, they will always have reason to chide themselves for not doing enough, and they will be moved to multiply their self-beautification efforts, unavailing though they are sure to be. For these women, narcissistic aims become superordinate psycho-corporeal demands and consuming life occupations. Their psychic/*psyché* economy overshadows other interests and constricts their agency. I would urge, then, that this form of narcissistic agency be distinguished from the cultivation of beauty, which I regard as a wholly legitimate and worthy project.

Still, many women are not so compulsive about their appearance that they fail to pursue other goals or pursue those goals less successfully than they otherwise might. Some may be sorry that they devote so much time to appearance maintenance or that they are not more comfortable with their looks. But pangs of regret are by no means wrecking their lives. Why not concede, then, that because the value of attractiveness depends on others' responses and because *beautiful* is a superlative, there will always be a measure of insecurity built into the psychodynamics of narcissistic agency? Moreover, individual taste varies. Yet, if the values of beauty and attractiveness are culturally defined, as I believe they are, the scope for self-determination in setting appearance standards must be circumscribed. It is inevitable, then, that individual taste will seldom stray outside culturally set boundaries. Although it seems to follow that women who are not suffering from diagnosable pathologies have as much autonomy in this arena as anyone can reasonably expect, I argue that the cultural legacy discussed in previous sections contravenes this conclusion.

My skepticism stems from the way in which European and American pictorial and narrative traditions represent feminine narcissism. On the one hand, these representations conflate women's identity with their mirror reflections: "You and your worth are registered in me," women's mirrors decree. On the other hand, these representations dissociate women from their reflected images: "Your image will never match the one you look for in me," the mirrors taunt. Women's mirrors are not the most companionable alter egos. They install a psychic/*psyché* economy of eroticized self-estrangement.

Woman-with-mirror images and narratives of feminine narcissism collapse the self into the mirror. The representation—the external image—is not psychologically differentiated from that which it represents—the woman. Unlike Narcissus, who believes he is in love with a beautiful, submerged Other, women are positioned to believe that they will perish if the image in the glass disappears. Indeed, as Elizabeth Taylor's novel, *The Sleeping Beauty*, convincingly illustrates, women are so identified with their looks that different types of beauty are not interchangeable for them. In the book, a great beauty, Emily, is disfigured in an automobile accident. After extensive reconstructive surgery and a long period of recuperation, she is finally healed, and her proud doctor hands her a mirror. A beautiful face returns her anxious gaze. Still, she is devastated: "The moment in my life when I felt really destroyed was the moment when everyone else thought I was well again. . . . I knew *I was lost*. . . . In that looking-glass there was no vestige of me" (quoted in La Belle 1988, 110 – 111; emphasis added).[28] Although the present writer is not beautiful enough to ever face Emily's predicament, I find her response entirely believable, for I, too, very much want to continue to look like me.

I certainly wish I was beautiful, but I'm strangely attached to the way I actually look, ordinary as it undeniably is. I suspect that most other average-looking women feel the same way. Suppose you could actually look like your favorite beauty idol. Would you want to? Would you enter the wish-upon-a-star, dream-come-true transformation chamber? I do not think I would, even if I could make up my mind which form of beauty I liked best. What are we to make of this paradoxical state of mind?

Although Western representations of narcissism conflate the feminine self with its mirror double, they also portray the mirror as holding in its depths an image of perfection that women's reflected images cannot possibly match—the spectral image that gives Venus a scare and makes her watch her back. The message of woman-with-mirror discourse is contradictory: You are how you look, and you are how you will never look. This incoherent form of narcissistic subjectivity, which long predates consumer capitalism, is plainly incompatible with women's authentic selfhood. I may not be willing to abandon the way I look in order to achieve the stunning appearance that is also inextricable from my identity, but refusing this self-improvement opportunity does not make me the least bit less dissatisfied with the way I look. I am forsaking my better me, as it were. Notice, too, that a woman with more élan who would jump at the chance to undergo a radical beauty makeover would be no better off from the standpoint of authentic agency. She would be living a lie, for, her spectacular new appearance notwithstanding, her pre-makeover appearance remains constitutive of her identity. This dual narcissistic identity explains the contempt conventionally reserved for the "bottle blonde" and the derisive paparazzi photos of celebrity body profiles before and after breast implants. Norms of femininity and feminine prudence counsel artifice, but hyperartifice brings on charges of vanity and fakery.

A more troubling kind of falsity is guaranteed, however, by feminine narcissistic identity. Being true to one's actual looks entails being false to one's beauty ideal, and being true to one's beauty ideal entails being false to one's actual looks. The psychic/*psyché* economy of feminine narcissism subverts self-determination, for the inescapability of self-betrayal prevents the individual from making any coherent set of the desires, values, and goals her own.

Whether self-beautification is a major concern for a woman or not, Euro-American cultural constructions of feminine identity ensure a disconnect between mirror-constituted identity and narcissistic agency. Two ways to resolve this dilemma of femininity occur to me. One approach would aim to liberate women to self-beautify to the hilt and to do so without the slightest qualm about vanity or self-betrayal. The other would aim to liberate women to take narcissistic pleasure in their appearance whatever choices they make about self-beautification. I favor the latter approach, but I shall first outline my objections to the former.

In theory, gender parity in regard to narcissism would provide a direct route to the goal of uninhibited feminine self-beautification. The stigma of vanity and triviality poses a significant obstacle to women's narcissistic aspirations and enjoyment. If men, who are in fact equally vain, were perceived that way, narcissism would seem normal, and narcissistic women would not be subject to humiliating gibes.

Culturally assimilating masculinity to the psychodynamics of mirror-constituted narcissism does not seem wholly improbable. Since the feminine market for beauty products and services is gradually becoming saturated, it makes sense for the industry to try to recruit men as customers. Recent U.S. advertising campaigns in which male bodies are objectified in ways comparable to the traditional objectification of female bodies in commercial discourse suggest that this effort to exploit the male market is already under way (for related discussion, see Bordo 2000). Indeed, many young men in my undergraduate classes report that they are feeling the pressure of an ascendant masculine beauty imperative.[29]

I have doubts, though, about the scope and impact of these cultural developments. Young men have always been granted a good deal of latitude in matters of appearance cultivation, for a phase of narcissistic preoccupation is thought to be part of settling into a masculine sexual identity. Gays, working-class men, and minority men have been stereotypically branded narcissistic for a long time. Only mature, white, middle-class men have never been integrated into cultural discourses of narcissism. They are the ones, we recall, who in Freud's narrative forgo narcissistic satisfactions and experience complete object-love. Since Freud never took up issues of class, race, and ethnicity, we have no way of knowing whether he would have argued that heterosexual men from other social groups are also nonnarcissistic. But, if he followed cultural stereotypes, as he did in other gender matters, he would have attributed a narcissistic psychology to them. What is certain, though, is that he pins rampant narcissism on gays. Entrenched imagery and narratives insulate elite men from the inferiorized realm of narcissism. Capitalist expansionist schemes notwithstanding, I predict that great-looking, successful, white, heterosexual businessmen, politicians, and professionals will continue to pass as nonnarcissistic—as "natural beauties," so to speak.

One reason to be pessimistic about the gender parity strategy, then, is that high-status men's immunity to being perceived as narcissistic makes it unlikely that such equality will ever come about. If narcissism remains confined to Others, these men's projects and conduct will remain paradigmatic of agency. In Freud's terms, sublimation is the key to authentic agency, and sublimation transcends pre-Oedipal narcissism along with taboo Oedipal love. Authentic narcissistic agency remains as elusive as ever.

A more serious reason for pessimism, however, concerns the nature of the proposed objective and its exclusionary implications in regard to self-determination. It seems to me that conceiving authentic narcissistic agency as untrammeled self-beautification hands women and the vast majority of men over to the profiteering of consumer capitalism. Bordo anticipates this ominous consequence: "In a culture that proliferates defect and in which the surgically perfected body . . . has become the model of the 'normal,' even the ordinary body becomes the defective body" (Bordo 1997, 55). As more and more types of physical flaws are "discovered" and as body-type fashions fluctuate, "cures" for nonconforming bodies are publicized. If self-determination is identified with unfettered narcissism, beauty industry product development and marketing will supplant individual taste and judgment. There is no reason to believe, then, that this conception of narcissistic agency will anchor self-beautification in authentic desires, values, and goals.

Another problem is that this conception abandons people who are repelled by flamboyant narcissism, for it (implausibly) denies that a preference for minimal grooming or strictly hygienic self-care could be authentic. Worse still, this proposal strips the concept of narcissistic self-determination of any dissident potential, for, by definition, authentic narcissistic agents are individuals who revel in the endless self-beautification possibilities that advanced technology and their affluence make available to them. Naysayers become neurotic killjoys. But surely a tenable account of narcissistic agency must respect individuality and preserve the capacity for critique. I very much doubt, therefore, that narcissistic gender parity and the celebration of limitless narcissism heralds a glorious new freedom for anyone.

In my view, this approach to depathologizing narcissism is fundamentally misguided because it does not address the root problem of the psychic/*psyché* economy, namely, the conflation of women's identities with their mirror images and the eerie double presence—an actual and an ideal self—they find in the looking glass. Instead of dethroning the silvered alter ego, this approach recommends disidentifying with the actual mirror image—seeing it as an image of mere flesh or raw material—and identifying with the spectral ideal image. No longer prey to a schizoid alter ego, well-off women can euphorically buy and be beautiful.

The alternative approach aims to expand the range of viable narcissistic options by reconfiguring dominant cultural representations of feminine narcissism. The idea is to restructure feminine narcissistic subjectivity and sustain authentic narcissistic agency by reconstructing the normative relationship between women and their mirrors. Both feminist psychoanalytic theorists and feminist artists have taken the initiative in pursuing this goal. Although none of this work has gained the cultural currency that Freud's narrative and conventional woman-with-mirror pictorial imagery have, it vividly articulates the shortcomings of "Just Do It!" narcissism, and it offers heartening glimpses of an alternative to the calamitous psychic/*psyché* economy.

5. Narcissa in Rehab *(a Free Translation)*: Feminist Artists *Revision the Woman at Her Mirror*

A compelling image "embodies a fantasy that answers *needs*" that viewers already have (Bordo 1997, 130). My experience studying ballet convinces me that women have an unacknowledged need to reconstruct their relations with mirrors and that this reconstruction is possible. My survey of feminist art convinces me that these artists have been struggling to meet this need for quite awhile.

A visual critical discourse is indispensable to conquering the psychic/*psyché* economy, for the immediacy and the sensuous appeal of extant woman-with-mirror imagery limits the effectiveness of other critical methods. The history of woman-with-mirror imagery reveals that this pictorial conjunction has been used to represent surprisingly disparate themes — prudence, as well as vanity and mortality. The remarkable versatility of this imagery and its crushing impact on women have stirred many feminist artists to appropriate the woman-with-mirror motif and use it to subvert the hegemony of misogynist treatments of this material. Discerning women's need for an alternative mirroring discourse to disrupt perceptual biases, emotional tropisms, and interpretive habits, first-wave feminist artists, notably Mary Cassatt and Claude Cahun, took major strides in reconfiguring woman-with-mirror imagery, and many contemporary women artists — I shall limit my discussion to Carrie Mae Weems, Orlan, and Sam Taylor-Wood, but there are many others — have extended this transgressive tradition. Some of these artists depict mirrors in their work but reconstruct women's relations to them. Others take an indirect approach and symbolically represent and critique women's relations to mirrors.

MARY CASSATT   Mary Cassatt (1845–1926), an American painter with ties to the U.S. suffrage movement, spent most of her adult life in Paris, where she embraced the concerns of impressionism and exhibited with other members of this group. Unlike other prominent impressionists, however, Cassatt's feminist beliefs shaped her artistic sensibility, and this difference is evident in her dissident woman-with-mirror imagery. Cassatt often repositioned mirrors in relation to female figures, placing them behind women instead of shoving them in front of women's faces. One might understand Cassatt's relegating mirrors to the background as a fortuitous consequence of the modernist turn away from mythological, allegorical, and history painting. Taking up everyday life as subject matter entails depicting the decor of the sites one paints, and mirrors often adorned the walls of the well-appointed homes and tony places of entertainment that Cassatt frequented. However, close examination of Cassatt's pictures suggests that this naturalistic turn does not fully explain the role of mirrors in her work.

Two of Cassatt's paintings—one a portrait, the other a theater scene—explode scopic gender conventions. In *Women in a Loge* (Figure 5.4),[30] two young women are seated in their box, intently watching whatever is taking place on the stage. Behind them, a large mirror pane (its edges are outside the picture frame) reflects the back of one of the women as well as the sweeping, gilded balconies opposite them and the luminous, crystal chandelier suspended above them. The women are pretty, and they are prettily dressed. They carry tokens of femininity—one holds a fan, the other a bouquet. But Cassatt does not cast them as ornaments in the space they visit. They are engrossed in the performance and betray no awareness of the impression they might be making on other members of the audience. In another loge picture, Cassatt underscores the theme of women's indifference to male appraisals while attending public performances by depicting a man using opera glasses to spy on a female figure whose own opera glasses are trained steadily on the stage (*At the Francais: A Sketch*; for related discussion, see Barter 1998, 49–51).[31] There are no prying eyes discernible in *Women in a Loge*, but the concentration evident on both women's faces argues that they are at the theater for their own edification and enjoyment. Although they probably are being watched, neither of them allows the chance to charm an eligible young stranger to distract her.

The presence of the mirror in the background highlights the contrast between these women's looking—their intellectual and aesthetic engagement with a performance—and the looking so prevalent in woman-with-mirror imagery—that is, narcissistic gazing. This image of women looking at something other than themselves while in the company of a mirror is refreshing, for it endows them with nonnarcissistic agency in the shadow of the master symbol of narcissism. The mirror device also enables Cassatt to render the social import of female theater going in the late

FIGURE 5.4 *Women in a Loge*, Mary Cassatt, 1882,
National Gallery of Art, Washington, D.C.

nineteenth century. By including the large space of the auditorium in her picture, she implies that the apparently unaccompanied, yet plainly respectable young women are out in public on their own. Again Cassatt uses the mirror to attest to their self-determination, for it seems they are calmly defying traditional norms of domestic confinement and masculine patronage. The mirrored wall's reflection of one of the women's backs also enhances the illusion of her physical three-dimensionality. This augmentation of her volume endows her body with a solidity that undercuts the cultural presumption of feminine fragility. In a series of cunningly subtle and wickedly ironic strokes, then, Cassatt enlists the mirror to disavow the stereotype of feminine narcissism along with norms of feminine objectification and subordination.

Another of Cassatt's woman-with-mirror images reiterates and extends some of the themes from *Women in a Loge*. The sitter in *Portrait of a Lady* is Mary Cassatt's mother, Katherine Kelso Cassatt.[32] At home, seated comfortably in an overstuffed chair, the sitter is wearing pince-nez, and she is occupied reading *Le Figaro*. The mirror behind her and to her right reflects little more than one of her hands holding up the newspaper. The rest of the wall is unembellished, and no other furniture is included. In this picture, too, the figure's gaze transports her into the realm of ideas, not into the echo chamber of vapid narcissism.[33] A serious woman is taking in the events of the public world. Cassatt's composition reinforces this impression. It accents the sitter's hand holding the newspaper by doubling these elements in the mirror. Unmistakably, this is a woman who spends her leisure moments reading and thinking, not gazing and primping. As in the other painting, the mirror is moved to the background and used to overturn the feminine stereotype of fatuous vanity that woman-with-mirror imagery traditionally represents. That the sitter is Cassatt's mother challenges the one-dimensional maternal stereotype of devotion to children, as well.[34] As Linda Nochlin observes, "This is a portrait-homage not to the maternal body, but to the maternal *mind* . . . a loving but dispassionate representation of the mother not as nurturer but rather, the mother as logos" (Nochlin 1999, 191). In both of the Cassatt pictures under discussion, mirrors recede into the background and become mere furnishings. Spacially and psychologically repositioning the mirror in this way refits woman-with-mirror imagery to serve as a vehicle for simultaneously portraying the value women place upon intellectual stimulation and their repudiation of narcissistic frivolity.

**LOOKING INTO THE MIRROR, THE BLACK WOMAN ASKED,
"MIRROR, MIRROR ON THE WALL, WHO'S THE FINEST OF THEM ALL?"
THE MIRROR SAYS, "SNOW WHITE, YOU BLACK BITCH,
AND DON'T YOU FORGET IT!!!"**

FIGURE 5.5 *Mirror, Mirror*, Carrie Mae Weems, 1987–1988,
collection of the artist.

CARRIE MAE WEEMS   Carrie Mae Weems (b. 1953) imports issues of
race into her woman-with-mirror photographs. *Mirror, Mirror* (Figure 5.5)
is from Weems's *Ain't Jokin* suite—a group of captioned black-and-white
photographs in which the artist exposes racist humor and probes the
stereotypes and attitudes that undergird it.[35] The photograph in *Mirror,
Mirror* shows a young African-American woman wearing a gauzy, white
slip. Although she is standing squarely in front of a good-sized mirror, it
does not return the young woman's image. Instead, it houses an older

woman who is swathed in diaphanous white veiling and whose insignia is a glittering starburst. The caption reads: "Looking into the mirror, the black woman asked, 'Mirror, mirror on the wall, who's the finest of them all?' The mirror says, 'Snow White you black bitch, and don't you forget it!!!' "

This work obviously alludes to the clairvoyant mirror in *Snow White*, which punctures the ego of the evil queen, sweet Snow White's disgracefully unmotherly stepmother. I would stress, though, that such oracular mirrors (inner voices) have a long history in cultural representations of feminine narcissism. Titian and Velazquez also insert figures in Venus's mirror who have bad news to relay. In the Titian, Venus's distraught mirror image confronts her with her unacknowledged insecurity about her looks. In the Velazquez, Venus's coarse mirror image confronts her with the vulgarity of her desire. This more recondite allusion should not be missed, for, unlike in the fairy tale, the recipient of the harsh judgment both in the Renaissance woman-with-mirror images and in Weems's work is a beautiful woman. Weems invokes these cultural references, however, in order to interrogate the earlier imagery and racist beauty ideals.

I see the figure in the mirror as a priestess/mother. Her shimmering starburst is reminiscent of the wands that fairy godmothers wave. But hers is not a wand. She holds it up as if she were a police officer showing her badge to a suspect, and she has no magical power to fix society. She is merely a medium releasing bulletins from higher authorities. Also in contrast to smiling images of fairy godmothers, her expression is stern, and her direct look commands attention. Is she a revered, world-wise mother insisting on keeping her pretty young daughter in touch with reality?[36] The young woman has arranged her hair, but she is still in her slip. Perhaps she is getting ready to go out. Perhaps she has high-flying dreams of love or achievement. Perhaps the priestess/mother is trying to shield her from severe disappointment later by getting her to modulate her hopes now. Whatever the oracle's motives may be, the young woman listens closely. Still, her face is turned away from the mirror as if she were recoiling from the hectoring, epithet-laced reply the mirror spits back: "Snow White you black bitch, and don't you forget it!!!"

Venus with a Mirror and *The Rokeby Venus* construe the mirror as a truthful, reliable instrument of self-scrutiny. Weems's mirror tells truths and lies in one breath. It is true that the dominant culture devalues African-American women's beauty, but it is also false that they are less beautiful. Insofar as African-American women internalize these skewed standards, the spectral ideal image in their mirrors blocks their ability to see their own beauty. But, whether or not they internalize these standards, they need to know about the social realities they reflect in order to understand the constraints that frame their choices. Weems revives the use of woman-with-mirror imagery to illustrate the virtue of prudence. A woman, especially an African-American woman, is well advised to consult the mirror because she needs to grasp the disparity between her looks and the mirror's spectral, white, ideal image as well as the meaning of that disparity for her life. At the same time, Weems critiques the conflation of women's identities with their mirror images by accentuating the contradiction between what the mirror says and how the supplicant looks.[37] The mirror is not where a woman can find her true worth, for the spectral image it holds inferiorizes her, and doubly so if she is not white.

Combining the immediate emotional impact of an ingeniously staged visual image with the pointedness of a literary text, Weems's mordant work invokes the familiar only to explode it. Fond memories of the delectable childhood pleasures of fairy tale fabulism record one's induction into the racialized psychic/*psyché* economy of feminine narcissism. No woman's mirror is a blank glass. Every mirror is culturally inscribed—inhabited by the alien voices of racism and misogyny. The satisfaction that a woman's intimacy with her mirror affords is offset by the humiliation and despair that the mirror's spectral ideal image portends as well. For African-American women in particular, the cultural freight of the psychic/*psyché* economy too often contracts "Just Do It!" narcissistic agency into "No Can Do" disempowerment.

ORLAN Performance artist Orlan (b. 1947) centers her work on the problematics of self-beautification. Arguably, no one has carried woman-with-mirror imagery to a higher pitch than she has, for her staged events enact the full implications of the specular ideology of feminine narcissism in all their gory palpability. In a series of physician-assisted artworks, *The Ultimate Masterpiece: The Reincarnation of St. Orlan*, Orlan remodels her face guided both by cultural beauty ideals and by feminist values.

Through cosmetic surgery, Orlan "reincarnates" masterpieces from the history of art: Diana's nose from a school of Fontainebleau sculpture, chosen because the goddess was aggressive and refused to submit to the gods and men; the mouth of Boucher's *Europa*, chosen because she looked to another continent and embraced an unknown future; the forehead of Leonardo da Vinci's *Mona Lisa*, chosen because of her androgyny; the chin of Botticelli's *Venus*, chosen because of her association with fertility and creativity; the eyes of Gerome's *Psyché*,[38] chosen because of her desire for love and spiritual beauty (Hirschhorn 1996, 111). Orlan's ironic martyrdom to feminine narcissism and feminist critique takes place in operatically staged, video-transmitted surgical performances. In the operating theater, Orlan, her surgeon, and his assistants wear unorthodox hospital gowns, for instance, spangled costumes designed by Paco Rabanne; the set is decorated with assorted pop-cultural and art-referential props; music accompanies the choreography of the surgical solos and ensemble passages; and Orlan reads aloud from a psychoanalytic treatise on appearances and masks. This spectacle is beamed live by satellite to art galleries where audiences witness it and can even participate by putting questions to the performers. In addition to these events, Orlan produces artifacts and less operatic ancillary events. Her surgical performances are recorded on video; she saves waste tissue from her procedures and makes "reliquaries" to house it; her bruised, sutured, postoperative face and her healed, reconstructed face are photographed; she gives interviews in which she airs her intentions and experiences. Replicating the cultural script for the life of a saint, Orlan provides proof of her devotion by enduring mutilating ordeals and leaves remains for later veneration.

It is tempting, of course, to dismiss Orlan's work as sick folderol—grisly self-endangerment akin to Hollywood horror pictures but not make-believe. Still, neither the ghastliness of witnessing her operations nor speculation about the psycho-social roots of her art should disqualify her performances from cultural and political significance. Her work, I argue, is a dramatic demonstration of the double bind that the psychic/*psyché* economy imposes on women. Orlan's surgical performances enact conformity to orthodox feminine beauty standards, for the models for her transformations are ordered from the cultural catalogue of ideal beauty imagery. Yet, they simultaneously enact feminist resistance to these norms, for she chooses particular beautiful traits because they are associated with mythic female figures who personify feminist values. For St. Orlan, to capitulate to feminine norms that require unlimited self-sacrifice in pursuit of beauty is a martyrdom, but to stand up for feminist principles by emulating antipatriarchal role models is a martyrdom, too. Either way, Orlan ends up effaced and de-faced.[39]

The relation between *The Ultimate Masterpiece: The Reincarnation of St. Orlan* and familiar woman-with mirror imagery is not immediately evident. Orlan does not showcase mirrors in her performances. Yet, as a mir-

FIGURE 5.6 *Second Operation, Post-Operative,* Orlan, 1993,
photograph by Sichov, SIPA Press, New York.

ror transmutes flesh into an image, so too Orlan sculpts her flesh into an
image. Watching videos of her facial surgery, one sees that her "face is *detachable*"—"pure exteriority" (Adams 1995, 143, 147). Orlan's face becomes
an image-copying image that signifies no inwardness and expresses no
identity. Her art makes her face a mirror of her culture. In this post-op
photo, for instance, Orlan displays her swollen, bruised face while coyly assuming the pose of a reclining Venus (Figure 5.6). In addition, Orlan's repeated surgical reconfigurations create a succession of Orlan doubles—
each corporealized art-historical image is Orlan, and each is an Other. She
thus creates in time an analogue of the infinite series of images that a pair
of facing mirrors creates in space. Phenomenologically, Orlan reports, this
allusive morphing has deprived her of any sense of "narcissistic recognition" through her body (Hirschhorn 1996, 122). She has tricked herself out
of the psychic/*psyché* economy and entered "the pure subjectivity of
speech" (Adams 1995, 154). "Being a narcissist," she remarks, "isn't easy
when the question is not of loving your own image, but of re-creating the
self through deliberate acts of alienation" (Orlan, quoted in Hirschhorn
1996, 111). Orlan's oeuvre is, then, a demonstration of the impossibility of
a self-affirming narcissism based on the psychic/*psyché* economy.

I would add that her work supplies an elegant reductio of the logic of cosmetic surgery within the psychic/*psyché* economy. To debunk the "myth of magical transformation," Orlan makes a point of exposing audiences to close-ups of surgical incisions, excisions, and sutures during her performances and also to her discolored, swollen appearance in the aftermath of her performances (Hirschhorn 1996, 117). Moreover, Orlan denies that cosmetic surgery can deliver on the promise of ideal beauty. She claims to be creating a unique composite (Hirschhorn 1996, 116). Contrary to the goals of inauthentic narcissism, individuality is inescapable. Orlan's successive incarnations cannot duplicate the models she selects because surgery combines her preexisting anatomical structures with these images of perfection. It is impossible to fabricate an "ideal woman" by technologically synthesizing a real body with aesthetic ideals, for the idiosyncrasies of real flesh and bone place limits on what can be achieved through surgical intervention (Hirschhorn 1996, 116). Cosmetic surgery cannot bring a woman's actual mirror image into conformity with her mirror's spectral ideal image. In fact, it may confound the patient's narcissistic aspirations. "I'm much less pretty than before," observes Orlan (quoted in Fox 1993, 8).

Instead of speaking of self-improvement or self-beautification, Orlan speaks of "woman-to-woman transsexualism" (Adams 1995, 144). But whereas female-to-male and male-to-female transsexuals undergo transformative procedures in order bring their bodies into alignment with their sense of their gender identity, the procedures Orlan elects detach her from her body and prevent her from recognizing herself in her body. Like the psychic/*psyché* economy she critiques, Orlan's carnal art is anchored in an aesthetics of desexualization, not resexualization. To adapt her statement of the dilemma of feminine narcissism, being sexual isn't easy when the question is not of loving your own image, but of re-creating the body through deliberate acts of alienation. The project of trying to perfect one's looks according to cultural ideals, if carried out relentlessly, severs one's identity from one's body and hence from one's sexuality. As with poor, accursed Echo, Orlan's identity is reduced to her voice. It is doubtful, moreover, that a "Just Do It!" narcissist can hold onto a voice of her own. Michelle Hirschhorn points out that Orlan's body-alienating artistic practice takes her to the brink of insanity (Hirschhorn 1996, 129). More generally, if one's body shapes one's subjectivity, and if one's voice expresses one's subjectivity, the voice of a zealous narcissist whose face and body have been molded to maximize their convergence with her culture's ideals is in danger of becoming an echo of her culture's decrees. Perhaps my seemingly perverse desire to continue to look like my ordinary-looking self and my unwillingness to enter the turbo-charged beauty makeover chamber stems from an unconscious fear of desexualization and conformism.

CLAUDE CAHUN *Claude Cahun* is the nom de guerre of Lucy Schwob (1894–1954). The masculine first name, *Claude*, affirms her lesbianism, and her Jewish mother's surname, *Cahun*, allies her with womanhood without disavowing her Jewish heritage. This paradoxical cluster of identifications is evident throughout Cahun's life and work. She participated in the highly sexist surrealist movement. She was a feminist and an outspoken opponent of heterosexism. She was active in antifascist organizations during World War II. Her photographic oeuvre embodies her lifelong fascination with issues of identity. Through Cahun's lens, woman-with-mirror imagery becomes by turns funny, poignant, and uncanny.

The visual joke is one of Cahun's aesthetic strategies. For example, in *Self-portrait*, c. 1939, everything is topsy-turvy.[40] The top half of the image is upside down—a woman (Cahun) looks directly at the camera while she sits on a rock with a lake or bay and a range of mountains in the background and tropical foliage in the foreground. The bottom half is right side up, but in this ostensible reflection, only the scenery is isomorphic. (Actually, the scenery is only approximately isomorphic because the two shots were not taken from identical angles.) Although the woman in the lower part of the image (Cahun again) also looks directly at the camera, she stands on the rock instead of sitting, and she wears different clothing. In addition, the spatial relations defy the conventions of reflection depiction. Unless there is a reflecting surface in the sky, the upper figure and landscape should be right-side up, and the lower figure should be upside down. In two respects, this pseudo–woman-with-mirror image sends up conventional images of feminine narcissism. Not only does the woman ignore the watery reflecting surface and address her onlookers—she is no devotee of Narcissus's pond—but also the similacrum of a reflection that Cahun contrives is awry—women cannot expect veracity from mirrors.

The trope of mismatched figures and mirror images, which is all the more jarring because her medium is photography, is typical of Cahun's work. " 'To mirror' and 'to stabilize'—these are words that have no business here," she writes (Cahun's *Aveux non avenus*, quoted in Krauss 1999, 37). Her photographs consistently eschew the mirror as a guarantor of identity. However, not all of her photographs share the piquant humor of *Self-portrait* (c. 1939). Many evoke a meditative mood tinged with a trace of melancholy. In this vein, *Self-portrait*, c. 1928 (Figure 5.7), is a woman-

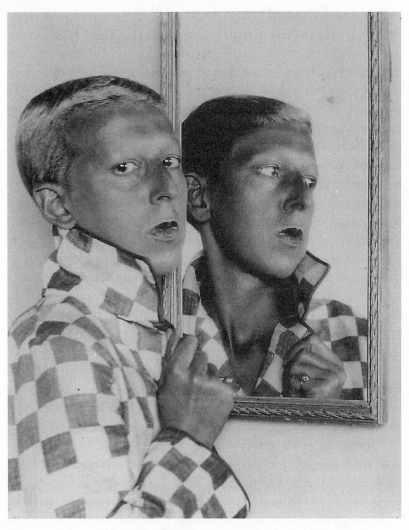

FIGURE 5.7 *Self-portrait*, Claude Cahun, c. 1928, Musée des
Beaux-Arts de Nantes, France.

with-mirror image that violates every convention of that genre to disrupt
both heterosexist and sexist norms.[41] The angle from which Cahun shoots
her scene proliferates perceptual ambiguities and interpretive conundrums. Cahun poses very close to the mirror, yet she is looking at the
viewer/camera rather than at the mirror. Because the viewer/camera
"sees" Cahun's face almost frontally but "sees" an oblique mirror image of
her face, Cahun seems to bear two different facial expressions. The face
turned toward the viewer is level and "does not flinch from eye contact,"

but the face in the mirror is cocked back and "averts her eyes gazing glass-ily into the unknown" (Kline 1998, 69–70). Cahun's upper body and its mir-ror image read differently, too. Her "real" jacket's collar and lapel are turned up and conceal her neck, but in the reflected image her throat is exposed. The "real" aspect of the figure looks steady and unintimidated, whereas the reflected aspect registers vulnerability, apprehension, and diffidence.

It might be tempting to interpret Cahun's image as a descendant of Ti-tian's *Venus with a Mirror* and Velazquez's *Rockeby Venus*. In both Renais-sance works, Cupid presses a silvered glass upon Venus, but the image in the glass clashes with the portrayal of the "real" Venus. Cahun's picture is not a variation on these themes but rather an invalidation of them.

No one—and certainly no personification of love—presents the mirror to Cahun. It is merely a furnishing and not a particularly eye-catching one at that. A thin, simply carved frame barely differentiates the glass, which looks white in the photograph, from the white plaster wall. Unlike the Re-naissance love goddesses who pose in dishabille and exude feminine charm, Cahun's appearance is androgynous, and her face is impassive. Her costume in this work is a concerted assault on 1920s gender/sexual-ity norms. *Self-portrait* (c. 1928) refuses heterosexuality by presenting Cahun in a close-cropped, boyish coif and a tailored but rakish checker-board jacket. This defeminization effect is magnified by the lighting. The gleaming highlights on the smooth planes of Cahun's skin impart a hier-atic quality to the image that calls to mind the stylized gender ambiguity of Etruscan statuary. Cahun's photograph also spurns traditional woman-with-mirror imagery inasmuch as she does not contemplate her image. Both because Cahun's sporty, loose-fitting clothing, masculine hairstyle, and androgynous physiognomy violate the canons of feminine allure and because she is not consulting her glass and does not see her reflection, it is impossible to read this image as a confirmed narcissist's traumatic mo-ment of disillusionment. This mirror is no harbinger of the perils of fem-inine narcissism—the perils of identifying with a schizoid silver alter ego.

Katy Kline constructs a narrative context for *Self-portrait* (c. 1928). She imagines a scenario in which Cahun has been communing with her own image until a visitor arrives, grabs her attention, and interrupts her nar-cissistic interlude (Kline 1998, 69–70). This account is premised on a fan-tasy that Cahun might or might not have entertained, a story she might or might not have acted out as she set up her shot. What is certain, however, is that at the moment Cahun released the shutter, she was posed between a mirror and a camera, and she was looking at the camera. Since the rest of Kline's narrative is conjectural, I would urge that her interpretation of this photograph does not fully appreciate Cahun's radicalism. The trouble is that Kline's view relies on a culturally entrenched understanding of a woman's mirror as the Other in which she finds herself—that is why she presumes that Cahun has been absorbed in her mirror image before the intrusion—and it relies on an anthropomorphic conception of the camera as a beholder—that is why she presumes that Cahun is responding to another person.

I would like to propose an alternative interpretation of this work. My suggestion is that it represents an unfathomable agentic capacity in exquisitely economical pictorial terms. In my reading, Cahun deposits her fears and weaknesses in her mirror while she auditions or rehearses a self-possessed persona before her camera, her mirror with a memory. The complete scene—the mirror holding Cahun's image, the "real" Cahun, and Cahun's unseen camera/mirror—represents the capacity to fashion a poised, self-assured countenance for the social world without forgetting or denying other dimensions of one's identity.

The way Cahun wears her collar and the fact that her hand gesture emphasizes that feature of her attire lends support to this reading. Cahun's turned-up collar is both self-protective and casually chic. This detail of dress encodes the vulnerability and reticence manifest in the mirror image in her style of self-presentation without parading these sensitive points before strangers. Thus, it preserves the connection between the material left for safekeeping in the mirror and the "real" figure's appearance.

What Cahun represents, then, is not a rift between psycho-corporeal modules. On the contrary, she represents a multilayered and networked agentic subjectivity that enables individuals to divulge less than they know about themselves without severing their conduct from their larger sense of self. This capability is indispensable to self-determination in most social settings, for indiscriminate trust is seldom warranted. If this interpretation of *Self-portrait* (c. 1928) is tenable, Cahun is refiguring the mirror as a self-determination appliance—on the one hand, a repository of inner feelings that the individual sometimes prefers to keep private and, on the other hand, a receptacle for testing out modes of social self-presentation. Abrogating the laws of light refraction, Cahun's pair of mirrors does not create a visual echo chamber that traps her in the psychic/*psyché* economy of feminine narcissism. Together, the literal and the metaphorical mirror create a breathing space in which she can experiment with and personalize a novel gendered and sexed look. For Cahun, the mirror is not the instrument of the phony "Just Do It!" agency of untrammeled narcissism. It is the instrument of the unheralded, everyday chore of authentic self-enactment.[42]

SAM TAYLOR-WOOD A recent diptych by photographer Sam Taylor-Wood (b. 1967) projects women's desire and pleasure beyond the confines of the psychic/*psyché* economy. Taylor-Wood claims quattrocento Italian altar pieces as one inspiration for her *Soliloquy* series (Taylor-Wood 1998, 137). Thus, all of these works are composed of two framed photographs: a very large upper panel with a predella beneath it. Taking a page from surrealism's exploration of the unconscious, fantasy, and dreaming, the upper panel of each work shows a lone individual who is deep in reverie or asleep, and the lower, oneiric panel depicts the individual's subjectivity.

The upper panel of *Soliloquy III* (Figure 5.8) is a photographic recreation of *The Rokeby Venus* in modern undress.[43] Apart from Cupid's absence and the updated bedroom furnishings, there are three notable differences between *Soliloquy III* and *The Rokeby Venus*. First, Venus's mirror image is 1990s supermodel beautiful—a face befitting the svelte, pampered body lounging before us. Second, Venus's reflected face is unruffled and betrays no agitation. Third, Venus's reflected eyes look straight back at her and pay her beholders (viewers of the artwork) no mind. This panel envisages a sublime, private, narcissistic idyll.

The lower panel is a panoramic view of a brightly lit, sparsely appointed loft space. It is populated mainly by fourteen naked people, who are lolling about, posing suggestively, talking on the phone, and having perfunctory sex. Two clothed figures are present: a man in a business suit who is working at a cluttered table and a woman in a red dress who sits primly, her knees locked together and her eyes shut, in a red leather chair at the back of the room. Although nearly everyone has disrobed and two couples are having sex, this is no bacchanal. No liquor or food is being served. Everyone, except the woman in red, seems content and at ease, but no one is in transports of ecstasy. The mood is closer to ennui than to lust—a depiction of the banality of sex, it would seem.

The nude Venus in the top panel is the same woman as the woman in the red dress in the bottom panel. Venus's gaze is pinioned to her reflection, but it is the dreamy gaze of someone whose thoughts are elsewhere. Her fantasy double, however, refuses vision and wills her own blindness to the debauch around her. What are we to make of the contrast between Venus in solitude and Venus among acquaintances?

In the predella, Venus is decked out in the color of passion. Yet, every-

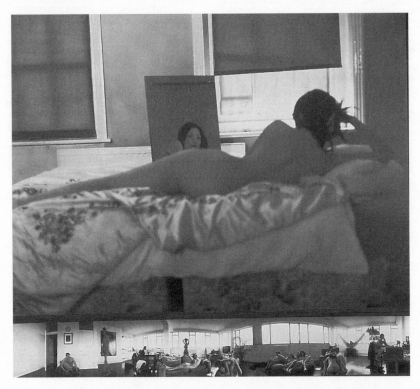

FIGURE 5.8 *Soliloquy III*, Sam Taylor-Wood, 1998, collection of
the artist. Photograph courtesy of Jay Jopling/White Cube,
London; photograph by Attilio Maranzano.

thing else about this figure—the demure cut of her dress, her military erect posture, and her closed eyes—shuns passion. In this guise, Venus is an unmistakable figuration of repressed desire. Still, it is doubtful that Venus's sexuality is repressed. Like the imperturbable nudists disporting themselves below, the nude Venus betrays no arousal. Yet, her come-hither eyes stare fixedly at her reflection because her own looks turn her on and trigger her erotic fantasies. So far as a beholder can tell, she is enjoying herself as much as anyone in the group-sex gang. The only difference is that she takes her pleasure alone. In *Soliloquy III*, Venus has not lost her desire to the mirror, nor has she sacrificed her pleasure to the mirror's tyranny.

The woman in the red dress raises the key question of the lower panel: What does this image of repressed desire tell us about the nude Venus's desire? Whether the goddess of love has abdicated her throne or been deposed, she no longer presides over the kingdom of sex. Everyone ignores the uptight woman at the edge of the scene, and none of the other women are fetishized. It is just as well, for one price Venus always pays for being the sex goddess is the erasure of her own desire. In the company of heterosexual men, she becomes a desireless symbol of their desire. Like the woman in the red dress, her unseeing eyes do not objectify her partner, and her rigid, still body is condemned to passivity. But in Venus's fantasy, women are no longer goddesses—the naked women represent a wide variety of body types, each attractive in its own way—and the men are no longer scopophillic maniacs—they neither worship nor despise the women. The pay-off of this imaginary era of sexual democracy is the emancipation of feminine narcissism. The nude Venus's mirror is Rubens's flattering mirror. The end of Venus's reign, Taylor-Wood seems to be saying, would free women to see themselves as beautiful, for the cultural specter of ideal beauty would no longer menace them from their mirrors. At last, women's autoerotic libido would flow freely and sustain a robust feminine narcissism. The goddess is dead! Long live beautiful women!

Many feminists would object to *Soliloquy III*. It fails to entertain a lesbian alternative. It relies on a conventional conception of beauty to represent women's ability to appreciate their own beauty. It invokes a questionable conception of the natural body to represent gender equality among heterosexuals. I would like to set these criticisms aside, though, in order to examine another worrisome dimension of *Soliloquy III*'s vision.

None of the naked people in the predella is self-conscious about being nude or embarrassed to be with other nude people, but these naked bodies do not seem to carry the slightest charge. Taylor-Wood's predella, which is Venus's fantasy, envisions a heterosexuality that is so blasé that it seems numb. Sex has little savor for anyone. But, Taylor-Wood might retort, bad as that may sound, at least women are not any worse off than anyone else. Heterosexual relations are chummy and egalitarian, and women enjoy narcissistic pleasure without fear of the mirror's vengeance. If Venus could descend from Olympus and loosen up—that is, if men stopped idealizing women and turning them into overvalued goddesses—she could have a satisfying narcissistic economy and a male lover who would not dominate her. Although *Soliloquy III* leaves the question of authentic narcissistic agency unexplored, it appropriates and recontextualizes a classic woman-with-mirror image to reclaim women's narcissistic desire and pleasure.

6. Narcissa Unbound: *Anticipating an Authentic Narcissism for Women*

Feminist woman-with-mirror imagery is discomfiting. It does not permit viewers to fall back on culturally entrenched interpretive templates. It disrupts accustomed cognitive and emotional schemas. Griselda Pollock maintains that successful political art impels the audience to ask: "What knowledges do I need to have in order to share in the productivity of this work?" (Pollock 1988, 183). I would add that such art must also bring audiences to ask: What ostensible knowledges do I need to *suspend* in order to participate in the productivity of this work? Posing these questions in response to the art of Mary Cassatt, Carrie Mae Weems, Orlan, Claude Cahun, and Sam Taylor-Wood displaces the modus operandi of the psychic/*psyché* economy. From within a patriarchal culture, it is impossible to anticipate fully what authentic narcissistic agency would be like for women. However, these artists' woman-with-mirror imagery points to some of the liabilities that such agency would avoid, as well as some of authentic narcissistic agency's advantages.

Authentic narcissistic agency is suppressed, Weems, Orlan, and Cahun warn, in cultural milieux that systematically denigrate the bodies of historically subordinated social groups—female bodies are castrated; lesbian genitals are outsized; black bodies are dirty. Such distortions are offensive apart from their consequences for agency. Moreover, their obverse—narrow and exclusionary beauty ideals—defeats authentic narcissistic agency, for when these ideals govern narcissistic agency, it is driven by fear of ostracism and loneliness or by hatred of one's own distinctive physical qualities instead of by self-love and a desire to care for oneself. Fueled by such anxieties, narcissistic concerns easily degenerate into obsessions — devouring, taunting desires that war with self-determination. Although the desires, values, and goals that give rise to authentic narcissistic agency are lasting commitments, Cassatt's images remind us that they are nonetheless compatible with equally serious commitments to other projects. Indeed, Cassatt's and Weems's images advise women not to rely exclusively on looks for narcissistic gratification (for further discussion of the dangers of a purely looks-centered narcissistic economy, see Chapter 6). Since the form of narcissism that feminist artists represent would fit into a balanced life, there is no reason whatsoever to condemn authentically narcissistic agents as vain or to ridicule their self-beautification practices.

It is at this point, I believe, that we can see a place for gender parity in a theory of narcissism. Since authentic narcissistic agency is pleasurable for the individual, and since it also creates aesthetic and erotic value for others, I would think that privileged men would want access to this form of agency as much as anyone else. The intrinsic appeal of a well-crafted conception of authentic narcissistic agency may yield a happy bonus — fostering gender equality in the looks economy.

Orlan and Taylor-Wood call attention to another obstacle to authentic narcissistic agency. Both hypernarcissistic agency and narcissistic apathy desexualize the body. "Artificial" looks alienate the individual from her own body, but "natural" looks make for humdrum sex. Plainly, the narcissistic compass must fix on a different polestar — the unique *and* individualized face and body.

To detoxify narcissism, the regimentation of narcissistic agency that currently prevails must be relaxed in two crucial respects. First, cultural representations broadcast a homogenized feminine beauty ideal and ensconce it as the universal goal of women's narcissistic agency. In my view, fixing on beauty as the aim of narcissistic agency is disastrous for women. Attractiveness is a more appropriate value to privilege. Not only is attractiveness attainable for virtually everyone, but also it is a heterogeneous concept. Beauty is one among many ways to look attractive (for complementary strategies to pluralize our conception of beauty, see Chapter 6, Section 2). An appearance can also be attractive because it is thought-provoking or approachable or amusing. There is a vast range of possibilities because attractiveness is clearly a matter of personal taste. Whatever sociobiologists evangelizing about the survival of the most beautiful may say, it is indisputable that people differ enormously in judgments of attractiveness. There is no other explanation for the staggering diversity of the individuals whose sexual partners delight in their looks. Also, many people find a variety of looks pleasing. This aesthetic eclecticism makes sense since there are so many great looks: pert, dainty, dreamy, swank, sportive, glamorous, flamboyant, defiant, diminutive, vivacious, merry, mischievous, soulful, scintillating, allusive, enigmatic (the list could go on and on). Each pleases some people; none pleases everyone. This indeterminacy makes room for self-determination. If the spectral ideal image in women's mirrors were an image of attractiveness rather than beauty, it could be individualized. It could be an image selected by the individual, not imposed by a uniform cultural code, and it could be gauged to the individual's actual physical endowment and coordinated with her other desires, values, and goals.

Second, cultural representations currently posit narcissism as one of two preeminent feminine concerns (the other, as we saw in Chapter 2, is motherhood). Thus, narcissistic agency is mandatory for women in two respects. First, feminine norms oblige them to work at their appearance. Second, the stereotype of the narcissistic woman guarantees that most women will be perceived as narcissists, whether self-beautification is a priority for them or not, and that those who are not perceived as narcissists will be considered aberrant and unfeminine. As long as cultural representations of womanhood bond women's identity to their mirror images, many women will have difficulty obtaining fair recognition of their agency and accomplishments in other arenas (Valian 1998, 136–139).[44] Moreover, few women will be capable of ignoring or resisting the ubiquitous reminders of narcissistic norms. If women are to gain authentic narcissistic agency, then, both the degree of a woman's commitment to narcissistic values and the centrality of narcissistic projects in her life must be a matter of individual preference. Not really wanting to "Be All You Can Be" must be imaginable as a credible option, but it will remain unimaginable for most women unless their identities are culturally and psychically distanced from their mirror images. As in Cassatt's and Cahun's imagery, women's mirrors must be relegated to the status of tools and furnishings. How much one uses or notices other utilitarian and/or decorative appurtenances is optional, and how much women use or notice mirrors must become optional, too.

Emancipating women from the psychic/*psyché* economy of narcissism requires renovating the cultural storehouse of woman-with-mirror imagery.[45] To deflate the exalted status of mirrors in women's subjective lives and to ensure that feminine subjectivity allows women to define their own narcissistic commitments, it is necessary to symbolize a less intimate, less dependent relationship between women and their mirrors in regnant discourses. New woman-with-mirror imagery must authorize women to turn their backs on mirrors. Likewise, new woman-with-mirror imagery must terminate beauty's monopoly on the spectral ideal image in women's mirrors and authorize women to define their own attractiveness—that is, their own narcissistic goals. Admittedly, the existing supply of beauty-idolizing and identity-collapsing woman-with-mirror imagery seems inexhaustible and unassailable. However, if mirrors are to stop functioning as obtrusive alter egos—sometimes surly, sometimes congenial, always noisy, and usually in the way—and if women are to achieve authentic narcissistic agency, culturally recoding women's narcissistic subjectivity is vital, and feminist artists are showing the way.

CHAPTER SIX	Miroir, Memoire, Mirage:
	Appearance, Aging, and Women

There is nothing lovely about the sight of me. I have been taught that firm and un-lined is beautiful. Shall I try to learn to love what I am left with? I wonder. It would be easier to resolve never again to look into a full-length mirror.
—Doris Grumbach, "Coming into the End Zone"

Straddled hands and knees over the silvered glass I caught sight of my face. Stopped shocked. I watched the crawling creature warily. . . . This was not me.
—Janet Burroway, "Changes"

 The trick has always been to look only selectively into the mirror. To see the bright eyes, the shining hair, the whispered print of the blouse falling open to reveal soft tanned cleavage, the shapely curve of a taut muscular calf.
—Pam Houston, "Out of Habit, I Start Apologizing"

Actually, it's far from easy to resolve never to look in a mirror. Reflecting surfaces are everywhere—in our homes, on the streets, in stores, restaurants, and theaters. Presumably, decorators install mirrors not only because they create illusions of greater space but also because many people enjoy glimpsing themselves or feel the need to glimpse themselves at frequent intervals. Indeed, we have seen that Euro-American culture makes women into mirror junkies, and we have seen, too, how hard it is to kick the specular narcissism habit (Chapter 5).

This chapter concerns an experience familiar to many aging women—meeting a stranger in the mirror. Instead of encountering the face one has identified with, however ambivalently, one confronts an alien image. This face is disconnected from one's sense of self—it's not the face with which one entered long-standing, treasured interpersonal relationships and embarked on valued, enduring projects; it doesn't reflect one's continuing zest for life. Worse, it is an object of scorn and a constant reminder of mortality. With this "death mask vivant" permanently sealed in place, women feel shortchanged and stuck. Social possibilities dry up. Economic opportunities are cut off. Self-esteem plummets.

My question is how women can live with this reflected phantasm. And I do not mean grieving, enduring, and soldiering on. I mean *live* in the richest sense of the term—appreciating, enjoying, even loving this time-altered visage. How can women salvage their face-esteem? How can they embrace the stranger in the mirror?

In pursuing these questions, I develop three main lines of thought. First, it is well known that women are commonly plagued with dissatisfaction about their looks throughout the life span, and I capitalize on that continuity. Some younger women seek surgical solutions to correct their perceived flaws, and, like aging women, they face a stranger in the mirror once the bandages come off. I present some strategies used by younger women who have undergone cosmetic surgery to reconnect with their radically transformed faces, and I explore parallel strategies that aging women might adopt (Section 1). Second, I argue that three assumptions about the self, the expressivity of faces, and the nature of beauty undergird these self-recognition strategies. After showing how these commonplace assumptions conspire against aging women, I propose some ways in which they could be modified to accommodate women's lifelong needs (Section 2). Finally, I take up the symbolic association between death and the changes women's faces undergo as they age (Section 3). Why do women's aging faces, but not men's, betoken mortality? And how does this macabre misogynist symbolism structure women's choices?

1. Miss Lonelyhearts' Guide to Identifying with the Stranger in the Mirror

In trying to think about how aging women might assimilate their changing appearance, I thought I might find some clues in the cosmetic surgery literature. Many aging women find it impossible to identify with the face they see in the mirror. Similarly, people who undergo cosmetic surgery on their faces emerge from their bandages and find a stranger returning their gaze from the mirror. Pursuing this avenue of inquiry, I examined Kathy Davis's account of the experience of a woman, Diana, who became the target of merciless teasing and harassment because of her protruding teeth and who submitted to a major surgical procedure and endured a long, severely painful recovery to correct this problem. Apparently, the operation changed Diana's face so dramatically that some colleagues at the school where she taught did not recognize her afterward.

There are a number of parallels between Diana's testimony and some of the excerpts from interviews with the aging clients of a beauty parlor that Frida Furman reports in her book *Facing the Mirror*. First, these women condemn their appearance in hyperbolic terms. For example, Diana and one of Furman's subjects, Evelyn, invoke metaphors of congenital disability to symbolize their assessment of their appearance:

> Diana: "I looked retarded." (Davis 1995, 100)
> Evelyn: "I look like a birth defect." (Furman 1997, 95)

Whatever we may think about the ableist prejudices implicit in these tropes, these two women clearly mean to convey an absolute horror at their own appearance, a horror that I find poignant. A second similarity between Diana and Furman's subjects is what I would refer to as their synecdochic psychology, their tendency to fixate on a single flaw and to condense the whole horrific problem into that flaw (Furman 1997, 57; Davis 1995, 99–100). By localizing all of their disaffection with their appearance in a single facial feature—Diana's teeth, an elderly woman's wrinkles—they shrink their problem to manageable proportions, but they vastly exaggerate the hideousness of that feature. Third, women who have had cosmetic surgery and aging women affirm continuity through physical change by appealing to an inner, unchanged, attractive self. Diana declares that her postoperative self is the same as her childhood self—a self that was "petted and hugged" (Davis 1995, 107). Similarly, when asked to respond to a recently taken photograph of herself, one of Furman's subjects, Clara, declares, "I see an old lady. . . . [But] I just brush it off. It isn't me. Because the me is inside, here [pointing to her chest]. And I'm still younger than springtime" (Furman 1997, 105). Through cosmetic surgery, Diana gains a face that fits her inner nature. Through passing time, Clara loses the face that fit her inner nature. But both are convinced that they have a core self that persists and that is well or ill represented by their outward appearance.

Davis's study of women who choose cosmetic surgery and Furman's study of elderly women converge on several themes: (1) the enormity of the perceived appearance problem, (2) the containment of dissatisfaction by concentrating it on one "ghastly" flaw, (3) the affirmation of an ongoing core self that is not disavowed, and (4) the complaint that an unattractive face conceals a likable self. In light of these overlapping approaches to self-understanding, I wondered whether Diana's strategies for coming to terms with and coming to identify with her surgically reconstructed, initially alien face might provide clues about strategies that could be deployed to acclimate oneself to a face gone strange as a result of aging. Diana's three principal strategies are: (1) externalizing identity continuity, (2) affirming the congruence between her strange face and her authentic identity, and (3) selective self-alienation. As I present these strategies, I consider how they might be adapted to aging women's situation. Then I show how pioneering aging theorist Margaret Morganroth Gullette uses these very strategies to come to terms with her own aging appearance.

To offset her difficulty recognizing the face in the mirror as her own, Diana cites two kinds of constancy—her personality and her friendships—and she explains the latter in terms of the former. People, she says, always liked or disliked her for her personality, not for her appearance, and so her improved appearance hasn't made any difference to her close interpersonal ties (Davis 1995, 111). Telling herself that she has changed only superficially, Diana finds her surgically reconstructed face less disorienting.

Many of Furman's subjects also insist that their inner self persists despite the changes their bodies have undergone. But, as people age, the continuity of their relationships becomes increasingly tenuous (for insightful and moving discussion of this problem, see Bartky 1999). Friends and family members may relocate, or one may move away oneself. The older one gets, the more likely it gets that friends and family members will die. Age segregation in residences, lifestyles, and attitudes commonly blocks the formation of lasting, intimate intergenerational relationships. Consequently, many aging women will not find it easy to minimize the importance of their changed appearance by projecting their sense of inner continuity and self-worth onto a stable and valued social network. Nevertheless, one can imagine how women might collectively undertake to break down socially constructed barriers to using this strategy and how individuals might improvise ways to avail themselves of it.

Diana's second strategy, which is another variant of the idea that one's inner self secures continuity, is to affirm a better fit between her true, enduring self—the self that used to be "petted and hugged"—and her sur-gically altered appearance (Davis 1995, 107). She can feel comfortable with her unfamiliar visage because she is convinced that the face she sees in the mirror more accurately represents who she really is—a person who de-serves to be petted and hugged. Her new face is very different, yet it is more truly her.

Interestingly, aging women could not identify with their wrinkled, sag-ging faces on the grounds that there is now a better match between their identity and their appearance without shaking up quite a few seemingly firm assumptions about physical appearance and the self. If the true self is a constant self, as Diana assumes it is, and if one's identity is most accu-rately reflected in one's aged face, as Diana claims her identity is most ac-curately reflected in her postoperative face, one's true self has never been and would not now be well represented by an unlined, tautly contoured, dewy face. Either one's enduring, authentic self is well represented by a youthful face, or it is well represented by an aging face. The same char-acter and personality could not be well represented by such different appearances.

Supposing that one's true self is well represented by one's aging face and also that one has a good character and an agreeable personality, it fol-lows that our standards of female physical attractiveness and our conven-tions of representation vis-à-vis correlations between inner states and facial features are seriously off base. If appropriated by older women, Diana's second strategy would have the curious consequence that ad-mirable, congenial young women should yearn for the day when gravity and wear-and-tear finally leave their marks. Perhaps they would be well ad-vised to undergo cosmetic surgery of the sort Kathryn Morgan recom-mends (Morgan 1991). That is, if young women want their associates to be able to read their virtues off their faces, they should have wrinkles carved across their foreheads, bags implanted under their eyes, jowls attached to their jaw lines, and brownish blemishes splattered here and there. Adapt-ing Diana's second strategy to aging women's needs has disquieting im-plications: Either we must give up the constancy of the self—we could, for instance, enshrine unpredictable, surprising variability as a desideratum, or we could partition life into different stages correlated with different virtues—or else we must give up our conventions of representing virtues and values and replace them with heterodox standards of beauty.

Diana's second strategy seems unexceptionable until one draws out its implications for older women, but her third strategy is quite astonishing ab initio. Revisiting her history of humiliations, she excuses her harassers, saying she's just like them and it's normal to find ugliness repellent (Davis 1995, 110). Through a stunning reversal that amounts to selective self-alienation, Diana identifies with her tormentors' attitudes and behavior, and she disidentifies with part of her past—that is, the face they taunted and her suffering at their hands. Putting the past behind her and letting bygones be bygones, she strengthens her identification with her "new, improved," yet strange appearance. Diana's capitulation to self-hatred and her refusal to critique the cultural norms that foster the cruelty she endured are troubling. But I shall set these matters aside because adapting this strategy to the circumstances of aging women would not involve such problems.

Still, it is far from obvious how to adapt this strategy to the circumstances of aging women without becoming ensnared in yet another twisted logic. To embrace their present appearance, which by conventional standards is unattractive, by disidentifying with part of their past would be to repudiate the face that others thought pretty as well as their earlier pleasure at being admired for their looks. Whereas Diana embraces orthodox beauty norms and identifies with those who uphold them, elderly women would have to reject the equation of youth and beauty and create an alternative community of more discerning viewers who presumably would have a better grasp of the true nature of beauty.

Renowned portraitist Alice Neel deploys Diana's strategy of selective self-alienation. Asked why she never painted a self-portrait until she was eighty years old, Neel explains: "I always despised myself. . . . I hate the way I looked. . . . I was a very pretty girl and I liked to use that with the boys, but I wasn't like me. My spirit looked nothing like my body" (Castle 1983, 40). Neel eschews orthodox beauty norms and valorizes her octogenarian looks. It is clear, too, that her self-portrait draws admiration. Still, this strategy gives me pause, for, premised as it is on embracing a univocal conception of beauty rather than on appreciating various forms of physical attractiveness, it would require sacrificing the narcissistic needs of younger women to those of older women. Adhering to this logic, Neel's remarks sound a note of contempt for the pretty young woman whom men found alluring.

I doubt, moreover, that altogether abandoning ideals of beauty that accommodate youth is practically feasible or aesthetically credible. Neel's self-portrait tells hard truths about her aged body, but it banishes self-pity and resolutely affirms the life within her. Her rendering of her face reveals skepticism, boldness, and defiance tempered by familiarity with woe.[1] She holds the tools of her trade, a paintbrush and a rag, in her hands. Although seated on a couch, she is in the midst of her work—contemplating her subject, that is, herself as seen in a mirror. She gives an unabashed description of her aged body—her hunched shoulders, pendulous breasts, bulbous belly, lumpy legs. Yet, her body is not without tensility, for she looks as if she is about to rise and return to her canvas. Neel's image of her eighty-year-old self is undeniably inspiring. Nevertheless, it would be a pity to spurn an image like Joan Semmel's self-portrait, *Me without Mirrors*,"[2] which depicts her supple, curvaceous, youthful body caught in a moment of self-cradling and self-caressing as she towels herself off.

In many respects, Margaret Morganroth Gullette's approach to the stranger in the aging woman's mirror recapitulates the strategies I have derived from Diana's testimony. Gullette urges us to reject the progress/ decline dichotomy and the autobiographical templates that cast life stories either as tales of progress or as tales of decline (Gullette 1997, 11). Rather, we should figure out how social forces conspire to enlist us in narratives that equate advancing age and decline, and we should develop "complex idiosyncratic narrative[s] of age identity" (Gullette 1997, 15, 18). With respect to the miseries of disidentification with an aging face, Gullette suggests that we remind ourselves of how unhappy we were with our youthful faces when we were younger, how vital our personal and professional midlives actually are, and how sadly some forms of physical beauty have been neglected (Gullette 1997, 58, 60, 64–65). "Your story must be a *becoming*," she counsels (Gullette 1997, 61). But she stresses that a story of becoming is not the same thing as a progress story. Trying to counterbalance aged-face despair with a cheery progress narrative merely sets an emotional seesaw in motion: "You're beautiful. No you're not. Yes, you are." To escape from this syndrome, one must recognize that one's dissatisfaction with one's appearance stems from the poisonous ageist propaganda one has internalized, and one must reconnect with one's distinctive life story and unique subjectivity (Gullette 1997, 68).

Gullette's view rests on an uneasy admixture of social constructionism, which is particularly in evidence in her dismissive account of women's choices to undergo cosmetic surgery (Gullette 1997, 70), and classical individualism, which comes out in her optimism about women's ability to "decide what aging means to *me* at midlife, beyond decline ideology" (Gullette 1997, 12). However, I shall not pursue this difficulty. What I shall probe instead is Gullette's notion of a becoming—as opposed to a decline or progress—narrative and her endorsement of a more "democratic" conception of beauty.

A becoming narrative tells a story of acceptable, assimilable change: "I may not be getting better and better, but I'm not getting worse and worse, and I *am* okay." Yet, the face-narrative Gullette retails is in fact decidedly upbeat. She reports success in getting her career on track and finally dedicating herself to work she really wants to do (Gullette 1997, 60). Also, she tells of debunking the fantasy of youthful self-approval and, with the help of this more realistic view of her past, gaining emotional equilibrium (Gullette 1997, 57–58). Surely, these are distinct advances. Indeed, if we weren't self-consciously striving to overcome binary oppositions, we'd call them progress. When Gullette focuses specifically on her feelings about her midlife appearance, she adapts and blends Diana's strategies. She repudiates the pleasure she once took in being noticed as a young female, and she harshly indicts her youthful "beauty" and her former looks, which she characterizes as "blurry as to identity, banally pretty, uncertain, even frightened; and when not frightened, foolish" (Gullette 1997, 62). In the past, her appearance did not fit her inner self, but now it does. Her midlife self-presentation is more in keeping with her work and her feminist values—it strikes "a better balance between representing femaleness and 'me-ness'" (Gullette 1997, 63).

In one way, we would expect Gullette's thinking to depart from Diana's strategies, for she advocates a less exclusionary view of beauty. Yet, what Gullette actually does is to extol midlife beauty—she has learned to appreciate big, soft bodies and "interesting" faces with "well-defined features marked by intelligence and experience"—and to censure youthful beauty—slender, gym-trained bodies are "junior Cyborgs," and young faces are confined to a narrow repertoire of expressions (Gullette 1997, 64–65; also see Chapter 5, n.39).[3] By admiring isolated facial features and by not demanding that the whole face approximate an ideal, she finds more women of her age cohort beautiful (Gullette 1997, 63). In her view, however, the young are denied admission to the temple of beauty. Although her conception of beauty inverts beauty orthodoxy, it does not proliferate types of beauty.

2. The Self, Representation, and Beauty: A Trio of Dubious Postulates

Reconfigured for use by aging women, Diana's strategies for deflecting her attention from the strangeness of her face and for identifying with her transformed face raise fundamental questions about the self, representation, and beauty. The Diana-derivative strategies presuppose that people have stable, authentic identities—I call this the identity constancy postulate. They presuppose that people's inner nature can be deciphered from their outward appearance—I call this the facial legibility postulate. They presuppose that an attractive inner nature is embodied in an attractive face—I call this the goodness-goes-with-beauty postulate. These assumptions may seem unimpeachable until one notices the binds they get us into when we adapt Diana's strategies to the needs of aging women.

To compensate for the unfamiliarity of one's face, it seems sensible to reassure oneself of the stability and worth of one's self by projecting it onto stable and worthwhile relationships or projects. However, this strategy is less viable for aging women whose relationships are frequently derailed, curtailed, or terminated and whose health or other circumstances may interfere with their ability to sustain other pursuits. The complementary strategies of affirming a better fit between one's aging face and one's true self while disavowing one's youthful appearance involve disparaging the narcissistic pleasures of youth, dismissing the standards of attractiveness that undergird them, and replacing these conventional beauty ideals with counterideals of midlife beauty. This is a tall order. Not only does it seem psychologically perverse, but also it merely substitutes one exclusionary ideal for another. One must wonder, too, whether this counterideal will work for all aging women—octogenarians as well as fifty-year-olds; Asian-American, African-American, Native American, and Latina women as well as Euro-American women; and so on.

The identity constancy postulate gives rise to three dilemmas. First, this assumption undermines the ability of aging (and many other) women to see a correspondence between their inner self and their interpersonal relationships or their vocational or other projects. Thus, they cannot manage their anxiety about their changed and changing appearance by focusing their attention on their unchanged and unchanging commitments or activities. Second, assuming a normal U.S. life span, this assumption entails that one's appearance will fail to coincide with one's inner nature for at least part of one's life. If the true self is invariant (at least throughout one's adult lifetime), and if the face is a window onto the soul, a changing face cannot aptly represent this constant inner nature. If one's face misrepresents one's true self when one is young, passing years may eventually bring one's appearance into alignment with one's inner nature. However, if one's face accurately reflects one's true self when one is young, passing years will inevitably leave one's appearance out of whack with one's inner nature. In either case, one is doomed to spend a significant part of one's life distraught by the mismatch between one's inner nature and one's outer appearance—a living violation of the facial legibility postulate. Third, in conjunction with the goodness-goes-with-beauty postulate, the identity constancy postulate underwrites exclusionary beauty ideals. If an attractive, unchanging inner nature is most aptly represented by a certain type of conventionally pretty face, a youthful face and an aging face cannot both be attractive. Attractiveness at one stage of life ensures unattractiveness at another, and women are doomed to spend a significant part of their lives in despair over their ugliness or toiling to overcome it (and probably both).

I believe that for purposes of understanding identity and agency, a looser conception of the self would not only suffice, it would be better. Born into and formed by misogynist, heterosexist, racist, ethnocentric, ableist, and classist societies as we are, we need to understand the true self as an evolving self if we are to overcome internalized markers of domination and subordination and if we are to resist unjust social structures and practices without sacrificing authenticity (for extended discussion, see Meyers 1989, 2000a). I would add, moreover, that few of us have invariant identities, and yet many of us do not feel hopelessly adrift. We exert a good deal of control over our lives, and our lives make a tolerable amount of sense to us. For purposes of self-knowledge and self-determination, then, assorted, intermittent, unfolding identity continuities suffice. We do not have identity constancy, and we do not need to conform to the identity constancy postulate (but for critique of fracturing the self, see Chapter 4, Section 5, and Meyers 1989, 143–147).

Aging women need not be saddled with the deleterious consequences of this overly exigent postulate. A looser conception of the self will allow older women to see continuities in their style of interacting and living and in their values even in the midst of unsettling social losses and personal turmoil. Moreover, a looser conception that allows for the possibility that the virtues of youth may differ somewhat from the virtues of age would not preclude the possibility that a youthful face and an aged face could befit one's true self during different periods of one's life (for discussion of the virtues of age, see Ruddick 1999). Thus, the trauma of feeling that there is an irremediable disparity between who one is and who one appears to be could be alleviated.

Still, loosening up our conception of the self does not fully address the problem of exclusionary beauty ideals, for these seem to have a life of their own and show little sign of succumbing to critique. One may accept that one's older self differs from one's younger self and that the same face could hardly speak for both. Yet, there is a strong tendency to lapse into thinking that one's older face (and perhaps one's older self, too) is less attractive or else to defensively denigrate one's younger face (along with one's younger self). To address this bind, it is necessary to consider the question of representation—the facial legibility postulate.

The facial legibility postulate is not simply false. We must and routinely do read emotions, desires, and motives off facial expressions. Moments when a person is saying one thing, but her face betrays her and exposes her deception are familiar to everyone. For this to happen, of course, facial expressions must be revealing. Also, we seldom have trouble identifying emotions like sadness, anger, joy, or embarrassment on the basis of facial expressions. Indeed, facial expressions are called *expressions* because they normally express what people are feeling.

Nevertheless, it is important to recognize the limits of facial legibility. I doubt, for example, that people can reliably differentiate a face contorted by rage from a face contorted by agony without knowing anything about the context. Also, it seems clear that interpretations based solely on facial expressions are quite crude. We may be able to tell that a person is not happy simply by looking, but we cannot tell whether a person is experiencing grief or despair simply by looking. Without contextualization, people's facial expressions do not enable us to divine much about their passing subjective states, and, if we try to decode people's episodic inner states without the benefit of relevant contextual information, we are liable to go astray, possibly to run amock.

However, worse mischief stems from the remarkably persistent though peculiar belief that the way a person looks reveals something deep about who she is. This conviction is peculiar because it is counterbalanced by the belief that the face can mask a person's true nature and also because it is awfully mysterious how a person's character and personality are manifest on her face. Certainly, there is no natural or necessary correspondence between states of the soul and features of the face or their configuration. One can have the face of an angel and the soul of a Nazi. "Beauty is only skin-deep," mothers intone. Moreover, ostensible correlations between facial features or types of face and character or personality traits often track derogatory or honorific stereotypes far better than they track inner realities—for example, the Jew's big nose supposedly signaling his greed or deviousness or a creamy complexion supposedly signaling purity of heart.

The facial legibility postulate is suspect, then, for it memorializes a history of social stratification and bigotry.

Still, Diana thinks her reconstructed face fits her inner nature better, and Gullette thinks her midlife face fits hers better. Why do they think so? And why do they think it matters? Are these women captivated by some noxious fairy tale?

There seem to be several factors working here. First, because our culture furnishes a stock of face prototypes—the innocent face, the world-weary face, the honest face, the priggish face, the shrewd face, and so forth—we have a facial vocabulary and therefore the possibility of scrutinizing our own features and questioning their fit with what we know about ourselves. Second, presenting a face that does not fit one's character and personality carries a whiff of inauthenticity. So, one may feel derelict in some unspoken duty if one concludes that one's face is misleading. Also, since others form preconceptions about us based on their prototype-driven reading of our faces, we may want a good match in order to minimize misunderstanding and false expectations based on over- or underestimations of our character and personality. Third, the good fit we want may be less tied to specific traits of character or personality and more tied to an overall assessment of them. The idea might be that, if one thinks one has a decent character and an agreeable personality, one wants this self-esteem to be manifest in one's appearance. One wants to look as attractive as one feels one is inside. This does not seem to be about authenticity, however, since, so far as I know, people with odious characters and abrasive personalities never regret not having faces to match. Rather, people whose faces are considered ugly worry that few people will look beyond their appearance and notice their fine qualities, and consequently they fear social ostracism.

Two themes emerge from these observations, and they may pull in opposite directions. Insofar as people identify authenticity with the wholeness or unity of the self, a disparity between one's inner nature and one's outward appearance is inauthentic. An authentic individual's character and personality must be embodied in her face. So a person who values authenticity will want her face to fit her inner nature. Second, one's face is a social asset or liability. Since people prefer an asset, they may not care whether the asset accurately represents their inner nature or their feelings about themselves. Also, since some people have self-esteem although they lack decent characters or agreeable personalities, they may think that an attractive face accurately represents how they feel about themselves, and this match may overshadow any mismatch between their face and their actual character or personality traits.

I hope I have said enough by now to convince you that this is all smoke and mirrors. If we want to know who someone is, as opposed to how someone is feeling at the moment, we'd better listen to what they say and notice how they act in a variety of situations. Facial prototypes are poor indicators of enduring character and personality. The facial legibility postulate must be circumscribed. Within limits, it works for subjective episodes, but it does not work for enduring traits at all. Ideally, then, we should delete the vocabulary of facial prototypes from our cognitive repertoire. This is not likely to happen, though, for these prototypes are deeply ingrained in each of us and continue to be culturally reinforced through the history of art as well as through commercial and entertainment imagery. So, it might be wise to shave down our ambitions and consider whether anything can be done to shake the goodness-goes-with-beauty postulate — the broad equivalency between inward goodness and outward attractiveness together with the contrary equivalency between inward wickedness and outward ugliness.

A moment's reflection discloses the sheer lunacy of the presumption that an estimable character and personality will be embodied in a beautiful, even an attractive, face. Yet, there is ample evidence that people commonly slide from seeing an attractive appearance to regarding the individual so perceived as more congenial, more intelligent, more competent, and more likely to be successful (Bersheid and Walster 1974, 168–171; Cash 1990, 54–56).[4] It is also worth noting that critical reflection does nothing to expunge the positive correlation between beauty and erotic appeal. And erotic response undoubtedly colors our perception of character and personality. Evidently, perceiving physical beauty primes people to notice good qualities, to place a positive construction on average ones, and to overlook mediocre or bad qualities. Despite the overwhelming evidence to the contrary, people persist in presuming that the Good and the Beautiful go hand in hand.

Nevertheless, I think it is possible to install some cognitive and emotional ballast to offset the pernicious tendencies that the goodness-goes-with-beauty postulate aids and abets. To disabuse ourselves of the various associations between facial appearance and traits of character and personality, mental exercises in radical materialism might be salutary. Try to look at faces and concentrate on their biological functions — see eyes and noses as organs, mouths as orifices, skin as a protective sheath. Once you've reached the point where you're looking at a mere organism, allow yourself to endow it with nonphysiological meanings and notice how arbitrary, and even bizarre, these physiognomic attributions are. It's eerie, but try this cleansing ascetic discipline on yourself.

Of course, we would not want to do without aesthetic pleasure. So we also need a discipline to refurbish our aesthetic sensibilities. It helps to bear in mind that beauty is not an inborn property and that ideals of beauty are culture-bound and historicized. Thus, it is useful to ponder stories like Hanan al-Shaykh's recollection of being despised for being too skinny in a culture that valorizes fleshy voluptuousness (al-Shaykh 1994) and Renaissance images like Titian's and Rubens's zoftig Venuses (Figures 5.1 and 5.3). Although we are trained to find this or that beautiful, we can study other conceptions of beauty and learn to recognize and relish beauty on those terms. This discipline would undercut the tendency to rush to dismiss people—ourselves included—who are unusual looking or who are ordinarily deemed ugly.

These exercises in the disenchantment and reenchantment of the face might help us suspend judgment about people until we have interacted with them for a while and gotten to know them a bit. If one forms a favorable opinion of someone, one's positive response to their character and personality would then influence one's perception of their physical qualities. We idealize those we love. Mothers are notorious for thinking their sons far more handsome than most of their sons' prospective mates do. Nor are mothers alone in this harmless aggrandizement. Few of us have gorgeous partners, but our love magnifies their attractiveness. If your grandmothers were elderly when you were a child, try remembering how you perceived them back then. They probably did not look like witches, hags, or crones to you. If we could form emotional attachments with minimal static from prejudicial cultural imagery and ill-considered first impressions of people's faces, we would discover more forms of beauty.

Pam Houston (see epigraph) and Gullette (1997, 63) suggest another way to diversify our conception of beauty. When encountering a person, focus on a single (conventionally) good feature and then let your appreciation of that feature infuse the composite. Maybe we routinely do this without realizing it. After all, few of us demand that our friends measure up to exacting criteria of beauty. Heightened consciousness of how latitudinarian our aesthetic standards really are might serve as an antidote to overzealous self-criticism and self-contempt. Deliberately working to foster our awareness of beauty in its many guises would augment our enjoyment of others along with our acceptance of ourselves. Notice, too, that these exercises would benefit younger women who violate current criteria of beauty as much as they would benefit aging women, which is to say that they would benefit virtually all women!

As a cure for the specific pathology of automatically deeming aging features ugly, I propose assembling a portrait gallery of women whom one admires. Gather photographs of them taken in their later years, and display them where you'll see them often. The idea is to link respect for their accomplishments to enjoyment of their aging faces. Depending on your predilections, you might include Simone de Beauvoir, Janet Flanner, Coretta Scott King, Golda Meir, Louise Nevelson, Gertrude Stein, Virginia Woolf, Eleanor Roosevelt, Hannah Arendt, Jeanne Moreau, Rosa Parks, Mary McCarthy, Bella Abzug, Colette, Indira Gandhi, Katharine Hepburn, Toni Morrison, Margaret Mead, Iris Murdoch, or Georgia O'Keeffe. Would it be so horrible (is it so horrible?) to look more like them? Just as one may seek to emulate them in one's life, so one might hope eventually to resemble them in one's appearance. Thus, one might become reconciled to, even pleased with, one's own aging face. Better still, start your portrait gallery when you're a girl, and you may never become displeased with your aging face.

If we got rid of an unduly stringent view of identity continuity, and if we opened up the concept of beauty, the facial legibility postulate would be more benign. Still, the reframings I have proposed may seem like palliatives, for I have said nothing about the relation between aging facial features and the aging body. One does not just see a less beautiful face in the mirror. One sees a face that is a harbinger of impending death—the ultimate Other that one's appearance now personifies and that one feels impelled to flee. I now turn to the problematics of gender, mortality, and aging faces.

3. Facing up to Scary Heterogeneity: The Limits of Becoming and the Feminization of Death

Feminism has had an important role in articulating complex, nonstatic conceptions of the agentic self. Typically, feminists view the subject as heterogeneous and thus as to some degree opaque to itself and to some extent in conflict with itself. But, by and large, they have seen heterogeneity as an impetus for change—for personal insight and development as well as for social critique and political activism. In other words, the self is construed as evolving—as capitalizing on heterogeneity to gradually gain under-standing and enhance effective functioning. Since *evolution* carries con-notations of improvement, Gullette would charge that feminists are build-ing an autobiographical progress template into their account of the self, and she would be right. To some extent, this is an artifact of the questions that have been salient for feminist scholars. They have tried to discern women's agency in everyday life, often under severe economic and emo-tional constraints. Also, they have sought to understand how women can extricate themselves from repressive socialization and ideology and how they can take bold emancipatory action. Aiming to explain how women re-tain a measure of control over their lives despite male dominance and how women can resist and overcome their subordination, feminist accounts of the self accent the propitious side of heterogeneity.

162) 163

A quick scan of the feminist literature suggests that this orientation has led to tunnel vision where the body is concerned. The preponderance of feminist work on the body focuses on women's bodies insofar as they pre-sent problems that cultural critique and social policy could ameliorate. There are, for example, vast feminist literatures on reproductive freedom, on sexual violence and other forms of woman battery, and on eating dis-orders. Insofar as feminist thought has included the body as a dimension of the subject's heterogeneity, it has seen bodily heterogeneity as remedi-able. If only laws were changed, services provided, sexist attitudes and practices forsworn, women would stop experiencing their bodies as alien sites of danger. Women would be able to live in harmony with their bodies.

It seems to me that, despite a core of good sense, Gullette's proposal to replace progress and decline narratives with becoming narratives and my proposals to loosen the identity constancy postulate, to discredit the facial legibility postulate, and to defang the goodness-goes-with-beauty postulate do not escape this blithe mindset. Even if we acknowledge the formidabil-ity of the cultural and psychological obstacles to implementing these pro-posals, a hint of Pollyanaish falsity lingers. I trace this suspect aura to the failure of these proposals to confront an intractable form of heterogeneity associated with the body—the eventuality of death.

Feminist discussions of heterogeneity pay scant attention to cruel, vio-lent unconscious material—to the death drive, as Freud would say. They emphasize relatively tame unconscious material—material that can be ac-cessed and used as a resource for critique, as opposed to material that is best left repressed or disguised through sublimation. Likewise, feminist discussions of the body sidestep its unassimilable aspects—unrelievable, insupportable suffering stemming from incurable disease or irremediable impairment, not to mention death itself. Bodies do not evolve forever. The fatal potentiality—vulnerability to accident and disease—dwells within every body. If one is not killed suddenly when one is still young, one's body will deteriorate. It will require more attention all the time, and it will become stiff, brittle, and weak regardless of how much attention one lavishes on it. Then death comes. But this fate awaits male bodies, too (by actuarial calculations, usually earlier). Why, apart from discrimination in medical research and health-care delivery, is eroding health and death a feminist issue?

I submit that it should be a feminist concern because of the symbolic nexus that links death to femininity. Insofar as mortality is embedded in theology, and death is conceptualized as a deity plucking a life, the agent of death is represented as gender congruent with the life-conferring, life-taking androdeity. No doubt, the symbolic system that links femininity to beauty and motherhood reinforces the theological rationale that binds death to an active, masculine agent. Since feminine imagery repels associations between womanhood and the "ugliness" and dreaded finality of death, the bipolar logic of gender seems to entail a masculine representation of life's end. Yet, figured as the Grim Reaper, death is depicted as an emaciated, skeletal male—as vestigially masculine and thus as a feminized male.

A shift in psychodynamics and imagery accompanies the scientization of life and death, and this shift brings the symbolic link between womanhood and death into full view. Life is reduced to a piece of biological luck, while death is conceived as an inborn eventuality and an unredeemable terminus. Medicalized, death is internalized—it is a consequence of genetic susceptibility, bad habits, or toxic infestation. Secularized, death is a personal tragedy—the annihilation of individual subjectivity. Gray hair, wrinkles, and the like are not symptoms of any malady, much less imminent death. Still, women's aging features have been commandeered as figurative vehicles for decline and demise. As feminist scholars have pointed out, patriarchal cultures not only identify Woman with nature and Man with culture, but also they prize culture over nature. The cunning of a thriving patriarchal gender symbolism is that it contrives to load the entire natural life cycle into feminine imagery.[5] So powerful is the association of womanhood with youthful beauty and motherhood that when a woman's looks cease to inspire ardor and her ovaries cease to produce eggs, womanhood is identified with death.

Feminine beauty ideals and matrigyno-idolatry are complementary symbolic systems. Fair Venus is the goddess of love, to be sure, but she is also Cupid's mom. Beauty is tied to fecundity as well as to sex appeal and romance. The consequences of this linkage can be blatant and devastating. In the aftermath of the 1999 Kosovo war in which Serb soldiers captured and raped many Muslim women, very few women would accuse their torturers and testify to having been raped. Listening to the voices of Muslim Kosovar men explains why these women are so reticent about the appalling abuse many of them endured. Here are the words of a Muslim Kosovar husband who believes, despite his wife's denial, that she was raped: "Kissing her is like kissing a dead body" (New York Times, June 22, 1999, p. A1). If women are deemed soiled and unsuitable for childbearing, they cannot personify love and life. No longer emblematic of love and life, they are marked by morbidity and personify inborn death.

Unconscious fantasies, as psychoanalytic theorists Julia Kristeva and Luce Irigaray remind us, associate death with lack and dissolution and associate lack and dissolution with the "castrated" female body and the engulfing maternal body (for further critique of castration and fusion imagery, see Chapter 2, Sections 3–4; Chapter 3, Section 2; and Chapter 4, Section 3). These associations gain psychic momentum in a disenchanted universe where death is a feared but natural phenomenon. Though repressed, this metaphoric background structures perception of women's aging faces and imbues them with symbolic significance, just as it structures perception of an allegedly impure woman whose culture reviles her as unfit to bear children. Because death is symbolically linked to the female body, and because a postmenopausal woman cannot also symbolize the capacity to create life and thereby mute that unconscious link between her body and death, an aging female face issues a particularly sharp rebuke to cherished illusions of invulnerability and immortality.

Here we have another instance of the treachery of the facial legibility postulate. Although I am not sure that we can altogether sever the potent (and hardly inapt) symbolic link between time-altered features and the realities of decline and death, I am confident that feminists should be working on severing the symbolic link between *women's* aging faces and these disturbing bodily heterogeneities. There is no reason that women's aging faces should bear the whole burden of anxiety about death.

Now, it is worth pointing out that Ann Ferguson's suggestion that we substitute an aesthetic of health for an aesthetic of loveliness is on a collision course with these underlying symbolic associations (Ferguson 1996,

116). Not only is it mystifying what health looks like—do my friends who look fine but who are undergoing chemotherapy for cancer look healthy? But also this proposal solidifies, when it should be resisting, the facial legibility postulate—health and healthy looks pass as surely as youth and youthful looks. Moreover, by itself, this proposal is futile, for it denies the symbolic connection between the aging female face and deteriorating health and death without subverting this well-entrenched figuration and the misogynist discourse in which it is embedded. No alternative aesthetic of the aging feminine face has any chance of succeeding until women's bodies and the concept of femininity have been freed from their phantasmatic coupling with death and its medically mediated portents. It is imperative, then, that feminists undertake a counterfigurative politics aimed at defeating this figurative regime.

The cultural background I have sketched explains why aging women are compelled to refuse their faces—why so many of us know the face in the mirror is ours but still identify with a facial image frozen in our twenties. It's tough enough being the feminine Other. Nobody wants to become the ultimate Other. It explains, as well, why aging women do not consider their painstaking grooming and grueling fitness routines frivolous or vain and why they depict their efforts at self-beautification as virtuous (Furman 1997, 54–55, 70). If aging women do not hide the signs of age, conventional beauty ideals and the facial legibility postulate authorize us to read their faces as a mark of inner corruption—the Grim Reaper lurking within. Laboring to stay young looking is a way of shunning devolution and defilement. Jo Anna Isaak is right: "Contrary to Sartre's claim that after forty we get the face we deserve, women after forty get *the face they have the courage to present*" (Isaak 1996, 150; emphasis added). No meaning is inherent in any face, and likening the aging female face to a death mask is a vicious slander. Yet, it is far from clear how a courageous woman is to respond. If discretion is the better part of valor, keeping one's aging face and its symbolic reminder of death under wraps is the courageous response to aging. On this interpretation of courage, women should redouble their efforts to conceal their age and dedicate themselves to self-beautification. But if surrendering to misogyny's symbolic tyranny is cowardice, women should follow Susan Sontag's stirring advice—they "should tell the truth" (Sontag 1979, 478). On this interpretation, courage demands repossessing our purloined faces and wearing them unrepentantly.

CHAPTER SEVEN

Live Ordnance in the Cultural Field:
Gender Imagery, Sexism, and the Fragility
of Feminist Gains

Women's self-determination, I have argued, presupposes their ability to articulate their lives in their own way. They need their own voices, for personal sorrows and moral pitfalls await those who speak the language of patriarchy. Recounting the past and anticipating the future in culturally authoritative but patriarchally tainted terms do violence to women's needs, values, and aspirations. Of necessity, then, they resort to survival strategies, either rationalizing the disparity between who they are and how they are living, or deluding themselves that there is no disparity. Both of these self-deceptive disciplines are emotionally costly. Both can devolve into moral culpability. Both interfere with women's control over their fortunes. Neither contributes to women's fulfillment or increases their self-esteem.

These liabilities notwithstanding, many women will continue to use distorted and distorting images of womanhood to frame their self-concepts and their commitments as long as patriarchal cultures are bombarding them with such imagery. It is extremely difficult for an individual to do otherwise in these cultural contexts. Since gender dissidence is personally taxing and socially penalized, women who overcome the hazards attendant on silence and self-alienation marshal exceptional courage and ingenuity. Being estranged from oneself is usually painful. Yet, fashioning language to close the gap between one's subjectivity and one's life story strains many women's powers of invention. Embracing an unconventional autobiographical plot or an idiosyncratic account of a conventional plot line and braving others' mystification or disapproval outstrips many women's confidence in their self-representations. In my view, then, feminists must launch a sustained public critique of culturally entrenched gender imagery, and they must strive to make alternative emancipatory imagery widely available and generally accepted. They owe this to women, for women's self-determination depends on it.

But, of course, women's self-determination depends on much more than their discursive resources. Their social, economic, and political environment is no less crucial. One cannot lead the life one would like to live if one cannot make it intelligible to oneself and others, but neither can one lead the life one would like to live if repressive or exclusionary institutions defeat the ventures one holds dear. Analyzing what sorts of opportunities, incentives, and supplementary goods and services facilitate women's self-determination and how institutions can best deliver them is beyond the scope of this work. However, my concern with misogynist gender imagery is not irrelevant to these more concrete matters. Thus, I shall close by examining a little-noticed intersection between orthodox gender discourses and social structures.

Specifically, I shall consider a dual problem that all progressive social movements face—how to prevent lingering prejudice from eroding institutional gains and how to hang onto institutional gains and protect them from backlash movements. It is my view that feminist neglect of the gendered imagery encoding sexuality, beauty, maternity, and mortality leaves unexploded ordnance littering the discursive field. A favorite battle plan of the forces of resurgent misogyny is to outflank feminists, retrieve the patriarchal rhetorical ammunition left behind, and fire it off to halt women's progress. Traditional representations of womanhood normalize the unconscious sexist attitudes that motivate everyday practices of subordination. Moreover, they connect the reversals that backlashers support to powerful emotions at the same time as they give these retrograde programs a veneer of reasonability.

To understand the role of orthodox gender imagery in subverting feminist advances, it is necessary to examine the relationship between cultural representations of womanhood and sexist attitudes and behavior. There are currently two major approaches to sexism and similar prejudices—cognitive psychology (Section 1) and psychoanalysis (Section 2). Students of sexism from both schools of thought agree that this prejudice functions as a tonic for men's self-esteem and that the tonic does not work without an infusion of male bonding. However, cognitive psychologists and psychoanalytic theorists propose radically different solutions for this problem

(Section 3). Unfortunately, none of their recommendations would suffice to wipe out sexism. Neither cognitive psychology nor psychoanalysis adequately integrates culturally entrenched representations of womanhood into its account of the genesis of sexism, and consequently all of the remedies for sexism derived from these theories bypass one of sexism's major contributing causes. Since men in male dominated societies internalize a sexist cultural patrimony, a feasible and effective program for resisting and subduing sexism and for securing men's self-esteem without it must include a discursive politics aimed at replacing this heritage of misogynist imagery with emancipatory gender imagery (Section 4). As long as feminine stereotypes remain integral to our mythologies of selfhood and human purpose, unconscious sexism will flourish, and women's social and economic gains will be fragile.

1. Sexism According to Cognitive Psychology: Conceptualization and Inference

Cognitive psychologists assimilate stereotypes to the broader concept of the schema. A schema is a small-scale theory that explicates a category (Fiske and Taylor 1991, 98). People have schemas for the major components of experience, including one's self, other persons, events, and social roles (Fiske and Taylor 1991, 118–120). Each of these theories is comprised of hypotheses that prime perceivers to generate pertinent explanations and predictions (Valian 1998, 106). The schema for the concept of woman, for example, leads individuals to expect women to be easy to influence and to attribute women's behavior to this malleability. Relying, as schemas do, on generalizations about large batches of particulars, schema-based judgments about actual individuals and their conduct can miss the mark (Basow 1992, 3; Valian 1998, 107, 118–120, 127–128). In fact, plenty of women are stubborn. Still, cognitive psychologists maintain that schemas are necessary because people have neither sufficient time nor sufficient brain power to approach every moment afresh (Valian 1998, 2). Crude though some schemas may be, they work well enough most of the time. If this were not true, people would be functioning much less successfully than they are.

Some proponents of cognitive psychology's approach to gender reject the term *stereotype* because of its negative connotations (Valian 1998, 2). If stereotypes are bad, it seems we should be trying to get rid of them. But since schemas, including gender schemas, are indispensable to thought and action, this is a forlorn hope. For the sake of efficiency and expediency, people must depend on the rough-and-ready presuppositions that these schemas furnish.

In my view, cognitive psychology's thesis that people need interpretive cues and shortcuts is correct. It does not follow, however, that people should be satisfied with whatever schemas their culture happens to inculcate. Indeed, feminist cognitive psychologists have catalogued many of the misleading inferences that current gender schemas authorize, and they have gauged the harm these schemas inflict on women (for a comprehensive review of this work, see Valian 1998). Cognitive psychologists can and should recommend gender schema refinement and reform. Where such modification is called for, I consider the term *stereotype* perspicuous, for its negative connotations signal the schema's cognitive and moral failings. It may be true that we cannot get rid of gender schemas, but we should be contesting gender stereotypes. Unfortunately, recent psychological research demonstrates that there are formidable barriers to schema—and hence stereotype—change.

Research in cognitive psychology shows that schemas function as intellectual filtration systems. Schemas organize memory and perception, and they cause people to overlook anomalous cases (Hamilton 1981; Rothbart 1981; Snyder 1981). Since people do not notice when a schema does not jibe with reality, they have no reason to revise it. A complementary mechanism magnifies this schema-reinforcing effect. In addition to filtering out disconfirming evidence, schemas underscore confirming evidence. Since schema-compatible evidence is more prominent in perceivers' minds, their schema seems empirically unimpeachable. Still, data selectivity is only one of the ways in which schemas are self-ratifying. Research also shows that gender stereotypes elicit behavioral conformity. When one individual has schema-based expectations about another individual's gender, it is likely that the target of those expectations will fulfill them (Skrypnick and Snyder 1982). Thus, schemas mobilize self-confirming evidence by inducing people to voluntarily enact them.

Conspiracy aficionados should find cognitive psychology's account of gender altogether congenial. In this view, purely cognitive processes minimize people's access to information that would justify modifying gender stereotypes. Then, just in case anyone might be alert enough to notice some counterevidence, schema-based interaction drafts women and men into willingly creating a schema-compliant social world, which verifies the schema. Thinking and behaving through this conceptual and inferential infrastructure, people register as rational and socially competent subjects when they reproduce the relations of domination and subordination that their cognitive apparatus encodes.

The prospects for gender stereotype transformation already look exceedingly bleak. Nevertheless, cognitive psychology provides further reason for pessimism, for people's emotional needs also obstruct gender stereotype reform. Although remembering not to lapse into old patterns of thought is inconvenient and bothersome, this annoyance hardly accounts for people's stalwart allegiance to gender stereotypes nor for the anger and/or anxiety that critiques of gender stereotypes stir up. To fill in this explanatory blank, some cognitive psychologists attribute people's emotional investment in invidious social role schemas to in-group versus out-group dynamics. The idea is that people readily distinguish among and construct conceptions of social groups because they want a positive self-image and because they can secure one by identifying with an in-group that has admirable attributes (Fiske and Taylor 1991, 161, 166; Oakes et. al. 1994, 83; Brown 1995, 170–173). Although this theory does not entail that out-groups must be assigned despicable attributes, the logic of self-esteem amplification increases the probability that out-group schemas will be disproportionately derogatory. Conversely, in-group schemas are likely to be disproportionately laudatory. Since gender stereotype change would detract from men's self-esteem, self-interest puts an emotional lock on established gender stereotypes. Men's control over the engines of culture positions them to translate this emotional lock into a cultural lock.

No doubt, this esteem-enhancing strategy is feasible for and attractive to many members of privileged social groups (but for evidence of the limits of self-esteem's role in schema formation, see Fiske and Taylor 1991, 166–167). More surprisingly, cognitive psychologists contend that members of subordinated groups also adopt it at the personal level. By focusing on trivial advantages that they enjoy—for example, men open doors for women—and by identifying with those virtues and talents that are ascribed to them—for example, empathy, altruism, and interpersonal skills—women sustain their self-esteem (Valian 1998, 152; Cudd 1998, 199–200). It seems to me, however, that this account conceals the ferocity of patriarchy's attack on women's self-esteem. Women's internalized oppression gives rise to a great deal of frustration and suffering. Its damage to women's self-esteem is recorded in high rates of depression and eating disorders, overinvestment in infertility treatments, and rocketing demand for cosmetic surgery. Plainly, in-group self-identification is not working all that well for women.

I doubt that cognitive psychology's thin theory of gender-related emotion tells the whole story for men either. It is de rigueur for psychologists who countenance the term *prejudice*, which is colloquially associated with strong, sometimes turbulent affect, to abstract the feeling out of the concept in their discussions of experimental results.[1] Thus, contemporary psychology figures women as collateral damage of universal cognitive dispositions. Women are subordinated, it seems, without sexism or misogyny. No animosity. No acrimony. No harm intended.

In light of the glaring social inequity that in-group/out-group theory masks, I find this account of the relation between self-esteem augmentation, gender stereotyping, and sexism psychologically farfetched and inordinately exonerating. It glosses over daily news reports of brutality against women. Men are not merely inflating their in-group image. They are also pummeling women, physically as well as discursively. Moreover, they are doing their best to recruit their victims into a sinister ideology of masculine superiority and feminine inferiority that lurks behind a reassuring ideology of liberal equality. People need self-esteem, to be sure, and I agree that misogyny forges male-to-male bonds and pumps up men's self-esteem. But I doubt that men's in-group image maintenance fully explains the prejudice that fuels patriarchy's systemic outrages. Sexist assaults on women's well-being, which range from rape, woman battery, and sexual harassment to casual derision and unthinking marginalization, are statistically commonplace. They are not committed by a few sociopaths. Although it is true that much discrimination and other subordinating treatment of women occurs without conscious malice toward women as a group and that large numbers of men publicly disclaim sexism, the persistence of unconscious sexist attitudes and practices together with the virulence of many men's attitudes toward women and the savagery of many attacks on women suggests that sexism's emotional wellspring is deep and poisoned.

2. *Sexism According to Psychoanalysis: Desire and Emotion*

Psychoanalytic theory maintains that all children consolidate their gender identity as they develop a sense of self. But it holds that girls develop feelings of inferiority at the same time as they consolidate feminine identity, and boys develop feelings of contempt for women at the same time as they consolidate masculine identity.[2] We have seen that in-group/out-group theory confirms the link between masculine identity and sexism. Research in cognitive psychology also confirms the psychoanalytic claim that gender and selfhood are intimately connected. Reviewing the literature on femininity and masculinity, Kay Deaux notes that women and men usually describe themselves as very feminine or very masculine, respectively, regardless of the cultural gender coding of their other self-reported attributes (Deaux 1987, 298). Apparently, most people are willing to avow gender-inappropriate traits and conduct, but they cannot tolerate identifying with the "wrong" gender label. One explanation for this paradoxical result is that females and males fixate on the gender-appropriate attributes that they do possess, and they regard these attributes as sufficient to qualify for femininity or masculinity (Deaux 1987, 297). If so, they customize their conception of the gender to which they belong in order to safeguard their own gender identity.

Still, there appear to be severe restrictions on people's license to customize their conception of gender, and people's hyperproprietary feelings about gender attest to intense, complex, and obdurate passion at the core of femininity and masculinity. The guilt and shame that mothers often experience when they cannot (or prefer not to) conform to traditional nurturer/homemaker responsibilities and the shame and humilia tion that men often experience when they cannot (or prefer not to) conform to traditional warrior/breadwinner responsibilities show that gender's emotional onus encumbers people's basic desires and their major, ongoing undertakings. Women's lifelong anxiety about measuring up to beauty ideals and the devastation aging women suffer as their looks change and they lose their procreative ability points up the obsessional quality of women's ties to gender identity. Likewise, the rage heterosexuals often vent at lesbians and gays whom they classify as gender violators is symptomatic of churning emotion and acute defensiveness about gender normativity. Psychoanalytic theory explains people's fervent attachment to gender identity by telling a story about the emotionally charged interaction between children and their parents and the psychological mechanisms through which these relationships are in some respects internalized and in other respects defended against.

Perhaps the best-known feminist psychoanalytic account of masculinity and sexism is Nancy Chodorow's. Chodorow traces sexism to the sexual division of labor in the family—women are primarily responsible for child-rearing, whereas men are expected to work outside the home. Because fathers are absent most of the time (and because mothers who work outside the home typically employ other women to care for their children), virtually all infants and young children receive most of their care from women. As a result, both girls and boys form their first attachment to a woman and strongly identify with her. The development of a girl's gender identity is continuous with this original bond (Chodorow 1980, 13–14). To become feminine, all girls need to do is persist in identifying with their mothers.[3] However, the development of a boy's gender identity requires rupturing the maternal bond and emulating a father who is emotionally and physically distant. This paternal void in the household obliges boys to define masculinity in reaction to their mothers—"I am not like her"—and to look to popular culture for a code of masculinity. According to Chodorow, that boys who are parented exclusively by women must form their gender identity by negating feminine identity and by discerning general rules of masculine conduct entails that their gender identity is fragile (Chodorow 1980, 13). They achieve masculinity by repressing a deeply embedded part of themselves—those aspects of their mothers that they internalized during the earliest stages of life—but this repressed feminine material forever threatens to crop up and expose them as "sissies." It is understandable, then, that they exaggerate the differences between themselves and girls/women and that they come to hate that which imperils their sense of their own masculinity, namely, the feminine.

In Chodorow's view, the logic of fortifying masculine identity in a society in which only women do childcare pushes men into misogyny. By shunning their mothers and despising the Other within, boys/men secure their gender identity. But in denying the despised Other within and pinning this dangerous, despised Otherness on women, boys/men become sexists. Rigid social structures combine with pressing psychological needs to forge an inherently sexist form of masculinity.

Chodorow focuses on a salient aspect of the feminine stereotype that is linked to a common form of sexism. Her narrative recounts how men come to fear the qualities of emotional warmth, empathy, and nurturance and to disdain those who are supposed to have them. These are the maternal qualities male infants have internalized but need to expel later on. Still, it might be objected that her narrative accounts for too little, for aversion to and devaluation of these straightforwardly admirable qualities is only one of sexism's many manifestations. There are also sexists who idealize women, sexists who demean women's intelligence, and sexists who consider women loathsome. Sexuality, race, and class further complicate sexist attitudes. In *The Anatomy of Prejudices*, Elizabeth Young-Bruehl seeks to examine the full spectrum of sexisms. With that end in view, she establishes a taxonomy of sexisms that differentiates sexism from sexist racism/classism and sameness sexism from difference sexism, and she invokes Freud's theory of narcissism to analyze each of these psychic positions.[4]

Young-Bruehl construes sexism as stemming from a "fantasized originary condition"—namely, primary narcissism—and an "elemental experience"—namely, the "bewilderment and exasperation" caused by the "*irreducible* fact" of sexual difference (Young-Bruehl 1996, 136, 131). Primary narcissism is the fantasy of fusion with an omnipotent, devoted mother— a phallic mother (also see Chapter 2, Section 3; Chapter 3, Section 2). By projecting his phallus onto his mother, a boy ensures that the individual who holds power over him is someone like him—not a potentially hostile Other—and also that he is one of the powerful since he has a phallus like hers. But it is inevitable that boys will discover sexual difference, for, the shared humanity of women and men notwithstanding, mothers do not have phalluses. This revelation arouses an "elemental anxiety": How can someone be so like me and yet so different from me? And this anxiety threatens narcissism: What if powerful people are different from me? What if I am defective? (Young-Bruehl 1996, 131). The upshot is an "inability to tolerate difference" that is silenced by an "elemental denial": Women and men are really the same! (Young-Bruehl 1996, 131). The psychic function of sexism, according to Young-Bruehl, is to conceal the clash between men's desire for anatomical uniformity and the reality of sexual dimorphism. Misogynist attitudes, doctrines, and practices are elaborations of unconscious fantasies of unisexuality. Sexism satisfies men's narcissistic needs—it assures them that they are anatomically intact and that they are powerful—by keeping the boy's "hope of sameness alive" (Young-Bruehl 1996, 131–132). How does each of the sexisms that Young-Bruehl identifies accomplish this aim?

Sameness sexism preserves men's dream of genital monism by splitting off the idealized, worshiped woman from actual wives and mothers. Goddess figures festooned with insignia of sexual allure and fecundity sustain men's denial of difference by standing in for the phallic mother (Young-Bruehl 1996, 419). But since real, corporeal women threaten to explode the illusion of sameness, this form of sexism installs an ideology that occludes their bodily difference (Young-Bruehl 1996, 419). One such ideology is the reproductive theory that men make babies whereas women merely incubate them, which implies that women have no valuable capacity that men lack—that, in all important respects, they "really are men, even if imperfect men" (Young-Bruehl 1996, 419). Unfortunately for women, sexists advert to these minor feminine departures from the male standard of excellence to rationalize treating women as menial domestics (Young-Bruehl 1996, 419). With women and their distinctive capabilities and experiences out of the psychodynamic picture, nothing casts doubt on men's bodies or on their social dominance.

Difference sexism is a backup maneuver. If sexual difference is a basic and inescapable fact, sameness sexism's outright denial strategy is always on the verge of crashing. To compensate for sameness sexism's shakiness, difference sexism goes overboard making concessions to "reality" and asserts hyperdifference: Women are so different from men that they hardly belong to the same species. Unlike those men who are called on to make cultural, economic, and political contributions, women's sole purpose in life is bearing and caring for children (Young-Bruehl 1996, 420). Unlike men, who are by nature sexually aggressive, women have no erotic needs or pleasures—they are chaste, self-sacrificial mothers (Young-Bruehl 1996, 421).[5] While trumpeting flagrant gender difference, this form of sexism neutralizes it through derogation and exclusion. Women are inhuman both because they are nothing but baby breeders and, curiously, because they are otherworldly saints. By decreeing men the only real human beings, this ideological regime fabricates the unisexual, masculine psychic reality that underwrites men's self-esteem.

Still, lesbians constitute a fifth column that anxious males need to vanquish, and sameness and difference sexism have divergent attitudes and policies regarding this phantasmatic menace.[6] In cultures where sameness sexism flourishes, lesbian sexuality is considered disgusting because it is not phallic, yet it is not rigorously suppressed provided that it stays out of public spaces (Young-Bruehl 1996, 425). Since extirpating lesbianism presupposes acknowledging the lesbian's nonphallic body and sexuality, it is safer for the sameness sexist to pretend that there are no lesbians by ignoring closeted lesbianism. In contrast, difference sexism regards lesbians (and other nonreproducing women) as abominations, for they shun difference sexism's womanhood-motherhood equivalency (Young-Bruehl 1996, 427). Because their unavoidably public nonmotherhood likens them to men while their anatomy disqualifies them as men, the very existence of these women flies in the face of the difference sexist's postulates.[7] For this reason, difference sexism mandates zero tolerance for lesbians.

So far, I have been sketching forms of sexism as opposed to sexist racism/classism. Young-Bruehl stipulates that she will reserve the term *sexism* for prejudice directed against women from one's own social group —women "of the mother's kind" (Young-Bruehl 1996, 414). *Sexist racism/ classism* refers to prejudice against women who belong to a less-privileged race or class than one's own—women who are "not-mother" (Young-Bruehl 1996, 414). That sexism varies depending on the victim's race and class cannot be gainsaid. However, it is not altogether clear that the distinction between intra- and intergroup prejudice—sexism toward "one's own" women and sexism toward "other" women—accounts for the difference.

Young-Bruehl models sexism toward African-American women on sameness sexism.[8] Figured as matriarchs and heads of households—in other words, as phallic mothers—these women are like men (Young-Bruehl 1996, 134). However, it is doubtful that this form of sexism is confined to African-American men. After all, it was a white man, Daniel Moynihan, who argued that African-American matriarchs had emasculated their men and wrecked the family in their own community (Young-Bruehl 1996, 92). Since this form of sexism traverses racial boundaries, it seems that Young-Bruehl's like-mother/not-mother distinction does not define the targeted population for every sexist attitude.

Turning to intergroup attitudes—sexist racism/classism—Young-Bruehl switches to the difference sexism model. Whites' racism prompts them to divide women into madonnas and whores and to assign out-group women to the latter category (Young-Bruehl 1996, 134). Middle-class people debase working-class women in the same way. Although Young-Bruehl acknowledges that women can share sexist racist/classist attitudes, she analyzes these prejudices from the masculine point of view, for she holds that the incest taboo governs madonna-versus-whore classifications (Young-Bruehl 1996, 134, 368, 414).[9] Women who could be one's mother are designated madonnas. Women whose race or class supposedly precludes a consanguineous relationship are designated whores.

I agree that misogynist cultures rely on imagery of women from subordinated social groups to represent the prototypical whore. Likewise, I agree that by exporting socially censured desires—desires condemned as violent or perverse—to "subhuman," out-group women—oversexed women who themselves have depraved desires—this form of sexism adds a soupçon of libidinal titillation to difference sexism's narcissistic balm. Sexist racism/classism condones erotic adventures and pleasures that no "honorable" man could permit himself were he bedding an in-group madonna. However, peer sexual harassment and acquaintance rape, both of which are prevalent, are not always aimed at out-group women. Some sexual harassment cases involve male clerical workers posting risque photographs in office spaces that female clerical workers must also frequent. Similarly, the victims of acquaintance rape are commonly the assailants' in-group dates and girlfriends. These practices raise doubts about the claim that the category *whore* is reserved for Other women who have been typed as dissolute and promiscuous. Again, the bright line between intra- and intergroup sexism blurs. Indeed, sexism appears to be so labile that it can activate opportunistically.

Young-Bruehl's assertion that sexism is not kindled by men's desire for Difference—psychologically significant Otherness—but rather by their nostalgic desire for "Before Difference" sharpens the contrast between her account of sexism and Chodorow's (Young-Bruehl 1996, 132). For Chodorow, gender difference and sexism are joint artifacts of a relational history in a particular familial structure. They are not biologically programmed, nor do they arise from an instinctive reaction to biological facts. If men become sexist, then, they must have a desire to be different from their female caregiver that subtends the process through which Difference becomes a preoccupation and this prejudice emerges. Young-Bruehl inverts this conception. For Young-Bruehl, the boy's perception of the biological reality of sexual difference "naturally" elicits an anxious response and presses him into a defensive posture (Young-Bruehl 1996, 131, 236). Just as Freud presumes that the anatomical distinction between the sexes has transparent meaning for girls—they are inferior—so Young-Bruehl presumes that the anatomical distinction between the sexes has transparent meaning for boys—they might be inferior. Consequently, there is no reason for her to posit that men desire Difference as such. Instead, the discovery of genital difference suffices to subtend the emergence of sexism.

This substantive disagreement notwithstanding, it is important to recognize the methodological congruence of these two theories. Both Chodorow and Young-Bruehl assimilate sexism to a xenophobic model— people hate what they fear. Because the dynamic of xenophobia is a matter of common sense, their narratives rest on a psychological truism. Because the sexual division of labor in the family remains widespread and the anatomical distinction between the sexes seems self-evident, their stories unfold in a cozily familiar social and biological world. Moreover, because most people experience gender identity as crucial to their sense of self, Chodorow's and Young-Bruehl's thematic intertwining of masculinity and sexism dispels the mystery of sexism's staying power and emotional urgency. Finally, because both of these theorists represent gender identity as formed in early childhood and subsequently experienced as second nature, their plot lines explain why sexist attitudes are seldom accessible to consciousness and why these attitudes seem unexceptionable to the sexist when they do come to light.

3. Overcoming Sexism?

Sexism is a chameleon endowed with prodigious powers of transformation and survival. The protean sprawl of sexism is unequaled. It reaches into every site of human endeavor and interaction—from bedrooms and nurseries to streets, schools, workplaces, stores, and recreational facilities. It runs the gamut of moods and modes: automatic to deliberate, gallant to violent, sour to arrogant, reverential to lewd, surly to gleeful, nonchalant to vindictive. It blends into the social scenery—always there, seldom noticed. When critical consciousness and institutional reforms threaten it with extinction, it reinvents itself.

Sexism's awesome adaptability stems in part from its relation to masculine narcissism. As Young-Bruehl remarks, sexist attitudes are " 'natural' (ego syntonic) for half the species" (Young-Bruehl 1996, 137). I know of no student of gender and sexism who disputes this sobering observation. Consequently, it comes as no surprise that cognitive psychology and psychoanalysis converge on two fundamental points: 1) sexism augments men's self-esteem, and 2) sexism and male bonding go hand in hand. Still, because these theories ascribe different roles to male bonding and depict sexism's contribution to self-esteem differently, they offer different advice about how to eliminate sexism.

Cognitive psychologists regard sexism as a byproduct of male bonding. By seeing themselves as belonging to the category *men* and allocating desirable attributes to that category, individual men gratify their need to belong to a valued group and secure their self-esteem. Alas, this kind of categorizing is a contrastive enterprise, and women become the out-group to men's in-group. Still, according to cognitive psychology, this othering is not infused with animus. Sexism is primarily a batch of intellectual errors that leads men to treat women unfairly. Since cognitive psychologists construe feminine stereotypes either as reasonable but overinclusive generalizations from experience or as generalizations based on faulty logic, they favor rationalistic remedies.

Paying more attention to how one is thinking is their principal weapon against bias (Banaji and Greenwald 1994, 69–70). First, society must discourage children from adopting gender stereotypes by educating them about the misinformation these stereotypes encode (Valian 1998, 307). Second, individuals must admit that their judgments are sexist. By conducting thought experiments in which the sexes of the participants are switched around, people can catch themselves using gender stereotypes and own up to their cognitive malfunctioning (Valian 1998, 305). Third, people need to take measures to reduce their reliance on gender schemas. They can familiarize themselves with common reasoning errors and learn to avoid them (Valian 1998, 310–314). Also, if they spend more time forming judgments and submit their judgments to others' review, they are less likely to accept stereotypical interpretations (Valian 1998, 307–308). In short, cognitive caution and vigilance should counteract sexism.

Other recommendations from cognitive psychologists would require reconfiguring social relations. Researchers who believe that stereotypes are rough replications of social reality contend that legislated social change is an effective antidote to prejudice, for social change presents people with a new set of data to generalize about (Banaji and Greenwald 1994, 68–69). On a smaller scale, some social settings derail stereotypical thinking. In personalized situations, individuals decategorize and recategorize the individuals with whom they are interacting, and stereotypes give way to particularized understandings (Brown 1995, 265). More specifically, the incidence of stereotype-based judgments decreases under circumstances of cooperative interdependence, equal status, and egalitarian norms (Neuberg 1994, 125).

None of these suggestions is particularly promising. Lessons about the inaccuracies of gender stereotypes face stiff competition in children's everyday lives. Other educational materials are replete with gender stereotypes. Moreover, children are inundated with "gender-appropriate" toys and regaled with sexist representations of women in the media. In this environment, well-intentioned corrective instruction cannot be counted on to mold future generations of nonsexist men. Another difficulty is that realizing that one is prone to bias does not give one the presence of mind to quash it in the flux and flow of real life. The fast pace of events and the seeming triviality of many situations easily overpower people's antistereotyping resolutions. Social change does not seem to take up the slack. Despite the fact that most U.S. women, including most mothers, now work outside the home, the stereotypical equivalence of womanhood and motherhood remains as influential as ever (see Chapter 2). If social change affects prevalent conceptions of femininity at all, there is such a long time lag between the social change and the cognitive uptake that it is impossible to track a causal relation between them. Finally, personal interaction structured to minimize stereotyping may persuade a sexist man that the woman he has gotten to know or worked with does not fit the feminine stereotype. Still, sexists need not generalize on the basis of such experience. Too often they conclude that this particular woman is the exception who proves the rule (Neuberg 1994, 126; Brown 1995, 265). Moreover, the mutually respectful settings that promote the perception of women as individuals are rare in patriarchal societies. Indeed, since it could be argued that such settings will never be common until sexism has been defeated, it seems doubtful that they could contribute much to a campaign to overcome sexism. Although rationality-enhancing tactics are sometimes beneficial, to rely exclusively on such strategies would be to ignore men's need for a replacement for sexism's contribution to their self-esteem and thus to underestimate the magnitude of the problem that sexism poses.

Since psychoanalytic theorists attribute sexism's intractability to its role in stabilizing masculine identity, they advocate preempting sexism by meeting this need through other means. Chodorow and Young-Bruehl agree that fear is the ultimate cause of sexism, but they indict different fears. In Chodorow's view, it is fear of the feminine Other within that unsettles self-esteem and that sexism relieves. Since boys do not internalize masculine identity through a close relationship with their father, they must find another route to manhood. Male bonding originates in the boy's need to ascertain the rules of masculinity by spending time with other males. In Young-Bruehl's view, sexism quiets the boy's fear that women are powerful and that he may be defective and weak. Because sexism stems from the fantasy that the beloved mother is phallic, male bonding is integral to the psychodynamics of sexism. In these relationships, men recreate the homoerotic bond between the boy and the imaginary phallic mother and reassure one another of their unassailable manhood. As a result of the disparate roles that male bonding plays in these two accounts of sexism, Chodorow's proposal for easing the anxieties that develop into sexism focuses on childcare practices, whereas Young-Bruehl's focuses on accessing and owning the needs that male bonding meets.

Chodorow's solution restructures boys' early relationships. One of her reasons for endorsing shared parenting is that a caregiving father would eliminate boys' need to define themselves as not-feminine, reduce their insecurity about masculinity, and quell their defensive scorning of femininity (Chodorow 1980, 12–16). Male bonding would not undermine women's interests if boys became masculine and developed self-esteem by identifying with a caregiving father.

In contrast, Young-Bruehl's interventions are aimed directly at the intrapsychic economy of sexism. She celebrates ex-"homosexuals" as models of category busting (Young-Bruehl 1996, 435). By *ex-"homosexuals,"* she means gays and lesbians who deny that one's sexuality makes one a definable kind of person and who refuse homosexuality as an identity. Following Judith Butler's account of the disenchantment of the naturalness of sexuality and gender, Young-Bruehl champions parodistic, ironic performances of gender norms and getting comfortable with fluid, multiple identities (Young-Bruehl 1996, 530–531, 534). In addition, ex-"homosexual" gays who cultivate lean, muscled physiques and men who openly admire these bodies reenact the homoeroticism of the fantasy of the phallic mother instead of repressing it (Young-Bruehl 1996, 535). Likewise, some gays self-consciously idolize (and may emulate) the phallic mother whom sexist heterosexuals fear and repress (Young-Bruehl 1996, 535). The Judy Garland, Bette Davis, Mae West, and Maria Callas cults wryly air the fantasy of the phallic mother and allay the narcissistic need for sexism.

Young-Bruehl also examines ways for women to opt out of sexist contexts. Since both sameness and difference sexism give rise to systems of control over women's reproduction, women can avoid some of the deleterious effects of sexism by gaining control over their reproductive lives (Young-Bruehl 1996, 419–421). She refers to one option as "Nordic marriage" but points out that a version of it is widespread among young, middle-class Americans (Young-Bruehl 1996, 429–430). In this system, unmarried adults cohabit by mutual consent. Dissociating sexuality from reproduction, they value sexual relations for intimacy and pleasure. Many couples marry only if they decide to have children. Young-Bruehl is convinced of the emancipatory impact of this approach to sexuality and reproduction because it is standard practice in Scandinavia, and sexist domination has been greatly reduced there (Young-Bruehl 1996, 430). The disadvantage of Nordic marriage, however, is that it perpetuates the nuclear family, an institution with a poor record of fostering women's equality. Thus, Young-Bruehl turns to African-American family structure in search of a better model. Although Young-Bruehl acknowledges that poverty and lack of opportunity often prevent African-American women from enjoying the full benefits of their extended kinship units, she emphasizes the potential advantages of households in which younger women work outside the home, grandmothers or elderly aunts care for children, and fathers love their children but reside elsewhere. If it were not for race and class oppression, she claims, this arrangement would afford women more control over their reproductive lives than the nuclear family ever could (Young-Bruehl 1996, 431).

There are moral as well as practical reasons to be skeptical of Chodorow's position on shared parenting. Since it directs fathers and mothers to raise children together, it valorizes a heterosexist system of childrearing (as does Nordic marriage), and it implicitly blames single mothers and lesbian couples for prolonging sexist attitudes. From a practical standpoint, the trouble is that shared parenting is not economically feasible for most cohabiting heterosexual parents, nor is it likely that the work world will be reorganized to accommodate shared parenting in the foreseeable future. Unpaid family leaves do not enable both earners to take time off when a baby is born or adopted, and, since most U.S. men still earn more than their female partners, there is a financial incentive for the mother to stay home if anyone does. Daycare centers are staffed overwhelmingly by women both because women are willing to accept substandard wages and because homophobic fears of male pederasty skew hiring decisions. All things considered, few boys (or girls) are likely to experience equally dedicated male and female caregiving.

Young-Bruehl's views about Nordic marriage and intergenerational female households attack symptoms of sexism rather than causes. Sexist men exert control over women's reproductive lives, and the arrangements Young-Bruehl describes would insulate women from this regulation. But there is no reason to believe that boys raised in either of these settings would not become sexist. Indeed, if Young-Bruehl's contention that sexism is a defense against the fantasy of the phallic mother is correct, it seems that the anxieties this fantasy arouses would be heightened in an all-female household. In addition, it is not clear that Scandinavian societies have really conquered patriarchy, for gendered job segration remains widespread there. Nor is it clear that the African-American kinship structure that Young-Bruehl endorses can succeed in elevating women's status. For one thing, many upwardly mobile African-Americans gladly leave this family structure behind. For another, feminists should not forget that grandmothers may well have their own ideas about how to spend their time, and these ideas may not include raising more children.

As for the virtues of madcap ex-"homosexuals," their free-spirited antics do not provide solutions for many people. Most men whose everyday conduct makes a mockery of gender norms face ridicule and ostracism, if not physical assault. Admirable though gays' candor about their attachment to the phallic mother and their need for homoerotic pleasure may be, it is unrealistic to expect many heterosexual men to follow this cathartic recipe, for most heterosexual men are at least as homophobic as they are sexist. Also, it is by no means clear that gay men are immune to sexism's wily charms. In worshiping movie and opera divas who personify the phallic mother, they may fall prey to sameness sexism vis-à-vis ordinary women. It is not clear, then, that women would benefit if heterosexual men followed the lead of the gay avant-garde.

4. Culture, Sexism, and Feminism

In my view, none of the theories of sexism and remedies for sexism that I have discussed takes adequate account of ambient culture in the acquisition and perpetuation of sexist attitudes and practices. Ubiquitous, yet elusive, patriarchal gender discourse is a singularly potent and adaptable system of pictorial and literary representations that shapes psycho-corporeal life.[10] Individuals do not invent sexist conceptions of women on their own. Neither the attributes people associate with femininity nor the emotional and valuational tincture these attributes take on can be convincingly explained without analyzing cultural representations of womanhood and the processes through which they insinuate themselves into individual economies of desire. If this is so, feminist emancipatory programs that do not confront gender discourse head-on and that provide no alternative subsidies for men's self-esteem have little chance of making much of a dent in sexism.

Cognitive psychologist Virginia Valian maintains that the fact that mothers physically nurture babies accounts for the feminine stereotype (Valian 1998, 116). In her view, people move from experiencing and/or observing nurturant breast feeding to using this physical activity as a metaphor for psychological nurturance and finally to concluding that women have nurturant personalities (Valian 1998, 116). By supplementing this characterization with attributes that rationalize the sexual division of labor that they see all around them, people embellish the stereotype—

nurturance is yoked to warmth and expressiveness, but also to insecurity, illogicality, sentimentality, vulnerability, submissiveness, and the like (Valian 1998, 115–116). It is not clear, however, why exposure to the sexual division of labor would lead anyone to infer that women normally have these traits. As Valian points out, women do not need them to perform their designated household chores, nor do they need them to succeed in the occupations into which they are traditionally segregated. Feminine attributes are not necessary for cooking (I cannot think of a single famous chef who is submissive), nor are they necessary for clerical work (illogicality would seem to be a handicap there). Without cultural input, then, it seems unlikely that anyone would generate the feminine stereotype on the basis of personal experience.

As a learning theory, cognitive psychology recognizes that children acquire a repertoire of categories in the process of learning a language and that recited and dramatized stories provide learners with prototypes for social categories and information about how members of these categories think and behave. Yet, when cognitive psychologists investigate stereotyping, they proceed as if each person were starting from scratch. Although studies show that people will use the slenderest of pretexts to conceive and identify with unprecedented in-groups, most types of grouping have long social histories. Newly forming in-groups can try to modify the precedents they inherit. But, even in the case of ad hoc groupings, such as street gangs, high school cliques, intramural teams, and political caucuses, the work of self-definition is undertaken against a background of in-group/out-group paradigms.

Patriarchal cultures place more severe constraints on improvisation in regard to gender. Gender concepts permeate culture—they are used both literally and figuratively in discourses as disparate as shipbuilding, medicine, and romance. Because these multifarious usages regulate the cognitive dynamics of gender, it is far more difficult to gain acceptance for a revised gender schema than it is to gain acceptance for a modified street gang or political caucus schema. As a result, the rationalistic corrective strategies that cognitive psychologists recommend seem puny by comparison with the gargantuan task of rescuing our thought and conduct from the steely vise of cultural gender stereotypes.

Chodorow's claim that boys define themselves as masculine by defining themselves as not-mother presupposes that they can discern what makes their mothers feminine. But when they negate their mothers, why do they all converge on the same list of repudiated attributes? Why don't boys whose mothers are quick-witted, calm, well-organized, or funny regard these characteristics as essential to femininity and negate these attributes? Chances are they steer clear of these blunders because their cultural environment directs them to other attributes. Chodorow acknowledges that boys whose fathers do little childcare are obliged to flesh out their conception of masculinity by studying cultural representations of manhood. I would go further: Boys do not figure out that not-mother consists of detachment, rationality, and activity by themselves, either.[11] They glean a skeletal conception of femininity from cultural representations of womanhood, and this conception highlights their mother's attachment, warmth, and passivity.[12] Having acquired this culturally mediated understanding of their mother's personality, they are now cognitively and emotionally poised to derive their rudimentary sense of masculinity by negating it. Without cultural cues, though, boys would not know what to disavow and despise.

Young-Bruehl's line of thought poses a parallel problem. Boys fantasize a phallic mother and appropriate her attributes, including virility, mastery, and wholeness. But it is not obvious why boys consider these qualities masculine.[13] Plenitude is another salient attribute of the phallic mother, yet it is not incorporated into boys' conception of masculinity. Why do they set this attribute aside? Again, I would argue that boys are under the tutelary wing of a patriarchal culture. In the context of Young-Bruehl's theory, however, culture must instruct boys directly in the fundamentals of masculinity. In addition, I believe that cultural pedagogy has a hand in shaping men's relations to women. Men's individuality inflects their sexism. Still, it is no coincidence that so many men's feelings about women collect around certain themes and that the manner in which many men interact with women falls into characteristic patterns. We owe this uniformity to patriarchal cultures. Misogynist representations of femininity prompt men to assume corresponding ego-boosting attitudes toward women while complementary representations of manhood prompt them to enact these attitudes in ways that their community deems normal. In short, an array of ready-made sexist modalities grooms men to subordinate women.

Without patriarchal gender discourses, sexism would not exist as a social phenomenon—that is, as a prejudice. Neither observation of social practices nor the mother-child relationship suffices to generate feminine stereotypes or to instill prejudice against women as a group. In postpatriarchal cultures, *sexism* might name a neurosis stemming from dysfunctional mother-son struggles, but it would no longer reference a widespread social pathology. Sexism thrives not only because it satisfies the deeply human need for self-esteem but also because patriarchal gender discourse hotwires emotional circuitry that constantly renews and rejuvenates it. Patriarchal cultures package gender in iconography and mythology that most people find irresistible, and they ceaselessly reiterate gender ideology in the myriad gender tropes that suffuse altogether unrelated discourses. Delivered in this form, the edicts of patriarchal cultures leave room for individualization and social change. By furnishing a sizable stock of culturally approved gender imagery, and by representing gender in polysemous imagery that requires ongoing interpretation, patriarchal cultures ensure that boys/men have enough latitude to craft a form of sexism that is responsive to their personal needs and life circumstances. Thanks to the luminous pictorial and literary representations through which these cultures articulate the polyvocal meanings of gender, sexism stays alive, vigorous, and in sync with the times.

Because feminist politics has historically prioritized protecting women from violence, expanding their opportunities, and improving their material conditions, feminist initiatives have seldom centered on patriarchal gender discourse.[14] As a result, in the aftermath of a period of sustained feminist activism—when the movement has achieved some high-profile legal victories and then slipped out of the news and into abeyance—retrograde gender imagery enshrining male domination and female subordination remains in circulation. Making a modest concession to the changes that feminists have won, the patriarchal culture industry retrofits age-old gender messages in trendy, even daring contemporary garb, and the entertainment, news, and advertising media loudly proclaim the advent of this dazzling "new" vision of womanhood.

Always posing as a prowoman corporation, the manufacturer of Virginia Slims cigarettes can be counted on to produce zeitgeist-attuned advertising that epitomizes the slimy genius of the patriarchal culture industry. In the 1970s, flush with the excitement of second-wave feminism, Virginia Slims exulted: "You've Come a Long Way, Baby!" In a more subdued mood thirty years later, the company's sloganeers now proffer empathic encouragement by coopting a feminist theme. "Find Your Voice," their ads purr. But of course, the real message has never changed: "Stay Slender by Smoking Virginia Slims!" In patriarchal cultures, risking one's health is a small price to pay to be a Gorgeous Goddess. Beneath surface changes lies a remarkably resilient system of culturally certified feminine values. The "truly" feminine woman's desires in the so-called postfeminist era turn out to be identical to those she had in the feminist era, which are themselves indistinguishable from those of past centuries. She wants to fit the picture that pleases men.

Postactivist periods are especially perilous for feminist causes because cultural representations of gender steadily replenish unconscious sexism and supply backlash movements with rallying cries.[15] At such times, men may perceive women's recent social and economic gains as net losses for themselves. Scaled-back privilege may wound masculine pride. Admixed with indignation, men's feelings of embattlement may translate into resentment. All of these responses are corroborated by culturally entrenched gender imagery, and none of the resultant complaints lacks for culturally authoritative formulations. Sexism is never voiceless as long as patriarchal discourse is intact. The "emasculating woman" of decades past morphs into the "corporate bitch." Patriarchal discourse couples sexist conative zeal to a decided rhetorical edge. As a result, women's rights and women's social and economic status remain precarious, for backlashers can easily yank the political momentum away from feminists.

The repercussions of the hegemony of patriarchal discourse are dire. We need look no further than abortion politics during the decades following *Roe v. Wade* to see how vulnerable to retrenchment feminist triumphs are and how effective recycled gender stereotypes can be at arousing reactionary sentiment (Bordo 1993, 71–97). We need look no further than sex discrimination and sexual harassment litigation in the decades after the Civil Rights Act was passed to see how persistent sexist behavior is and how dependent it is on misogynist stereotypes (Valian 1998, 291–293, 297–301). Perhaps more disturbing, there is evidence that the vernacular is evolving to revive the pre–Civil Rights Act acceptability of discriminating against women in pay. The expression *girl money* refers to the typically lower salaries women earn, and male heterosexual dates who cite girl money as a reason to pick up the check make points for politeness (Dowd 2000).

To borrow from the argot of the advertising industry, patriarchal representations of women have much too big a "mind share." So I support bell hooks's call for feminist marketing firms to seize the initiative and show manufacturers and service providers that progressive messages are better vehicles for selling their products (hooks 2001, 56). Likewise, feminist public relations agencies could contribute to an emancipatory cultural climate by showing politicians and celebrities how to get favorable press and augment their approval ratings without relying on gender stereotypes.

Feminist have discounted the power of the figurational detritus of patriarchal culture too long. Important as they are, progressive institutional changes —equal opportunity in education and employment, family-friendly workplaces that permit flex time and provide on-site day care, and emergency services such as battered women's shelters and welfare payments—cannot do the whole job for women. Since these reforms do not force changes in patriarchal representations of gender, they neither neutralize the impact of patriarchal enculturation on individual identities nor raze the epistemological barriers to self-knowledge that patriarchal cultures erect. Since sexism piggybacks on patriarchal representations of gender, few men wholeheartedly support these reforms, and many men who do not openly oppose them abrogate them in spirit. As a result, far too many women continue to feel embattled and/or demoralized whether they try to conform to feminine norms or not.

Throughout this book, I have argued for a feminist discursive politics aimed at making imagery available to women that would help them shed the bonds of internalized oppression. But patriarchal cultures compound the harm of interfering with women's self-determination by putting men who do not want to be sexist in a double bind that interferes with their self-determination, too. Within patriarchal cultures, men face a choice between accepting sexism and protecting their self-esteem, or repudiating sexism and destabilizing their self-esteem. If sexism is to go away and stay away, then, feminist discursive politics must take into account men's narcissistic needs along with women's agentic needs. In earlier chapters, I defend a number of changes in gender discourse on the grounds that they meet women's agentic needs. Here I shall urge that the same discursive changes would also meet men's narcissistic needs.

The imagery of matrigyno-idolatry, as I have termed pronatalist discourse, channels men into sexism while channeling women into motherhood (Chapter 2). The multidimensional image of the phallic mother, which is central to matrigyno-idolatry, is threatening to men in several respects. As a feminine figuration of power, it calls masculine status and authority into question. As a maternal figuration of limitless giving, it creates an infinite, unpayable debt. As an interpersonal figuration of fusion, it represents mothers as overwhelming and individual selfhood as vulnerable to dissolution. As the paramount figuration of the parent-child relationship, it disenfranchises fathers. Much better are Ettinger's matrix imagery, which endows children with a primordial form of independence, and Irigaray's game-of-catch imagery, which positions children as equal participants in their relations with the people who parent them and which also empowers fathers and mothers equally with respect to children (Chapter 3). Likewise, Kristeva's poignant depiction of the emotional and somatic complexity of motherhood, which includes times of pain and helplessness as well as times of serenity and delight, deflates the megalomania of phallic mother imagery and humanizes mother-child interaction (Chapter 2). If imagery that was respectful of children and realistic about motherhood were culturally entrenched, boys and men would have less impetus to react defensively to women and to express that defensiveness as sexist aggression against the imaginary feminine attributes they unconsciously fear.

The Oedipal imagery that subsumes heterosexuality in patriarchal cultures complements the symbolism of the phallic mother and reinforces sexist attitudes. We have seen how the family romance frames women's memories, confounds their self-knowledge, and disrupts father-daughter relations (Chapter 4). In men's lives, this trope plays several parts in the etiology of sexism. In representing the father as the unitary subject who extricates the child from the engulfing phallic mother, the Oedipal trope reprises the distinction between independent, active warriors/breadwinners and relational, submissive nurturers/sex objects, and it binds this distinction to sexuality and gender. According to this story of psychological development, men cannot be real men unless women are confined to a subordinate position. Oedipal imagery is also implicated in the elaboration of sexism into heterosexism. Since it normalizes heterosexuality, it rationalizes hatred of lesbians and gays. Moreover, it introduces an element of illicitness into sexuality, for it grounds sexual identity in the incest taboo while positing mothers and fathers as ur-lovers for boys and girls, respectively. This melange of sexual ardor and transgression paves the way for the madonna/whore distinction, which sanctifies sexual relations with "pure" women while projecting "degraded" desires onto others. To amplify Young-Bruehl's taxonomy, the family romance encodes sexism, sexist homophobia, and sexist racism/classism in a succinct and enduring narrative. It is particularly urgent, then, that feminists construct counternarratives representing the full spectrum of tenable sexual and gender identities. Dephallicizing the pre-Oedipal mother is an important precondition for this new tale of nonsexist masculinity and sexuality/gender pluralism. But the rest of the story, in which children engage with this revisioned maternal figure and a yet-to-be-revisioned paternal figure, remains to be told.

Conjoined with the tale of Narcissus, the tale of Oedipus congratulates men for transcending narcissism and foists the vice of narcissism onto women. The results are the psychic/*psyché* economy, which cruelly reduces women's identity to their mirror images, and the vast system of woman-with-mirror imagery, which prompts many women to embrace inauthentic narcissistic values and desires (Chapter 5). Since the psychic/*psyché* economy of feminine narcissism colludes with the sexist objectification of women, feminist artists seek to reconfigure women's relation to mirrors. Their representations of women with mirrors critique exclusionary beauty ideals, advocate an elastic spectrum of individualized forms of feminine attractiveness, and integrate narcissistic goals into lives that include other pursuits (Chapter 5). With the aim of translating the messages this pioneering artwork conveys into personal attitudes and behavior, I recommend a series of self-help exercises designed to democratize the aesthetic standards by which women are judged and by which they judge themselves (Chapter 6). If feminist revisionings of feminine attractiveness gained cultural ascendance, women's self-esteem would not depend on resembling exemplars of resplendent beauty, and men's self-esteem would not depend on dating "eye candy" or acquiring a "trophy wife." Cultural acceptance of benign images of feminine narcissism would dislodge sexist attitudes toward women's appearance and replace them with appreciation of the unique beauty of individual women. But to eradicate sexism, feminist discursive politics must build on this counterimagery. Sexism will persist as long as norms of masculinity forbid men to cultivate their appearance and to take pleasure in the results. Thus, creating imagery that frees heterosexual men to avow their own narcissism and that simultaneously inaugurates a culture of reciprocal allure and enjoyment within all types of sexual partnership must be a key feminist objective.

A feminist discursive politics could have sweeping benefits. Not only could it expand the scope of women's and men's self-determination, but it also could bring an end to the seesawing between women making tangible progress under the banner of equality and sexists subverting these breakthroughs under the sponsorship of patriarchal culture. Since egalitarian gender relations needle sexist men, feminists must take action against sexist attitudes. Since feminist discursive politics is necessary to still sexist attitudes, activist agendas must address cultural issues along with the social and economic issues that have been the mainstay of feminist movements. If feminists took culture more seriously and worked at culture jamming more tenaciously, egalitarian demands would eventually meet less resistance, and egalitarian changes would be more lasting.

In my view, then, women need a feminist discursive politics that takes as its goal nothing less than fashioning and disseminating emancipatory gender imagery that is so responsive to narcissistic needs and so rich in agentic possibility—in a word, so compelling—that it disarms the entire patriarchal arsenal. The stakes could not be higher. If a society combining justice for women with comity between women and men is the goal—and it surely is—feminist counterimagery is politically vital.

CHAPTER ONE

1. Transsexuals may seem to be an exception to this rule. But their sexuality and gender are at best semivoluntary, for they are culturally defined as "deviant," and in choosing to change their sex and to align their gender with this new anatomy, these individuals presumably do not choose this stigmatizing label.

2. Subordination of social groups is not a uniform phenomenon. Different subordinated groups are assigned to different social positions, and the prejudices against different subordinated groups vary in form and content. Women, for example, are not an isolated minority. Yet, manhood is the cultural norm of humanity, whereas womanhood is culturally coded as a defective form of manhood. Moreover, gender segmentation persists in labor markets worldwide, and women wield little political power compared to men of similar backgrounds. Likewise, minority groups may be more or less isolated—in the United States, for example, Jews are more socially and economically integrated than African Americans or Latinos. Prejudices against different groups are not uniform—homophobia is significantly different from racial bigotry, which is significantly different from misogyny. These variations notwithstanding, we may ask whether there are continuities with respect to the relationship between membership in a subordinated social group and the constitution of individual identities, and that question will be the focus of this section.

3. I want to acknowledge that Benson realizes that oppressive socialization does not necessarily rule out autonomy in all aspects of the victim's life. He discusses the possibility that a person's critical competence can be compartmentalized—that is, one can exercise critical capabilities in one arena but be unable to exercise these capabilities in another (Benson 1991, 397).

4. I would like to refer readers to an intriguing psychological discussion of the experience of control that lends support to my skills-based approach to autonomy. Ellen J. Langer and Justin Pugh Brown observe that psychologists have generally identified experiences of control with the ability to dictate or predict an outcome, and they argue that this conception is misguided. Reflecting on the problematics of control and self-blame in the psychology of victims of sexual violence, they maintain instead that one experiences control when one is "mindful of the choice one was making," that is, when one regards oneself as an able decision maker and made one's decision in a thoughtful way (Langer and Pugh Brown 1992, 269, 273). Presumably, individuals who developed proficiency with respect to the agentic skills I have enumerated are more likely to view themselves as good decision makers, more likely to exercise those skills when confronted with choices, and therefore more likely to feel in control of their lives. If culture-transcending free will is an illusion (as I believe it is), there can be nothing more to self-determination than feeling in control as a result of competent decision making.

5. It might be objected that the premium that feminist voice theory places on articulateness betrays a racial and class bias. I do not believe, however, that articulateness is raced or classed. What I believe is that *styles* of articulateness are raced and classed and that these stylistic differences lead many middle-class whites to discount the articulateness of members of other social groups. Thus, I would deny that feminist calls for hearing women's voices are elitist and exclusionary. If anything, they oblige members of privileged social groups to acquaint themselves with unfamiliar rhetorics and to learn to recognize different forms of articulateness.

6. Feminist scholars have catalogued many of the ways in which gender has come to function as a "root metaphor, one that has become so deeply embedded in our thought that we no longer recognize it as such" (Rooney 1991, 87, 91–95; Lloyd 1993b, 10–17, 1993a, 74–83; Kittay 1988, 72–77; Gilman 1985, 76–108; W. Williams 1991, 20–24).

7. I am mindful that cultural representations of womanhood are not freestanding. They are matched and sustained by cultural representations of manhood. Thus, successfully refiguring womanhood requires refiguring manhood as well. Moreover, I am mindful that refiguring manhood and integrating emancipatory images of masculinity into the cultural imaginary may prove to be the more difficult task—Westerners adapt more readily to a woman in pants than to a man in skirts, although, as I shall point out, there are severe limits on the acceptability of women's assimilation of masculine norms. In Chapters 2–6, I occasionally touch on these questions, and in Chapter 7, I emphasize that feminist counterfigurations must take into account men's needs for self-esteem and agency as well as women's. However, for the most part, I focus on critiquing and replacing cultural figurations of womanhood.

1. I shall be concerned exclusively with autonomy in deciding whether or not to become a mother, and I shall not take up the question of autonomy in the activity of maternal caregiving, which raises very different issues. In this chapter, then, phrases such as *motherhood decisions* and *decisions about motherhood* refer only to women's initial undertaking. This decision typically involves a decision about childbearing. But I would emphasize that deciding to give birth to a child does not entail deciding to become a mother, for a woman may choose to put her child up for adoption, and also that deciding to become a mother does not entail deciding to bear a child, for a woman may choose to adopt. Although I shall sometimes use the expressions *procreative autonomy, reproductive autonomy,* and *having children* to refer to the decision about whether to become a mother, I do not mean to rule out becoming a mother through adoption.

194) 195

2. The feminist focus on reproductive rights, such as the right to an abortion, has prioritized self-direction—ensuring that women are free to do what they want—but neglected self-discovery and self-definition. I want to stress that nothing I shall say is meant to detract from the importance of self-direction and the rights that secure it.

3. For example, Anne Donchin cites a study of couples belonging to RESOLVE, a support group for the infertile, that found that many of the men were less receptive to the idea of adoption than the women and that the women were willing to undergo infertility procedures chiefly in order to please their male partners (Donchin 1995, 49). It seems unlikely that women would assert their own values and preferences more forcefully in heterosexual discussions of whether or not to embark on an attempt to have children.

4. Meyers 1989, 87–91, 170.

5. It is worth adding that I take to heart the psychoanalytic insight that "abnormal" subjects provide invaluable insights into "normalcy."

6. A conception of autonomy from medical ethics might be invoked here. In the cases in which women opt for motherhood while under the influence of culturally dispensed idealizations of motherhood, it might be argued that they have not given informed consent to motherhood.

7. It is perhaps worth emphasizing that what distressed this individual was the possibility that she might not be able to become pregnant and give birth, not the possibility that she might never have the opportunity to raise a child. Whereas the latter clearly is a way of realizing one's potential, it is doubtful that the former is.

8. Arlie Hochschild documents the extent to which employers have transformed workplaces into employee-friendly sites where workers feel more fulfilled and appreciated than they do at home and enjoy their interpersonal relationships more than they enjoy their spouses and children (Hochschild 1997). The net result, she claims, is that workers are increasing the time they spend at work and socializing with coworkers, while minimizing time spent with their families. It is not clear how this trend will play out. To date, people are still over-

whelmingly choosing to have children but cramming parent-child relationships into designated "quality" time slots. In the long run, the shift in the balance of incentives might lead more people to reject parenthood, but it might spark a critique of the demands of the workplace and a movement to reduce the time and energy invested there. Hochschild advocates the latter outcome.

9. Rogers and Larson cite a study in which 92 percent of the voluntarily childless couples affirmed that they made an active choice and nearly 63 percent of the childed couples affirmed that they made an active choice (1988, 50). I think the best explanation of the apparent conflict between these self-reports and my interpretation of the evidence I have presented is that what these respondents mean by an "active choice" does not coincide with any plausible understanding of an autonomous choice (see Chapter 1, Section 2, for discussion of implausible accounts of autonomy). It is also worth noting that the subjects in this study were couples. Consequently, it is not clear what the women would have said apart from their partners.

10. Susan Babbitt's discussion of autonomy and nonpropositional knowledge is relevant here (Babbitt 1993, 252–254; see Chapter 1, Section 3, for discussion of her views). People sometimes have intuitions, feelings, urges, and the like that signal their true values, needs, and desires but that cannot be articulated in any authoritative discourse. To gain autonomy, according to Babbitt, individuals must find concepts and language that give voice to this inexpressible self-knowledge. In Sections 3–4 below, I critique a discursive framework that mystifies women's desires about motherhood and that reduces women to inarticulateness when asked about their desires, and I propose some specific remedies.

11. Choosing not to become a mother leaves one more latitude for reconsideration. Even if one opts for irreversible tubal ligation, one could still adopt a child.

12. In fact, it is only in my most recent work that I have begun to adequately appreciate the embodiment of values and the body's role in autonomy. Thus, my remarks here revise the position I take in Meyers 2001.

13. For maternal mortality rates, see "Vital and Health Statistics," June 1995, p. 9 (U.S. Department of Health and Human Services, Public Health Service, Centers for Disease Control and Prevention, National Center for Health Statistics).

14. I was astonished to learn that the reproductive technology industry and its cruelly false promises predate the twentieth century. In the late eighteenth century, for example, Dr. James Graham operated an institution called the Temple of Health and Hymen, which provided "fertility treatments" involving an electromagnetic bed and a celestial chamber to wealthy, infertile, gullible English aristocrats (O'Conner 2000, 6).

15. For a review of the neglect of this topic in early second-wave feminist writing, see Gimenez 1983, 287–301. For an example of a feminist attempt to theorize childbirth as a model of human agency, see Held 1989.

   Perhaps pragmatic concerns have led to the neglect of this topic. Feminists might reasonably fear that accenting the option of forgoing motherhood would alienate the huge population of women who regard motherhood as a prime value and a core project. Also, if one believes that securing the interests of mothers is the more pressing objective, one might worry that emphasizing women's free choice in regard to becoming mothers could supply ammunition to opponents of policies and services beneficial to women who already are mothers. There is certainly reason to fear that opponents of feminist initiatives would sidestep the issue by counseling women to exercise their right not to have children if they expect to find motherhood onerous.

Theoretical objections to autonomy have undoubtedly played a role, as well. As I note in Chapter 1, Section 3, a number of feminists have urged that the autonomous individual is nothing but a middle-class, androcentric phantasm.

16. For insightful discussion of how these gender stereotypes infect the U.S. judicial process, see Wendy Williams's analysis of Supreme Court rulings bearing on women's role in the military, especially the combat exclusion (W. Williams 1991, 17–20).

17. I adopt the expression *matrigyno-idolatry* rather than relying on the more familiar expression *pronatalist discourse* because I want my language to convey the following points: 1) the fact that cultures systematically bond womanhood to motherhood in a single ideal, 2) the reverence this ideal inspires, and 3) the utter misguidedness, indeed, the downright sinisterness, of this reverence.

18. It is worth noting how jarring the term *childfree* still is, for it testifies to the intransigence of the cultural refusal to acknowledge that not having children is a legitimate and, for some individuals, a positive option.

19. For illuminating discussion of the linkage between fusion imagery and motherhood in the mind of a maternally inclined woman and the linkage between motherhood and disintegration imagery in the mind of a maternally disinclined woman, see Marianne Hirsch's reading of Toni Morrison's *Sula* (Hirsch 1989, 182–185).

20. There is an extensive literature on the psychological perils, both for the developing child and for the mother, associated with the trope of fusion. In addition to Bassin 1994, see Benjamin 1994; Chasseguet-Smirgel 1994; Chodorow 1980; and Chodorow and Contratto 1982. For discussion of these views, see Chapter 3, Section 2.

21. Men are obliged to contend with a set of related, but not congruent norms. Whereas women face a maternity imperative, men face a virility imperative. In some respects, these gendered demands complement each other, but the difference between them is worth noting. Matrigyno-idolatry in contemporary Western cultures consolidates fertility and nuturance into a lifelong relationship and social role. In contrast, paternity supplies evidence of virility, but it signals neither the advent of a consuming relationship nor induction into a mandatory social identity. However important male virility may be, men who forgo or disavow paternity pay little or no social or personal price. As a result, the virility imperative reinforces matrigyno-idolatry. Because virility often leads to biological paternity, the virility imperative ensures that many women

will become biological mothers whether they want to or not. Moreover, because biological paternity is culturally secondary to virility and because biological paternity is culturally compatible with exemption from social paternity, including childcare responsibilities, it is culturally necessary to assign someone other than men to raise children. This is the function of matrigyno-idolatry. It is crucial, then, for feminist critique to take aim both at overblown cultural representations of the value and importance of virility and at eviscerated representations of paternity, for these representations of manhood help to perpetuate matrigyno-idolatry and the damage it inflicts on women's self-determination.

22. In a similar vein, Chapter 4 examines the role of tropes in the epistemic obfuscation associated with memories of childhood sexual abuse.

23. Tragically, adoption is a motherhood scenario that is not subjectively available to many women. Women undergoing fertility treatment often are seen and see themselves as heroic—true devotees of the cult of motherhood. In light of the risk and expense of technology-assisted reproduction and the desperate need of many existing children for homes, it is a pity that women discount the adoption option so readily.

24. Bartky's discussion of sexual fantasies (see Section 2) seems especially germane to the question of motherhood in light of Nancy Friday's documentation of "earth mother" fantasies (Friday 1998). Women who indulge in these fantasies enhance their sexual pleasure by picturing fertility imagery. Although Friday gives no indication of how prevalent these fantasies are, their existence surely demonstrates how deeply embedded in one's psycho-corporeal economy motherhood imperatives can be. Notice, though, that just as fantasizing rape during consensual intercourse does not entail wanting to be raped, fantasizing impregnation during intercourse does not entail wanting to have a baby. Autonomy with respect to motherhood decisions remains feasible.

25. For a wonderful example of appropriating and adapting an allegorical tale that does not, however, concern the issue of motherhood, see Mahoney and Yngvesson 1992, 66–67.

CHAPTER THREE

1. I remind readers that radicalism in the best sense endeavors to get at the roots of problems. It is in that sense that I use the term here.

2. Unconventional household configurations, for example, single mothers, gay couples, or lesbian couples and their children, are stigmatized as deviant. Although they may consciously resist patriarchal norms (as can heterosexual couples with children), they cannot elude the curse of patriarchy.

3. In *Breaking the Abortion Deadlock* (1996), Eileen McDonagh does a masterful job of debunking this biological myth in the context of law. Focusing on the pregnancy relationship, that is, the relationship between a woman and a fetus, she accuses the U.S. Supreme Court of relying on sexist, scientifically bankrupt dogmas to characterize this relationship. According to McDonagh,

the key medical point is that fertilized ova cause pregnancy. Thus, the core legal questions concern how to classify this behavior and what rights and duties follow. If the fetus is legally protected human life, it is not merely a part of the woman's body, nor is it a force of nature. It is an independent human agent, but it lacks rational volitional faculties. For legal purposes, therefore, it most resembles a mentally incompetent human agent. If so, its self-implantation in the uterus of a woman who does not consent to be pregnant is best understood as an illicit bodily intrusion by a private party. This form of intrusion, McDonagh maintains, is serious enough to constitute wrongful pregnancy and to justify the woman's use of deadly force in self-defense.

As a result of the singularity of the pregnancy relationship, McDonagh observes, a vast cache of metaphor and myth has agglomerated around it. The fetus is depicted as innocent. The pregnant woman is depicted as beatific. Together, they are pictured luxuriating in an idyllic state of fusion. Displacing this imagery is a large part of the burden of *Breaking the Abortion Deadlock*. To accomplish this objective, McDonagh crafts a repertoire of leitmotifs that recur like incantations throughout her text. The fetus is legally protected human life. The fetus—not sexual intercourse, not the male sex partner or the syringe—is the cause of pregnancy. It's not what the fetus is that matters; it's what the fetus does when it implants itself in a woman's uterus. The fetus is innocent of intention; it is not innocent of aggression. The fetus is not helpless. It has the power to expropriate the resources of a woman's body and to transform her endocrinology, cardiovascular organs, and morphology. Indeed, it may have the power to kill her. The pregnant woman is a "captive samaritan."

4. Feminist commentators have called attention to the babyfication of the fetus in propaganda supporting the right-wing challenge to abortion rights, in routine obstetric tests performed on middle-class women, and in U.S. law regarding the duties of pregnant women vis-à-vis the fetuses they are carrying (Petchesky 1987; Bordo 1993). The prevalence of ultrasound testing for fetal defects in contemporary obstetric practice visually represents and medically sanctions the conception of children as property. Thus, it poses an additional obstacle to the emancipatory discursive work for which I am arguing. Many women are grateful for a sonographic peek at their fetuses, and, if all goes well, they gladly name their "babies" in utero and bond with them before giving birth (Petchesky 1987, 73–75). In other words, thanks to ultrasound, a mysterious, inner Other—a developing fetus—is refigured as "*my* baby" long before birth.

5. For relevant discussion of the problematics of representing the mother who is angry, see Hirsch 1989, Chapter 5, especially 192–196.

6. For my defense of the claim that discursive change must be reinforced by institutional and customary change, see Meyers 1994, 113–115.

7. In these remarks, I take a cue from Claudia Card, who argues that we should theorize the caregiver-child relationship primarily from the standpoint of children, not from the standpoint of caregivers (Card 1996b, 19–20).

1. For defense of Freud, see Laplanche and Pontalis 1968, 6; Brennan 1992, 29. For criticism of Freud, see Masson 1992, xxxiii and throughout; J. Herman 1992, 13–14.

2. These allegations are not exclusively against biological fathers. Stepfathers, cohabiting male partners, visiting boyfriends, and male relatives are often charged with sexual abuse of girls, as well. However, for the sake of parsimony, I shall use *father* to refer to all of these possible culprits.

3. Since it is not relevant to recovered memory, I shall leave aside the boy's Oedipus complex here. However, I take it up in Chapter 5, Section 3.

4. I find it an interesting sidelight that Freud also figures the mother as a child molester—in the course of routine bathing and dressing, the mother stimulates her baby's genitals and sexually arouses it. However, the image of the mother/seductress has never caught on. Perhaps, these two roles are too much at odds to fuse. As long as a sexualized childhood is seen as unhealthy and perverse, at least one parent's chaste relations to children must be preserved if anyone is to remain indisputably competent and reliable as a caregiver for children. If women's credentials as benign caregivers were figuratively compromised, who could be trusted to do this work? This suggests a second source of resistance to this image, namely, that it is highly threatening to the sexual division of labor. If women were figured as untrustworthy with small children, how could their continued subordination as designated unpaid caregivers be rationalized? Finally, women's supposed sexual passivity is threatened by this image; it does not sit well with women's submission to men in heterosexual relations. There is too much at stake socially and politically for womanhood to be figured as a sexually aggressive mother.

5. The hyperprivacy in which sexuality is shrouded in many cultures complicates matters. Not only are there usually no nonparticipating witnesses to sex acts, but also conventions of propriety and privacy bar many people from talking about their sexual experiences. To the extent that memory depends on rehearsal, then, sex memory is weak. In this connection, it is interesting that the typical abuser's efforts to create a conspiracy of silence around the incestuous acts may counteract the frailty of sex memory. In order to secure the child's silence, the abuser reminds the child not to tell. Thus, abusers may speak of incest more than people usually speak of sex, and, if so, memories of incest may be strengthened.

6. Notice, by the way, that if cultures are thought to be implanting suggestions by purveying figurations, hardly any perception or memory would be uncontaminated by suggestion. On this sweeping view of the scope of suggestion, the charge of suggestion that is pivotal to Crews's critique of recovered memory would lose all force.

7. I want to distinguish this claim from Hacking's account of memories constituted through semantic contagion (Hacking 1995, 238, 257). As Hacking points out, once people have categorized their experience (say, as child abuse),

they may proceed to fill in their memory of this experience with category-appropriate events (say, incidents of sexual molestation). If I understand Hacking correctly, his view is that semantic contagion is part of the phenomenon of veridical memory formation. Whether a memory derived from semantic contagion is veridical or not depends on the memory practices that are in force in a particular culture at a particular time, and these practices are shaped by memoro-politics. I agree that literalizing a self-figuration could yield a veridical memory. Memory is cued in many different, sometimes mysterious ways, and there is no reason to deny that self-figuration can prompt veridical memories. But contrary to Hacking's view, I am suggesting that literalizing figurations often confuses backward-looking memory with forward-looking self-direction and also that, although memoro-politics may determine what people count as a veridical memory, it does not determine what is a veridical memory. Suppose that a scenario of being subjected to clitoridectomy in childhood gained currency as a trope expressing certain psychic scars. It seems unlikely that there would be any temptation to literalize this figuration, but if there were, it is obvious that no memory practice could by itself transform a literalization of this trope into a veridical memory. Only a woman's discovery that her clitoris had been surgically removed (without her knowing it at the time or despite her having forgotten it in the meantime) could certify the accuracy of the memory. Why, then, suppose that whether a memory that literalizes a figuration of an event for which there is no lasting physical evidence is veridical or not depends entirely on memory practices shaped by memoro-politics? When Hacking affirms that he regards truth and factuality as basic and unproblematic (Hacking 1995, 250), he seems sympathetic to this line of thought, for in these passages he seems to be denying that memory reduces to a circumlocutious discourse of prospective self-definition. Yet, his predominant concern with the malleability of memory practices and the power of these practices to authenticate people's recollections seems to belie this sympathy.

It is clear, however, that Elizabeth Loftus and Katherine Ketcham share my concern with distinguishing between discourses of autobiographical memory and discourses of self-definition (Loftus and Ketcham 1994, 265–267). I strongly object to the tone of relentless skepticism about recovered memory that pervades their book, and I do not endorse their suggestion that psychotherapy abandon its concern with autobiographical memory—if a patient has suffered childhood trauma, remembering it may be crucial to her recovery. Nevertheless, I think it is important to recognize that the incest scenario can be appropriated as a self-figuration and that the aptness of this figuration does not depend on the individual's having been sexually assaulted in childhood.

8. Note, too, that since the sadistic incest trope is the latest flotsam on a deep cultural current, and since people tend to appropriate self-figurations from cultural resources, there is little reason to believe Crews's contention that the women who are accusing their fathers are being manipulated by unethical

therapists. Some may be. However, Crews's blanket accusation introduces an extra layer of explanation, and parsimony argues for the simpler account.

9. My critique of the family romance raises interesting questions about the history of this trope in Western culture. It is possible that Freud and his followers did women an unintended service by bringing this trope into cultural currency, for its presence in the figurative repertoire may have been instrumental in enabling many women to remember and testify to childhood incest. Thus, this trope may have helped to gain attention for this heretofore well-concealed harm. Whether or not this is so, I am convinced that this stock figuration has now outlived its usefulness from the standpoint of women's interests. In addition to the other problems I raise, it is clear that it is no longer (if it ever was) appropriate to symbolize the sexual abuse of girls exclusively as a father-daughter issue.

10. Elizabeth Young-Bruehl points out another major obstacle to effective prosecution of incestuous child abuse—heterosexism (Young-Bruehl 1996, 448). The fact that pedophilia is stereotypically ascribed to gay men despite statistics showing that sexual abuse of children is far more prevalent in the heterosexual population makes it needlessly difficult to persuade social service workers and courts that girls are being sexually abused by their fathers or other heterosexual men who frequent the household. Thus, feminist activists working on behalf of these victims need to challenge cultural representations that absolve heterosexual men of responsibility by casting gay men as paradigmatic child abusers.

11. It is worth noting here that a parallel line of argument could be developed with respect to women's heterosexual desire. If female heterosexuality means repudiating the castrated mother and pining for the forbidden father, as Freud's family romance would have it, feminists cannot reclaim heterosexuality unless it is refigured to express the possibility of affectional attachment to and erotic satisfaction with a beloved male individual. Though there is a rich critical literature on conventional psychoanalytic figurations of heterosexuality, feminist psychoanalytic theorists have done relatively little to figuratively redeem heterosexuality.

12. Elsewhere I have defended a version of the multiplicitous self (Meyers 1994, 146–147). For a promising proposal to model the dynamics of the multiplicitous self on strategies for forging responsible agency among the members of an oppressed community, see Card 1996a, Chapter 2. For my views on why feminists need to deemphasize the unity of the self, see Chapter 6, Section 2.

13. It is worth noting, though, that none of Scheman's alternatives to figuring multiplicity as multiple personality disorder stem from the dominant Euro-American culture that gave us the family romance. Scheman's alternative figurations originate in African, African-American, Latina, and lesbian cultures.

14. In conversation, she has assured me that she does.

15. It is illuminating to juxtapose Leys's trope with Ettinger's matrixial trope (see

Chapter 3, Section 3). I hope that Leys will not object to my characterizing her view as a counterfiguration of multiplicity. She positions her view as an explanation of why memories of childhood sexual abuse are not recoverable, but I think my reading is faithful to the spirit of her work. For my reasons for reading psychoanalytic developmental theory as an extended trope, see Meyers 1994, 12–14.

CHAPTER FIVE

1. For discussion of the bad fortune that comes to some girls and women in ballet studios and suggestions about how recently developed, alternative dance practices can transform ballerinas' relations to their bodies and to studio mirrors, see Summers-Bremner 2000.

2. Since the walls of my childhood bedroom were decorated with several framed reproductions of Degas's famed paintings of dancers, I was curious to learn whether he portrays them as mirror-obsessed narcissists. Reviewing his oeuvre, I find it heartening to discover that he did not. Although the studios he depicts are equipped with standing mirrors rather than the mirrored walls that are standard in today's studios, and the smaller studio mirrors do not present as great a temptation to the dancers, none of them takes any notice of the mirror at all. The ballerinas are busy dancing, not communing with their splendid reflections.

3. Thomas Bullfinch confuses matters by abbreviating and modernizing the narrative. Declaring that Narcissus "fell in love with himself," Bullfinch edits the problematics of selfhood and mirroring out of the story (Bullfinch ND, 86).

4. It is worth noting that beauty has often been explicated in terms of unity. This relation between the two concepts provides a link from the Narcissus myth to Lacan's account of the mirror stage.

5. I do not mean to suggest that the association between women and mirrors was first forged in the twelfth century. Etruscan women, never Etruscan men, were buried with mirrors (La Belle 1988, 58, n.2). But it is not known what this practice symbolized.

6. I leave aside the peripheral implausibilities of a male character who chatters so much that the gods deprive him of his own voice or of a spurned female character who violently kills herself on her beloved's doorstep.

7. Caravaggio, *Narcissus*, c. 1599–1600, Galleria Nazionale d'Arte Antica, Palazzo Corsini, Rome.

8. Salvador Dali, *The Metamorphosis of Narcissus*, 1937, Tate Modern Gallery, London.

9. I leave aside the question of whether this dearth results from repudiation of the Narcissus theme or from the loss of works over the centuries.

10. Before the twentieth century, there are comparatively few examples of artworks depicting women artists using mirrors to create self-portraits because the population of women artists was infinitesimally small. Still, there are some examples. The earliest ones, however, may not be the work of the

women artists themselves. For example, in a fifteenth-century illuminated manuscript of Bocaccio's *Concerning Famous Women*, the identity of the illuminator is uncertain. But a woman artist, Marcia, is shown holding a tiny mirror before her face while she concentrates on painting her own portrait (*Marcia Painting Her Own Portrait*, 1402, Bibliotheque Nationale de France).

11. Johannes Gumpp's *Self-portrait* (1646, Galleria degli Uffizi, Florence) is an example of the former; *A Man with a Mirror*, a work from the studio of Jose Ribera (seventeenth century, Derek Johns Ltd., London) is an example of the latter.

12. Titian, *Venus with a Mirror*, c. 1555, National Gallery of Art, Washington, D.C.

13. Diego Velazquez, *The Toilet of Venus*, 1647–1651, National Gallery, London.

14. Peter Paul Rubens, *Venus before the Mirror*, 1616, Collections of the Prince of Lichtenstein, Vaduz Castle, Vaduz, Lichtenstein.

15. Of course, the magic mirrors of literature, theater, and film are another matter. For more on those, see Section 5.

16. Interestingly, there is precedent for the link between censuring vanity and dedicating oneself to salvation in the Roman cult of Venus. The goddess of love has a death-dealing aspect. Her cult's initiates (Ovid was among them) believed that cultivating ritualized sexual techniques could lead to spiritual grace, and they likened orgasm to death (B. Walker 1983, 1043). Thus, the beautiful Venus was associated with proud sensuality and blissful mortality. No wonder, then, that prudish Christian appropriations of woman-with-mirror imagery, featuring mortal women instead of goddesses, shade representations of vanity into representations of vanitas.

17. Hans Baldung supplies examples of both types: *Vanity*, 1529, Alte Pinokothek, Munich, and *Death and the Woman*, 1517, Kuntsmuseum, Basel.

18. In view of this disvaluation of beauty and specular reflections of it, it seems ironic that the Virgin Mary is always portrayed as a pretty woman and, furthermore, that one of her attributes is the *speculum sine maculum*, the stainless mirror that symbolizes her purity.

19. Georges de La Tour, *The Penitent Magdalen*, seventeenth century, Metropolitan Museum of Art, New York. Not all memento mori images feature female figures. For example, in Salvator Rosa's *Self-portrait* (seventeenth century, Metropolitan Museum of Art, New York), the artist portrays himself wearing a cypress wreath, which is an emblem of mourning. In the painting, he is inscribing the warning "Behold, whither, when" on a skull. Interestingly, in his efforts to demonstrate his sensitivity and spiritual depth in the presence of this somber theme, the artist feminizes himself. We see a youthful artist with refined bone structure, long soft curls, and blood-infused lips. I have not been able to locate enough examples of paintings in which the vanitas theme is represented through a male figure to be confident that this picture is typical. If it is, however, it would lend credence to the psychoanalytic thesis that death is symbolically associated with the feminine. (For related discussion, see Chapter 6, Section 3.)

20. Ivan Albright, *Into the World There Came a Soul Called Ida*, 1929–1930, Art Institute of Chicago, Chicago.

21. Examples include Andrea della Robbia's *Prudence* (c. 1475, Metropolitan Museum of Art, New York) and Simon Vouet's *Allegory of Prudence* (c. 1645, Musée Fabre, Montpellier).

22. Examples of the sort of work Miller has in mind include Johannes Vermeer's *Woman with a Pearl Necklace* (c. 1664, Staatliche Museen zu Berlin, Gemaldegalerie, Berlin), Georges Seurat's *Young Woman Powdering Herself* (1888–1890, Courtauld Gallery, London), Edgar Degas's *At the Milliner's* (1882, Metropolitan Museum of Art, New York), and Pierre Bonnard's *Nude in Front of a Mirror* (1931, Galleria Internazionale d'Arte Moderna di Ca'Pesaro, Venice). It is worth noting, however, that some scholars do not see these works as innocent of moral messages (Wheelock 1995, 153–154; Chicago and Lucie-Smith 1999, 151).

23. The English term *psyche* and the French term *psyché* derive etymologically from the Greek term for breath, the animating principle in human life, or the soul or spirit. Thus, the French adaptation of this word to signify a woman's cheval-glass implicitly locates feminine identity in her mirror image. The French terminology is also of a piece with a curious bit of folklore. In medieval Europe, mirrors were associated with witchcraft, that is, with marginalized women, and mirrors were believed capable of capturing souls (Gregory 1997, 62). It seems to me that Western culture has managed to turn the tables on these dangerous women and take control of the power of reflection. Mirrors now capture women's "souls."

24. In characterizing psychoanalysis as a form of mythology, I do not mean to disparage psychoanalysis or mythology. Myths enshrine commonsense understandings of who we are, how we should live, and where we fit in the universe, and they articulate these views in vivid, memorable ways. Although they are not always benign, and they are not immune to criticism, they are effective, perhaps indispensable, instruments of cultural cohesion and self-understanding. To my mind, then, "Which myths should we circulate?" is a more realistic question than "Should we have a mythology?"

25. For useful discussions of the theme of narcissism in Lacan and Freud, see Grosz 1990, Chapter 5, and Benjamin 1998, Chapter 2.

26. Someone might take exception to my characterizing psychoanalytic theory as authoritative on the grounds that psychoanalysis has been discredited as science. I do not mean to suggest that psychoanalysis's authority derives from its evidential support. Rather, my suggestion is that, despite damaging criticism on empirical grounds, psychoanalytic tropes and narrative constructions remain so pervasive as to be unavoidable in contemporary culture. Their authority, then, is the de facto authority of cultural entrenchment, not the authority of scientific validation.

27. One of Bartky's most important insights is that women's very proficiency in self-beautification skills poses a major obstacle to their appreciating the force of feminist critiques of the objectification of women (Bartky 1990, 77). For someone who has mastered these skills and who exercises them well, feminist critiques of feminine body culture are unnerving because these arguments threaten to deskill them. Since what one knows and knows how to do

is part of who one is, such deskilling would dislocate women's sense of themselves, and it would be experienced (at least temporarily) as undermining their capacities to control their lives.

28. Women's battles for identity and self-esteem after their faces have been damaged are moving and inspiring. In an autobiographical memoir, Lucy Grealy describes her ordeal beginning with disfiguring surgery for cancer of the jaw at the age of nine and continuing through a long series of reconstructive procedures, none of which fully restored her face. To compensate for the futility of trying to repair her face, she struggles to find her value elsewhere: "On one level I understood that the image of my face was merely that, an image, a surface that was not directly related to any true, deep definition of the self. But I also knew that it is only through image that we experience and make decisions about the everyday world, and I was not always able to gather the strength to prefer the deeper world over the shallower one. . . . I strive for a state of awareness and self-honesty that sometimes, to this day, rewards me and sometimes exhausts me" (Grealy 1994, 71–72). One tactic Grealy used on herself to defeat the psychic/*psyché* economy was to terminate her relationship to the mirror. For an entire year she did not look into one, and, eventually she discovered that she could accept another person's interest in her and enjoyment of her company as a truer reflection of her self than mirrors provide.

    Jacqueline Auriol, who was a beautiful woman from a prominent French family, took a different route. At the age of thirty-one, her face was crushed in a plane accident. Thirty-three reconstructive surgeries in the following three years failed to restore her face. But having been defeated by aviation in one respect, Auriol set out to conquer aviation in another way. "Now that my beauty was gone," she said, "I would have to derive a reason for being from the plane which had taken it away" (quoted in Martin 2000, C25). Although another woman beat her to her goal of becoming the first woman to break the sound barrier, she set a number of speed records as one of the world's leading test pilots. Plainly, narcissistic satisfaction need not derive exclusively from looking good, but substituting other forms of narcissistic satisfaction is arduous for women in cultures that enforce a "normal" psychic/*psyché* feminine economy.

29. Some young men express no ambivalence about this permission to be narcissistic. Lisa Cassidy reports that one of her male undergraduate students announced in class that his favorite personal grooming implement/product is the mirror and went on to say how much he enjoys staring at his image (private communication). It is not clear to me, however, that he will feel as comfortable publicly reveling in narcissism as a thirty-year-old as he does in his late teens.

30. 1881–1882, National Gallery of Art, Washington, D.C.

31. 1877–1878, Museum of Fine Arts, Boston.

32. 1878, private collection.

33. It should be noted that the device of placing a mirror in the background of a portrait of a woman at home has precedents. Some of Ingre's portraits take advantage of this device to enlarge the space represented and to complete the

form of the sitter. However, in Ingre's work, the sitter's eyes meet the viewer's eyes. Her gaze registers her sociable feminine nature, not her intellectual interests.

34. Although many viewers (myself included) find much of Cassatt's maternal imagery sentimental, scholars have questioned this judgment. For useful discussion, see Barter 1998, 69–81, and Pollock 1998, 185–213; 1999, 201–213.

35. 1987–1988, collection of the artist.

36. Andrea Kirsh and Amy Mullin stress that *Mirror, Mirror* confronts internalized racism in the African-American community (Kirsh 1994, 13; Mullin 2000, 116). Since the mirror figure's facial features resemble those of a stereotypically white face, her reply can be understood as an affirmation of the superiority of her own looks relative to those of a stereotypically African-American woman. An implication of this view might be that the mirror figure is an undercover police officer enforcing racist beauty ideals. Although I agree that there is an element of enforcement in the mirror figure's bearing and in her pronouncement, I believe that the figure in the mirror is costumed and posed too ambiguously to justify reducing her to a tomming agent of the white beauty regime.

206) 207

37. In another woman-with-mirror image from the series *Not Manet's Type*, Weems points up African-American women's resistance to racist beauty standards. In this work, a boudoir mirror reflects an African-American woman dressed in a short black slip and sitting on her bed with her head held high and her eyes closed. The text beneath the photograph reads: "I knew, not from memory, but from hope, that there were other models by which to live." To judge by a 1995 study that found almost 90 percent of Euro-American teenage women dissatisfied with their bodies and 70 percent of African-American teenage women satisfied with theirs, Weems's hopefulness that there is not just one truth about beauty is helping African-American girls to displace the psychic/*psyché* economy (Parker et al. 1995, 105). Perhaps, the utter hopelessness of measuring up to culturally dominant criteria of beauty has helped to give rise to the African-American aesthetic culture of "using what you've got," which accents personal style and projecting a self-confident image (Parker et al. 1995, 107–108). Although many adolescent African-American women dismiss dominant beauty ideals and display a degree of self-acceptance and self-esteem that eludes their Euro-American peers, it remains to be seen whether African-American women who seek economic opportunities outside their communities are able to maintain their satisfaction with their appearance (Parker et al. 1995, 111).

38. This Psyche angers Venus because Venus's son, Eros, falls in love with her and refuses to give her up. The jealous goddess dispatches Psyche to Hades but relents and resuscitates her because of Eros's pleas. The French term *psyché* refers to a panel showing Psyche with a mirror in Raphael's Loggia di Psiche in the Villa Farnesina in Rome.

39. A *New Yorker* cartoon seconds Orlan's point. A group of upper middle-class, middle-aged women are having tea together. One, whose taut face betrays a re-

cent face lift, says to her friends, "When I actually was this age, I didn't have much facial expression anyway" (*New Yorker*, Nov. 15, 1999). Age-erasing cosmetic surgery effaces the individual's emotions by de-facing her.

40. c. 1939, Jersey Museums Service, Jersey.

41. c. 1928, Musée des Beaux-Arts, Nantes.

42. Statements such as "Under this mask, another mask. I will never finish removing all these faces" (Cahun, *Aveux non avenus*, quoted in Krauss 1999, 29) have made Cahun a darling of postmodern criticism. But postmodernist feminists will regard my conclusion as absurd, for although they do not repudiate the notion of agency, they regard authentic agency as a relic of modernism. In contrast, I agree with scholars who call into question Cahun's postmodernist credentials. For example, Katy Kline maintains that the "artist and the individual are present within each disguise" that Cahun dons—each represents an aspect of a complex self that bears endless exploration (Kline 1998, 68; also see Chadwick 1998, 7; Lippard 1999, 36). Kline adds, and I concur, "There is no *single* original Claude to be found. . . . authentic aspects of the original Claude are to be found in every one of her multiple manifestations" (Kline 1998, 76).

43. 1998, collection of the artist.

44. For related social psychological evidence, see Chapter 6, n.4.

45. It also requires reconceptualizing our narratives of the formation of individual identity. Current narratives revolve around sight—seeing one's mirror image and being mirrored by one's caregiver, seeing one's genital endowment or seeing one's genital lack. Feminist psychoanalytic theorists persuasively critique this scopocentric psychology, and they offer important suggestions for reconstructing our psychological narratives. For example, both Luce Irigaray and Bracha Lichtenberg Ettinger stress the role of touch and kinesthetic sensation in the process of identity formation (Irigaray 1985, 23–33, 205–218; Ettinger 1992, 197–202). Jessica Benjamin proposes that the metaphor of dancing replace mirroring as the metaphor for caregiver-child interaction (Benjamin 1988, 27, 127). See Chapter 3, Section 3, for further discussion of these contributions.

CHAPTER SIX

All epigraphs taken from autobiographical essays in Foster 1994.

1. *Nude Self-Portrait*, 1980, National Portrait Gallery, Washington, D.C.

2. Joan Semmel, *Me without Mirrors*, 1974, collection of the artist.

3. I would like to interject that I find Gullette's snide remarks about fit bodies insulting. My senior cyborg body enables me to climb mountains with ease and also to feel safe enough to relax on city streets. While I realize my strength and agility will not last forever, they have afforded me incalculable pleasure, which I refuse to disavow or to give up prematurely. So, I'm with Donna Haraway. I, too, "would rather be a cyborg than a goddess" (Haraway 1997, 525).

4. Cash documents some noteworthy qualifications of the presumption that

beauty entails goodness. When physically attractive people do not reciprocate social overtures, their behavior may be read as aloof and therefore as evidence of self-centeredness, although shyness or deficient social skills could explain their behavior equally well (Cash 1990, 53–54). Also, there is, not surprisingly, a gender factor. Attractive women who apply for jobs that are conventionally coded masculine or who are employed in such positions may lose their advantage and may even be discriminated against (Cash 1990, 56–57). Along similar lines, we are all familiar with the stereotype of the dumb blonde—pretty and sexy, but foolish and manipulable. In this regard, I would stress that beauty is not invariably linked to every imaginable good quality. Although the dumb blonde lacks intelligence, she is often portrayed as having a heart of gold. She is an excellent candidate for marriage and motherhood, although not for the corporate boardroom.

5. Packing nature into feminine imagery frees masculine imagery to represent culture, mind, reason, and free agency, which are core patriarchal values. Thus, masculine identities get a cultural boost, and feminine identities get a cultural whack.

CHAPTER SEVEN

1. For example, Zanna and Olson's *The Psychology of Prejudice* (1994) and Brown's *Prejudice* (1995) have no index entries for *emotion* or *affect*, let alone *hatred*. Apparently, scientific psychology studies cognition, whereas psychoanalysts speculate about feeling.

2. Many feminist philosophers dismiss psychoanalysis. Its methods are scientifically suspect, they claim, and the plausible conclusions about gender that psychoanalytic theory advances can be explained by a theory with better scientific credentials, namely, cognitive psychology (Cudd 1998, 191–192). Although I agree that psychoanalysis is a hermeneutic theory, I disagree that cognitive psychology adequately accounts for gender identity and sexism, and I believe it is important to consider depth psychologies of gender and sexism.

3. I am simplifying a bit here. In classic psychoanalysis and in Chodorow's view, girls also need to transfer their erotic desire to a male, a developmental task that is undertaken at the Oedipal stage. But even this profound change is compatible with the girl's ongoing identification with her mother. After all, the mother is (presumably) a heterosexual who desires the girl's father.

4. Young-Bruehl briefly notes that sexism takes two additional forms. Rooted in a hysterical character type, sexism represents women as overwhelmingly maternal and devouring (Young-Bruehl 1996, 239). Rooted in an obsessional character type, sexism represents women as impure and corrupting (Young-Bruehl 1996, 239).

5. There are numerous parallels between my views about matrigyno-idolatry and the anxieties that mother-child imagery arouses and Young-Bruehl's account of sexism (see Chapter 2, Section 3, and Chapter 3, Section 2). However, I am no more convinced that boys' discovery of the difference between male and fe-

male genitalia impels them to defend against the specter of their own inferiority than I am that girls' discovery of their anatomical "lack" instills penis envy in them.

6. I note that Young-Bruehl distinguishes sexism from homophobia and discusses homophobia at length. Thus, she has a good deal more to say about prejudice against lesbians than I present here.

7. I would imagine that infertile women are no less threatening to difference sexists, and in many patriarchal cultures, infertile wives forfeit their standing in practice if not by law.

8. Much of Young-Bruehl's discussion of prejudice against African-American women is situated in the context of her discussion of racism, which she treats as a hysterical prejudice rather than as a narcissistic prejudice. Nevertheless, I am making a point of noting the congruence of her accounts of prejudice against African-American women with her typology of sexisms in order to stress the confluence of racism and sexism and the admixture of the motivations for them.

9. White women, Young-Bruehl observes, see Other women as competitors—as "women who have phallic power [the black matriarch] or as women who are sexually loose and easily able to command male attention" (Young-Bruehl 1996, 370).

10. Parsing gender stereotypes as dry social scientific hypotheses or dull attribute rosters may clarify the content of those stereotypes, but people do not acquire their conceptions of femininity and masculinity in this form. Although children accumulate lots of handy information by memorizing lists and explanations—for example, the names of the months and the cause of rain—rote learning cannot teach children how they should feel about other people or how to interact with them. Moreover, one would be hard-pressed to explain gender's embeddedness in women's and men's affective/conative economies if cultures transmitted gender as a pair of minitheories or a pair of inventories.

11. In her most recent book *The Power of Feelings*, Chodorow countenances a much larger role for culture in psychological development than she did in the past (Chodorow 1999, Chapters 3 and 4). Thus, it is possible that she would now agree with my emendation of her earlier view. Still, her argument that unconscious fantasy generates "personal meaning from birth on" also makes it possible that she would stick with her 1980 account (Chodorow 1999, 64). Since she does not revisit the topic of sexism in *The Power of Feelings*, I am uncertain what her current position is.

12. Up to a point, Chodorow could meet my criticism by adopting Valian's theory that children equate physical nurturance with a nurturing personality. But notice that in the mother-child relationship, the boy experiences his own dependence, not the mother's. Thus, boys must get the idea that women are dependent from some other source. In my view, that source is culture.

13. It should be noted here that Lacanian psychoanalysis sees the consolidation of selfhood as coextensive with acquiring the capacity to speak a language and

becoming a subject of enunciation. Insofar as culture is encoded in language, then, individuals assimilate gender stereotypes in the process of establishing distinct identities.

14. One exception is early second-wave feminism's critique of the "generic" masculine pronoun and such slang terms for women as *chick*, *girl*, and *fox*. Although the former line of thought has been quite successful in reforming speech and writing, it only scratches the surface of patriarchal discourse. Another exception is the opposition to pornography that Catharine MacKinnon and Andrea Dworkin spearheaded (MacKinnon 1993; Dworkin 1989).

15. For a helpful account of the backlash phenomenon, see Cudd 1999.

REFERENCES

Abel, Elizabeth. 1990. "Race, Class, and Psychoanalysis? Opening Questions." In *Conflicts in Feminism*, ed. Marianne Hirsch and Evelyn Fox Keller, 184–204. New York: Routledge.

Adams, Parveen. 1995. *The Emptiness of the Image: Psychoanalysis and Sexual Difference*. New York: Routledge.

Addelson, Kathryn Pyne. 1994. *Moral Passages: Toward a Collectivist Moral Theory*. New York: Routledge.

Alcoff, Linda. 1994. "Cultural Feminism versus Post-Structuralism: The Identity Crisis in Feminist Theory." In *Culture/Power/History*, ed. Nicholas Dirks, Geoffrey Eley, and Sherry Ortner, 96–122. Princeton, NJ: Princeton University Press.

al-Shaykh, Hanan. 1994. "Inside a Moroccan Bath." In *Minding the Body: Women Writers on Body and Soul*, ed. Patricia Foster, 193–208. New York: Anchor Books/Doubleday.

Appiah, K. Anthony, and Amy Gutmann. 1996. *Color Conscious: The Political Morality of Race*. Princeton, NJ: Princeton University Press.

Babbitt, Susan. 1993. "Feminism and Objective Interests: The Role of Transformation Experiences in Rational Deliberation." In *Feminist Epistemologies*, ed. Linda Alcoff and Elizabeth Potter. New York: Routledge.

Baier, Annette C. 1987. "The Need for More than Justice." In *Science, Morality, and Feminist Theory*, ed. Marsha Hanen and Kai Nielsen, 41–56. Calgary: University of Calgary Press.

———. 1994. "Trust and Anti-trust." In *Moral Prejudices*, 95–129. Cambridge, MA: Harvard University Press.

Banaji, Mahzarin R., and Anthony G. Greenwald. 1994. "Implicit Stereotyping and

Prejudice." In *The Psychology of Prejudice: The Ontario Symposium,* vol. 7, ed. Mark P. Zanna and James M. Olson, 55–76. Hillsdale, NJ: Erlbaum.

Barter, Judith A. 1998. "Mary Cassatt: Themes, Sources, and the Modern Woman." In *Mary Cassatt: Modern Woman,* ed. Judith A. Barter, 45–107. New York: Abrams.

Bartky, Sandra Lee. 1990. *Femininity and Domination.* New York: Routledge.

———. 1999. "Unplanned Obsolescence: Some Reflections on Aging." In *Mother Time: Women, Aging, and Ethics,* ed. Margaret Urban Walker, 61–74. Lanham, MD: Rowman and Littlefield.

Basow, Susan A. 1992. *Gender Stereotypes and Roles,* 3d ed. Pacific Grove, CA: Brooks/Cole.

Bassin, Donna. 1994. "Maternal Subjectivity in the Culture of Nostalgia." In *Representations of Motherhood,* ed. Donna Bassin, Margaret Honey, and Meryle Mahrer Kaplan, 162–173. New Haven, CT: Yale University Press.

Beauvoir, Simone de. 1989. *The Second Sex,* trans. H. M. Parshley. New York: Random House.

Benhabib, Seyla. 1995. "Feminism and Postmodernism." In *Feminist Contentions,* by Seyla Benhabib et al., 17–34. New York: Routledge.

———. 1999. "Sexual Difference and Collective Identities: The New Global Constellation." *Signs* 24: 335–361.

Benjamin, Jessica. 1988. *The Bonds of Love.* New York: Pantheon.

———. 1994. "The Omnipotent Mother: A Psychoanalytic Study of Fantasy and Reality." In *Representations of Motherhood,* ed. Donna Bassin, Margaret Honey, and Meryle Mahrer Kaplan, 129–146. New Haven, CT: Yale University Press.

———. 1998. *The Shadow of the Other.* New York: Routledge.

Benson, Paul. 1991. "Autonomy and Oppressive Socialization." *Social Theory and Practice* 17(3): 385–408.

Bersheid, Ellen, and Elaine Walster. 1974. "Physical Attractiveness." In *Advances in Experimental Psychology,* vol. 7, ed. Leonard Berkowitz, 157–215. New York: Academic.

Bordo, Susan. 1993. *Unbearable Weight: Feminism, Western Culture, and the Body.* Berkeley: University of California Press.

———. 1997. *Twilight Zones: The Hidden Life of Cultural Images from Plato to O. J.* Berkeley: University of California Press.

———. 2000. "Beauty (Re)Discovers the Male Body." In *Beauty Matters,* ed. Peg Zelin Brand, 112–154. Bloomington: Indiana University Press.

Brennan, Teresa. 1992. *The Interpretation of the Flesh.* New York: Routledge.

Brison, Susan. 1997. "Outliving Oneself: Trauma, Memory, and Personal Identity." In *Feminists Rethink the Self,* ed. Diana Tietjens Meyers, 12–39. Boulder, CO: Westview.

Brown, Rupert. 1995. *Prejudice: Its Social Psychology.* Oxford: Blackwell.

Bruner, Jerome. 1994. "The 'Remembered' Self." In *The Remembering Self: Construction and Accuracy in the Self-narrative,* ed. Ulric Neisser and Robyn Fivush, 41–54. New York: Cambridge University Press.

Bullfinch, Thomas. ND. *Bullfinch's Mythology*. New York: Modern Library.

Calhoun, Cheshire. 1997. "Separating Lesbian Theory from Feminist Theory." In *Feminist Social Thought: A Reader*, ed. Diana Tietjens Meyers, 200–218. New York: Routledge.

Card, Claudia. 1996a. *The Unnatural Lottery*. Philadelphia: Temple University Press.

———. 1996b. "Against Marriage and Motherhood." *Hypatia* 11: 1–23.

Cash, T. F. 1990. "The Psychology of Physical Appearance." In *Body Images: Development, Deviance, and Change*, ed. T. F. Cash and T. Pruzinsky, 51–79. New York: Guilford.

Castle, Ted. 1983. "Interview with Ted Castle." *Art Forum*, 2(2): 36–41.

Cavell, Marcia. 1993. *The Psychoanalytic Mind: From Freud to Philosophy*. Cambridge, MA: Harvard University Press.

Chadwick, Whitney. 1998. "An Infinite Play of Empty Mirrors: Women, Surrealism, and Self-representation." In *Mirror Images: Women, Surrealism, and Self-representation*, ed. Whitney Chadwick, 2–35. Cambridge, MA: MIT Press.

Chasseguet-Smirgel, Janine. 1994. "Being a Mother and Being a Psychoanalyst: Two Impossible Professions." In *Representations of Motherhood*, ed. Donna Bassin, Margaret Honey, and Meryle Mahrer Kaplan, 113–128. New Haven, CT: Yale University Press.

Chicago, Judy, and Edward Lucie-Smith. 1999. *Women and Art: Contested Territory*. New York: Watson-Guptill.

Chodorow, Nancy. 1974. "Family Structure and Feminine Personality." In *Woman, Culture, and Society*, ed. Michelle Zimbalist Rosaldo and Louise Lamphere, 43–66. Stanford, CA: Stanford University Press.

———. 1978. *The Reproduction of Mothering*. Berkeley: University of California Press.

———. 1980. "Gender, Relation, and Difference in Psychoanalytic Perspective." In *The Future of Difference*, ed. Hester Eisenstein and Alice Jardine, 3–19. Boston: G. K. Hall.

———. 1995. "Gender as Personal and Cultural Construction." *Signs* 20: 516–544.

———. 1999. *The Power of Feelings*. New Haven, CT: Yale University Press.

Chodorow, Nancy, and Susan Contratto. 1982. "The Fantasy of the Perfect Mother." In *Rethinking the Family*, ed. Barrie Thorne and Marilyn Yalom, 54–75. New York: Longman.

Contratto, Susan. 1987. "Father Presence in Women's Psychological Development." In *Advances in Psychoanalytic Sociology*, ed. Jerome Rabow, Gerald M. Platt, and Marion S. Goldman, 138–157. Malabar, FL: Krieger.

Crews, Frederick. 1994a. "The Revenge of the Repressed." *New York Review of Books* 41 (19): 54–60.

———. 1994b. "The Revenge of the Repressed." *New York Review of Books* 41 (20): 49–58.

Cudd, Ann E. 1998. "Psychological Explanations of Oppression." In *Introduction to Multiculturalism*, ed. Cynthia Willett. Oxford: Blackwell.

———. 1999. "Analyzing Backlash to Progressive Social Movements." *APA Newsletter on Feminism and Philosophy* 99(1): 42–46.

Daniels, Norman. 1975. "Equal Liberty and Unequal Worth of Liberty." In *Reading Rawls*, ed. Norman Daniels, 253–281. New York: Basic.

Davis, Kathy. 1995. *Reshaping the Female Body*. New York: Routledge.

Deaux, Kay. 1987. "Psychological Constructions of Masculinity and Femininity." In *Masculinity/Femininity: Basic Perspectives*, ed. June Machover Reinisch et al., 289–303. New York: Oxford University Press.

De Lauretis, Teresa. 1986. "Feminist Studies/Critical Studies: Issues, Terms, and Contexts." In *Feminist Studies/Critical Studies*, ed. Teresa de Lauretis, 1–19. Bloomington: Indiana University Press.

DeParle, Jason. 1999. "Early Sex Abuse Hinders Many Women on Welfare." *New York Times* (Nov. 28): sec. 1, p. 1.

Donchin, Anne. 1995. "Reworking Autonomy: Toward a Feminist Perspective." *Cambridge Quarterly of Healthcare Ethics* 4: 45–55.

———. 1996. "Feminist Critiques of New Fertility Technologies: Implications for Social Policy." *Journal of Medicine and Philosophy* 21: 475–498.

Dowd, Maureen. 2000. "Freud Was Way Wrong." *New York Times* (June 11): 17.

Dworkin, Andrea. 1989. *Pornography: Men Possessing Women*. New York: Dutton.

Ettinger, Bracha Lichtenberg. 1992. "Matrix and Metramorphosis." *Differences* 4: 176–208.

Ferguson, Ann. 1996. "Can I Choose Who I Am? and How Would that Empower Me? Gender, Race, Identities, and the Self." In *Women, Knowledge, and Reality*, ed. Ann Garry and Marilyn Pearsall, 108–126. New York: Routledge.

Fiske, Susan T., and Shelley E. Taylor. 1991. *Social Cognition*, 2d ed. New York: McGraw-Hill.

Foster, Patricia. 1994. *Minding the Body: Women Writers on Body and Soul*. New York: Anchor Books/Doubleday.

Fox, Margalit. 1993. "A Portrait in Skin and Bone." *New York Times* (Nov. 21): sec. 5, p. 8.

Franzwa, Helen H. 1974. "Pronatalism in Women's Magazine Fiction." In *Pronatalism: The Myth of Mom and Apple Pie*, ed. Ellen Peck and Judith Senderowitz, 68–77. New York: Crowell.

Freud, Sigmund. 1990. *Freud on Women*, ed. Elizabeth Young-Bruehl. New York: Norton.

Friday, Nancy. 1998. *My Secret Garden*. New York: Simon and Schuster.

Friedman. Marilyn. 1993. *What Are Friends For?* Ithaca, NY: Cornell University Press.

Frye, Marilyn. 1983. *The Politics of Reality*. Freedom, CA: Crossing.

———. 1990. "The Possibility of Feminist Theory." In *Theoretical Perspectives on Sexual Difference*, ed. Deborah L. Rhode, 174–184. New Haven, CT: Yale University Press.

Furman, Frida Kerner. 1997. *Facing the Mirror: Older Women and Beauty Shop Culture*. New York: Routledge.

———. 1999. "There Are No Old Venuses: Older Women's Responses to their

Aging Bodies." In *Mother Time: Women, Aging, and Ethics*, ed. Margaret Walker, 7–22. Lanham, MD: Rowman and Littlefield.

Gerson, Deborah. 1989. "Infertility and the Construction of Desperation." *Socialist Review* 19: 45–64.

Gerson, Kathleen. 1985. *Hard Choices: How Women Decide about Work, Career, and Motherhood*. Berkeley: University of California Press.

Gilligan, Carol. 1982. *In a Different Voice*. Cambridge, MA: Harvard University Press.

———. 1987. "Moral Orientation and Moral Development: The Empirical Base." In *Women and Moral Theory*, ed. Eva Feder Kittay and Diana Tietjens Meyers, 19–33. Totowa, NJ: Rowman and Littlefield.

Gilman, Sander L. 1985. *Difference and Pathology: Stereotypes of Sexuality, Race, and Madness*. Ithaca, NY: Cornell University Press.

Gimenez, Martha E. 1983. "Feminism, Pronatalism, and Motherhood." In *Mothering: Essays in Feminist Theory*, ed. Joyce Trebilcot, 287–314. Totowa, NJ: Rowman and Allanheld.

Goldin, Frederick. 1967. *The Mirror of Narcisssus in the Courtly Lyric*. Ithaca, NY: Cornell University Press.

Govier, Trudy. 1993. "Self-Trust, Autonomy, and Self-Esteem." *Hypatia* 8: 99–120.

Graves, Robert. 1960. *The Greek Myths: 1*. Baltimore: Penguin.

Grealy, Lucy. 1994. "Mirrors." In *Minding the Body: Women Writers on Body and Soul*, ed. Patricia Foster, 53–73. New York: Anchor Books/Doubleday.

Gregory, Richard. 1997. *Mirrors in Mind*. New York: Freeman.

Grimshaw, Jean. 1988. "Autonomy and Identity in Feminist Thinking." In *Feminist Perspectives in Philosophy*, ed. Morwenna Griffiths and Margaret Whitford, 90–108. Bloomington: Indiana University Press.

Grosz, Elizabeth. 1990. *Jacques Lacan: A Feminist Introduction*. New York: Routledge.

Gullette, Margaret Morganroth. 1997. *Declining to Decline: Cultural Combat and the Politics of the Midlife*. Charlottesville: University of Virginia Press.

Hacking, Ian. 1995. *Rewriting the Soul: Multiple Personality and the Sciences of Memory*. Princeton, NJ: Princeton University Press.

Hamilton, David L. 1981. "Illusory Correlation as a Basis for Stereotyping." In *Cognitive Processes in Stereotyping and Intergroup Behavior*, ed. David L. Hamilton, 115–144. Hillsdale, NJ: Erlbaum.

Haraway, Donna. 1997. "A Manifesto for Cyborgs: Science, Technology, and Socialist Feminism in the 1980s." In *Feminist Social Thought: A Reader*, ed. Diana Tietjens Meyers, 502–531. New York: Routledge.

Hartsock, Nancy. 1997. "The Feminist Standpoint: Developing the Ground for a Specifically Feminist Historical Materialism." In *Feminist Social Thought: A Reader*, ed. Diana Tietjens Meyers, 462–483. New York: Routledge.

Haslanger, Sally. 2000. "Gender and Race: (What) Are They? (What) Do We Want Them to Be?" *Nous* 34(1): 31–55.

Haste, Helen, 1994. *The Sexual Metaphor*. Cambridge, MA: Harvard University Press.

Hekman, Susan. 1995. *Moral Voices, Moral Selves*. University Park, PA: Pennsylvania State University Press.

Held, Virginia. 1987. "Feminism and Moral Theory." In *Women and Moral Theory*, ed. Eva Feder Kittay and Diana T. Meyers, 111–128. Totowa, NJ: Rowman and Littlefield.

———. 1989. "Birth and Death." *Ethics* 99: 362–388.

———. 1993. *Feminist Morality: Transforming Culture, Society, and Politics*. Chicago: University of Chicago Press.

Herman, Barbara. 1991. "Agency, Attachment, and Difference." *Ethics* 101: 775–797.

Herman, Judith Lewis. 1992. *Trauma and Recovery*. New York: Basic.

Hirsch, Marianne. 1989. *The Mother/Daughter Plot: Narrative, Psychoanalysis, and Feminism*. Bloomington: Indiana University Press.

Hirschhorn, Michelle. 1996. "Orlan: Artist in the Post-human Age of Mechanical Reincarnation: Body as Ready (To Be Re-) Made." In *Generations and Geographies in the Visual Arts: Feminist Readings*, ed. Griselda Pollock, 110–134. New York: Routledge.

Hochschild, Arlie Russell. 1997. *The Time Bind: When Work Becomes Home and Home Becomes Work*. New York: Holt.

hooks, bell. 1984. *Feminist Theory: From Margin to Center*. Boston: South End Press.

Horowitz, Ruth. 1995. *Teen Mothers: Citizens or Dependents?* Chicago: University of Chicago Press.

Houseknecht, Sharon K. 1987. "Voluntary Childlessness." In *Handbook of Marriage and the Family*, ed. M. B. Sussman and S. Steinmetz, 369–395. New York: Plenum.

Ireland, Mardy S. 1993. *Reconceiving Women: Separating Motherhood from Female Identity*. New York: Guilford.

Irigaray, Luce. 1981. "And One Doesn't Stir without the Other." *Signs* 7: 60–67.

———, 1985. *This Sex Which Is Not One*, trans. Catherine Porter. Ithaca, NY: Cornell University Press.

———. 1991. *The Irigaray Reader*, ed. Margaret Whitford. Oxford: Basil Blackwell.

Isaak, Jo Anna. 1996. *Feminism and Contemporary Art: The Revolutionary Power of Women's Laughter*. New York: Routledge.

Jaggar, Alison. 1983. *Feminist Politics and Human Nature*. Totowa, NJ: Rowman and Allanheld.

Kant, Immanuel. 1965. *The Metaphysical Elements of Justice*, trans. John Ladd. Indianapolis: Bobbs-Merrill.

Kaplan, E. Ann. 1994. "Sex, Work, and Motherhood: Maternal Subjectivity in Recent Visual Culture." In *Representations of Motherhood*, ed. Donna Bassin, Margaret Honey, and Meryle Mahrer Kaplan, 256–271. New Haven, CT: Yale University Press.

King, Deborah K. 1988. "Multiple Jeopardy, Multiple Consciousness: The Context of Black Feminist Ideology." *Signs* 14: 42–72.

Kirsh, Andrea. 1994. "Carrie Mae Weems: Issues in Black, White, and Color." In *Carrie Mae Weems*, ed. Andrea Kirsh and Susan Fisher Sterling, 9–17. Washington, DC: National Museum of Women in the Arts.

Kittay, Eva Feder. 1988. "Woman as Metaphor." *Hypatia* 3: 63–86.

———. 1999. *Love's Labor*. New York: Routledge.

Kline, Katy. 1998. "In or Out of the Picture: Claude Cahun and Cindy Sherman." In *Mirror Images: Women, Surrealism, and Self-representation*, ed. Whitney Chadwick, 66–81. Cambridge, MA: MIT Press.

Krauss, Rosalind. 1999. *Bachelors*. Cambridge, MA: MIT Press.

Kristeva, Julia. 1986. *The Kristeva Reader*, ed. Toril Moi. New York: Columbia University Press.

———. 1987. *Tales of Love*, trans. Leon S. Roudiez. New York: Columbia University Press.

Landa, Anita. 1990. "No Accident: The Voices of Voluntarily Childless Women—An Essay on the Social Construction of Fertility Choices." In *Motherhood: A Feminist Perspective*, ed. Janet Price Knowles and Ellen Cole, 139–158. New York: Haworth.

La Belle, Jenijoy. *Herself Beheld: The Literature of the Looking Glass*. Ithaca, NY: Cornell University Press.

Lang, Susan S. 1991. *Women without Children*. New York: Pharos.

Langer, Ellen J., and Justin Pugh Brown. 1992. "Control from the Actor's Perspective." *Canadian Journal of Behavioural Science* 24: 267–275.

Laplanche, Jean, and J.-B. Pontalis. 1968. "Fantasy and the Origins of Sexuality." *International Journal of Psychoanalysis* 49: 1–18.

Lasker, Judith N., and Susan Borg. 1994. *In Search of Parenthood: Coping with Infertility and High-Tech Conception*. Philadelphia: Temple University Press.

LeVine, Robert A. 1984. "Properties of Culture: An Ethnographic View." In *Culture Theory: Essays on Mind, Self, and Emotion*, ed. Richard A. Shweder and Robert A. LeVine, 67–87. Cambridge: Cambridge University Press.

Leys, Ruth. 1992. "The Real Miss Beauchamp: Gender and the Subject of Imitation." In *Feminists Theorize the Political*, ed. Judith Butler and Joan W. Scott, 167–214. New York: Routledge.

Lippard, Lucy R. 1999. "Scattering Selves." In *Inverted Odysseys: Claude Cahun, Maya Deren, Cindy Sherman*, ed. Shelly Rice, 27–42. Cambridge, MA: MIT Press.

Lloyd, Genevieve. 1993a. "Maleness, Metaphor, and the 'Crisis' of Reason." In *A Mind of One's Own*, ed. Louise Antony and Charlotte Witt, 69–83. Boulder, CO: Westview.

———. 1993b. *The Man of Reason*, 2d ed. Minneapolis: Univeristy of Minnesota Press.

Loftus, Elizabeth F. 1993. "The Reality of Repressed Memories." *American Psychologist* 48(5): 518–537.

Loftus, Elizabeth F., and Leah Kaufman. 1992. "Why Do Traumatic Experiences Sometimes Produce Good Memory (Flashbulbs) and Sometimes No Memory (Repression)?" In *Affect and Accuracy in Recall*, ed. Eugene E. Winograd and Ulric Neisser, 212–223. New York: Cambridge University Press.

Loftus, Elizabeth, and Katherine Ketcham. 1994. *The Myth of Repressed Memory*. New York: St. Martin's.

Lorde, Audre. 1980. *The Cancer Journals*. San Francisco: Aunt Lute Books.

———. 1984. *Sister Outsider*. Freedom, CA: Crossing.

Lugones, Maria C. 1987. "Playfulness, 'World'-Traveling, and Loving Perception." *Hypatia* 2(2): 3–19.

Lugones, Maria, and Elizabeth V. Spelman. 1986. "Have We Got a Theory for You! Feminist Theory, Cultural Imperialism and the Demand for 'the Woman's Voice.'" In *Women and Values*, ed. Marilyn Pearsall, 19–31. Belmont, CA: Wadsworth.

Macdonald, Cameron L. 1998. "Manufacturing Motherhood: The Shadow Work of Nannies and Au Pairs." *Qualitative Sociology* 21: 25–53.

Mackenzie, Catriona. 2000. "Imagining Oneself Otherwise." In *Relational Autonomy*, ed. Catriona Mackenzie and Natalie Stoljar, 124–150. New York: Oxford University Press.

MacKinnon, Catharine. 1982. "Feminism, Marxism, Method and the State: An Agenda for Theory." *Signs* 7: 515–544.

———. 1993. *Only Words*. Cambridge, MA: Harvard University Press.

Mahoney, Maureen A., and Barbara Yngvesson. 1992. "The Construction of Subjectivity and the Paradox of Resistance: Reintegrating Feminist Anthropology and Psychology." *Signs* 18: 44–73.

Mann, Patricia S. 1994. *Micro-Politics: Agency in a Postfeminist Era*. Minneapolis: University of Minnesota Press.

Martin, Douglas. 2000. "Jacqueline Auriol, Top French Test Pilot, 82." *New York Times* (Feb. 17): C25.

Masson, Jeffrey Moussaieff. 1992. *The Assault on Truth: Freud's Suppression of the Seduction Theory*. New York: HarperCollins.

May, Elaine Tyler. 1988. *Homeward Bound*. New York: Basic.

McDonagh, Eileen L. 1996. *Breaking the Abortion Deadlock: From Choice to Consent*. New York: Oxford University Press.

Meyers, Diana Tietjens. 1989. *Self, Society, and Personal Choice*. New York: Columbia University Press.

———. 1992. "The Subversion of Women's Agency in Psychoanalytic Feminism: Chodorow, Flax, Kristeva." In *Revaluing French Feminism*, ed. Sandra Bartky and Nancy Fraser, 136–161. Bloomington: Indiana University Press.

———. 1993. "Cultural Diversity: Rights, Goals, and Competing Values." In *Jewish Identity*, ed. David Theo Goldberg and Michael Krausz, 15–34. Philadelphia: Temple University Press.

———. 1994. *Subjection and Subjectivity: Psychoanalytic Feminism and Moral Philosophy*. New York: Routledge.

———. 2000a. "Intersectional Identity and the Authentic Self? Opposites Attract!" In *Relational Autonomy*, ed. Catriona Mackenzie and Natalie Stoljar, 151–180. New York: Oxford University Press.

———. 2000b. "Marginalized Identities—Individuality, Agency, and Theory." In *Marginal Groups and Mainstream American Culture*, ed. Yolanda Estes, et al., 13–23. Lawrence, KA: Kansas University Press.

———. 2001. "The Rush to Motherhood: Pronatalist Discourse and Women's Autonomy," *Signs* 26: 97–135.

Miller, Jonathan. 1998. *On Reflection*. London: National Gallery Publications.

Moody-Adams, Michelle. 1994. "Culture, Responsibility, and Affected Ignorance." *Ethics* 104: 291–309.

Morgan, Kathryn. 1991. "Women and the Knife: Cosmetic Surgery and the Colonization of Women's Bodies." *Hypatia* 6(3): 25–53.

———. 1996. "Gender Rites and Rights: The Biopolitics of Beauty and Fertility." In *Philosophical Perspectives on Bioethics*, ed. L. W. Sumner and Joseph Boyle, 210–243. Toronto: University of Toronto Press.

Mullin, Amy. 2000. "Art, Understanding, and Political Change." *Hypatia* 15(3): 112–139.

Nedelsky, Jennifer. 1989. "Reconceiving Autonomy: Sources, Thoughts, and Possibilities." *Yale Journal of Law and Feminism* 1: 7–36.

Nelson, Hilde Lindemann, 2001. *Damaged Identities, Narrative Repair*. Ithaca, NY: Cornell University Press.

Neuberg, Steven L. 1994. "Expectancy-confirmation Processes in Stereotype-tinged Social Encounters: The Moderating Role of Social Goals." In *The Psychology of Prejudice: The Ontario Symposium*, vol. 7, ed. Mark P. Zanna and James M. Olson, 103–123. Hillsdale, NJ: Erlbaum.

Nochlin, Linda. 1999. *Representing Women*. New York: Thames and Hudson.

Nozick, Robert. 1974. *Anarchy, State, and Utopia*. New York: Basic.

Nussbaum, Martha C. 1990. *Love's Knowledge*. New York: Oxford University Press.

Oakes, Penelope J., Alexander Haslam, and John C. Turner. 1994. *Stereotyping and Social Reality*. Oxford: Blackwell.

Oakley, Ann. 1981. *Subject Women*. New York: Pantheon.

O'Conner, Patricia T. 2000. "Party Girl: Review of *Georgiana, Duchess of Devonshire*." *New York Times Book Review* (Jan. 23): 6.

Okin, Susan Moller. 1995. "Inequalities between the Sexes in Different Cultural Contexts." In *Women, Culture, and Development*, ed. Martha Nussbaum and Jonathan Glover, 274–297. New York: Oxford University Press.

Oliver, Kelly. 1997. "The Maternal Operation." In *Derrida and Feminism: Recasting the Question of Woman*, ed. Ellen K. Feder, Mary C. Rawlinson, and Emily Zakin, 53–68. New York: Routledge.

Omolade, Barbara. 1995. " 'Making Sense': Notes for Studying Black Teen Mothers." In *Mothers in Law: Feminist Theory and the Legal Regulation of Motherhood*, ed. Martha Albertson Fineman and Isabel Karpin, 270–285. New York: Columbia University Press.

Ovid. 1955. *The Metamorphoses*, trans. Mary M. Innes. Baltimore: Penguin.

Parker, Sheila, et al. 1995. "Body Image and Weight Concerns among African-American and White Adolescent Females: Differences That Make a Difference." *Human Organization* 54: 103–114.

Peck, Ellen. 1974. "Television's Romance with Reproduction." In *Pronatalism: The Myth of Mom and Apple Pie*, ed. Ellen Peck and Judith Senderowitz, 78–97. New York: Crowell.

Petchesky, Rosalind Pollack. 1985. *Abortion and Woman's Choice*. Boston: Northeastern University Press.

———. 1987. "Foetal Images: The Power of Visual Culture in the Politics of Reproduction." In *Reproductive Technologies: Gender, Motherhood, and Medicine*, ed. Michelle Stanworth, 57–80. Minneapolis: University of Minnesota Press.

Pollock, Griselda. 1988. *Vision and Difference: Femininity, Feminism, and Histories of Art*. New York: Routledge.

———. 1998. *Mary Cassatt: Painter of Modern Women*. London: Thames and Hudson.

———. 1999. *Differencing the Canon: Feminist Desire and the Writing of Art History*. New York: Routledge.

Pomeroy, Sarah B. 1995. *Goddesses, Whores, Wives, and Slaves*. New York: Schocken.

Rawls, John. 1971. *A Theory of Justice*. Cambridge, MA: Harvard University Press.

Rogers, Lisa Kay, and Jeffrey H. Larson. 1988. "Voluntary Childlessness: A Review of the Literature and a Model of the Childlessness Decision." *Family Perspective* 22(1): 43–58.

Rooney, Phyllis. 1991. "Gendered Reason: Sex, Metaphor, and Conceptions of Reason." *Hypatia* 6(2): 77–103.

Ross, Michael, and Roger Buehler. 1994. "Creative Remembering." In *The Remembering Self: Construction and Accuracy in the Self-narrative*, ed. Ulric Neisser and Robyn Fivush, 205–235. New York: Cambridge University Press.

Rothbart, Myron. 1981. "Memory Processes and Social Beliefs." In *Cognitive Processes in Stereotyping and Intergroup Behavior*, ed. David L. Hamilton, 145–181. Hillsdale, NJ: Erlbaum.

Ruddick, Sara. 1987. "Remarks on the Sexual Politics of Reason." In *Women and Moral Theory*, ed. Eva Feder Kittay and Diana Tietjens Meyers, 237–260. Totowa, NJ: Rowman and Littlefield.

———. 1997. "Maternal Thinking." In *Feminist Social Thought: A Reader*, ed. Diana Tietjens Meyers, 584–603. New York: Routledge.

———. 1999. "Virtues and Age." In *Mother Time: Women, Aging, and Ethics*, ed. Margaret Urban Walker, 45–60. Lanham, MD: Rowman and Littlefield.

Safer, Jeanne. 1996. *Beyond Motherhood: Choosing a Life without Children*. New York: Pocket Books.

Scheman, Naomi. 1993. *Engenderings: Constructions of Knowledge, Authority, and Privilege*. New York: Routledge.

Sen, Amartya. 1990. "Individual Freedom as a Social Commitment." *New York Review of Books* (June 14) 37(10): 49–54.

Silverman, Kaja. 1992. *Male Subjectivity at the Margins*. New York: Routledge.

Skrypnick, Berna J., and Mark Snyder. 1982. "On the Self-Perpetuating Nature of Stereotypes about Women and Men." *Journal of Experimental Social Psychology* 18: 277–291.

Smith, Bonnie G. 1985. *Confessions of a Concierge*. New Haven, CT: Yale University Press.

Snyder, Mark. 1981. "On the Self-perpetuating Nature of Social Stereotypes." In *Cognitive Processes in Stereotyping and Intergroup Behavior*, ed. David L. Hamilton, 183–212. Hillsdale, NJ: Erlbaum.

Sontag, Susan. 1979. "The Double Standard of Aging." In *Psychology of Women: Selected Readings*, ed. Juanita H. Williams, 462–478. New York: Norton.

Spelman, Elizabeth V. 1988. *Inessential Woman*. Boston, MA: Beacon Press.

Stern, Daniel N. 1985. *The Interpersonal World of the Infant: A View from Psychoanalysis and Developmental Psychology*. New York: Basic.

Suleiman, Susan Rubin. 1994. "Playing and Motherhood; or, How to Get the Most Out of the Avant-Garde." In *Representations of Motherhood*, ed. Donna Bassin, Margaret Honey, and Meryle Mahrer Kaplan, 272–282. New Haven, CT: Yale University Press.

Summers-Bremner, Eluned. 2000. "Reading Irigaray, Dancing." *Hypatia* 15(1): 90–125.

Taetzsch, Lynne. 1994. "Fighting Natural." In *Minding the Body: Women Writers on Body and Soul*, ed. Patricia Foster, 233–247. New York: Anchor Books/Doubleday.

Taylor-Wood, Sam. 1998. "Interview with Germano Celant." In *Sam Taylor-Wood*. Milan: Fondazione Prada.

Terr, Lenore. 1994. *Unchained Memories: True Stories of Traumatic Memories, Lost and Found*. New York: Basic.

Valian, Virginia. 1998. *Why So Slow? The Advancement of Women*. Cambridge, MA: MIT Press.

Veevers, J. E. 1980. *Childless by Choice*. Toronto: Butterworths.

Walker, Barbara G. 1983. *The Woman's Encyclopedia of Myths and Secrets*. San Francisco: Harper and Row.

Walker, Margaret. 1998. *Moral Understandings: A Feminist Study in Ethics*. New York: Routledge.

Weir, Alison. 1995. "Toward a Model of Self-Identity: Habermas and Kristeva." In *Feminists Read Habermas*, ed. Johanna Meehan, 263–282. New York: Routledge.

Weston, Kath. 1991. *Families We Choose: Lesbians, Gays, Kinship*. New York: Columbia University Press.

Wheelock, Arthur K., Jr., ed. 1995. *Johannes Vermeer*. New Haven, CT: Yale University Press.

Williams, Patricia. 1991. *The Alchemy of Race and Rights*. Cambridge, MA: Harvard University Press.

———. 1997. "Mirrors and Windows: An Essay on Empty Signs, Pregnant Meanings, and Women's Power." In *Feminist Social Thought: A Reader*, ed. Diana Tietjens Meyers, 332–340. New York: Routledge.

Williams, Wendy W. 1991. "The Equality Crisis: Some Reflections on Culture, Courts, and Feminism." In *Feminist Legal Theory*, ed. Katharine T. Bartlett and Rosanne Kennedy, 15–34. Boulder, CO: Westview.

Woolf, Virginia. 1963. *A Room of One's Own*. New York: Harcourt, Brace, and World.

Young, Iris Marion. 1994. "Gender as Seriality: Thinking about Women as a Social Collective." *Signs* 19: 713–738.

Young-Bruehl, Elizabeth. 1996. *The Anatomy of Prejudices*. Cambridge, MA: Harvard University Press.

Zanna, Mark P., and James M. Olson, eds. 1994. *The Psychology of Prejudice: The Ontario Symposium*, vol. 7. Hillsdale, NJ: Erlbaum.

NAME INDEX

226) 227

death, cultural representation of, 65,
102, 103–104, 106, 112, 149, 151,
162, 163–166, 204. *See also*
vanitas

Echo, 101–103, 104, 106, 136. *See also*
Narcissus
equality/inequality, gender, 3, 5, 8–9,
16–17, 26, 29, 33, 93–95, 72, 73,
143–144, 145, 189, 191. *See also*
oppression, internalized

family romance, the, 79, 84–85, 86,
89, 90–91, 92, 93, 95, 97,
116–117
sadistic incest scenario, 79–80, 86,
90–93
See also incest; memory, recovered
fantasy, 9, 43–47, 50, 52, 57, 66, 73,
78, 82, 85, 89, 121, 127, 141–143,
198, 210
fatherhood, 69–70, 74, 90, 91, 174,
197–198
cultural representation of, 27,
66, 67, 74, 79, 84, 116–117,
189–190
See also manhood, cultural representation of
femininity. *See* womanhood, cultural
representation of
feminism
counterfigurative politics, 56–57,
73–74, 93, 94, 97–98, 146–147,
164, 165–166, 168, 189–192
goals, 31, 45, 46, 92–94, 101,
126–127, 163, 187, 188, 192
values, 16–17, 47, 48, 90, 133–134,
155, 162–163, 192

heterosexism, 13, 40, 73, 100, 104, 115,
119, 125, 138, 143, 144, 157, 173,
176, 183, 184, 190, 202
heterosexuality, 6, 35, 48, 49, 67–68,
79, 104, 115, 137, 209
cultural representation of, 84, 85,
103–104, 117–118, 190, 202
counter figuration and, 93, 141–144,
202
homosexuality. *See* heterosexism

identity
gender, 5–11, 30, 32, 123, 124, 135,
136, 140, 146, 172–175, 179, 181,
205
individual, 7, 10, 28, 32, 44, 53–55,
80, 120, 123–124, 136, 140–141,
145, 146, 157, 189, 193, 206, 211
imagination, 14, 20, 52–53, 55, 59, 68,
82, 89
incest, 78, 82, 84, 89, 91–94, 96
counter figuration of, 93–94
incest taboo, 68, 116–117, 125, 177,
190
See also abuse, sexual
infertility. *See* reproductive
technology
internalization, 7–8, 41, 114. *See also*
oppression, internalized
introspection, 20, 51, 113
cultural representation of, 107, 113

love, 101–106, 107, 116–119, 161

male bonding, 171, 172, 179, 189. *See
also* sexism
manhood, cultural representation of,
103, 105–106, 114–115, 116–117,
118, 124–125, 143, 174, 184, 186,
190, 191, 197. *See also* heterosexuality; Narcissus
masculinity. *See* manhood, cultural
representation of
matrigyno-idolatry, 47–51, 165,
189–190, 197–198, 209
memory, 20, 75, 78–79, 80, 81,
82, 83–84, 86–90, 170,
200–201
recovered, 79, 80–83, 85, 86, 90,
93–94, 201
misogyny, 3–4, 29, 67, 101, 119, 133,
144, 157, 172, 174, 193. *See also*
sexism
motherhood, 60, 69, 73, 94–95, 114,
173, 181, 197
counterfigurations of, 56–57,
64–65, 70–75, 130, 132,
189–190, 199
cultural representation of, 32, 35,
40, 47–51, 65–68, 71, 73, 78, 84,